Sandr...

P9-APN-009

BORN FEMALE IS...

"enough to convince anyone that the superstition and restrictive prejudices on which our system of work is built are depriving the country of nearly half its talent."

—Gloria Steinem
The New York Times Book Review

"the kind of book that stirs opinion and changes ideas."

—Publishers' Weekly

"the greatest thing for women since the pill!"

—Jane Trahey, President
Trahey-Wolf Advertising, Inc.

BORN FEMALE
was originally published by
David McKay Company, Inc.

Also by Caroline Bird:

The Invisible Scar

Published by Pocket Books

 Are there paperbound books you want
but cannot find in your retail stores?

You can get any title in print in:
Pocket Book editions • Pocket *Cardinal* editions • Permabook editions or Washington Square Press editions. Simply send retail price, local sales tax, if any, plus 15¢ to cover mailing and handling costs for each book wanted to:

MAIL SERVICE DEPARTMENT
    POCKET BOOKS • A Division of Simon & Schuster, Inc.
    1 West 39th Street   •   New York, New York 10018
    Please send check or money order. We cannot be responsible for cash.
    Catalogue sent free on request.

Titles in these series are also available at discounts in quantity lots for industrial or sales-promotional use. For details write our Special Projects Agency: The Benjamin Company, Inc., 485 Madison Avenue, New York, N.Y. 10022.

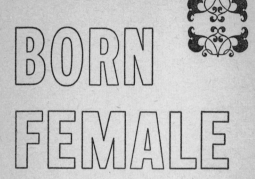

BORN FEMALE

The High Cost of Keeping Women Down

by
CAROLINE BIRD
with Sara Welles Briller

PUBLISHED BY POCKET BOOKS NEW YORK

BORN FEMALE:
The High Cost of Keeping Women Down

David McKay edition published June, 1968

A *Pocket Book* edition
1st printing...........May, 1969

This *Pocket Book* edition is printed from brand-new
plates made from completely reset, clear, easy-to-read type.
Pocket Book editions are published by Pocket Books, a division
of Simon & Schuster, Inc., 630 Fifth Avenue, New York, N.Y. 10020.
Trademarks registered in the United States and other countries.

L

Standard Book Number: 671-77070-5.
This *Pocket Book* edition is published by arrangement with
the David McKay Company, Inc..
Printed in the U.S.A.

To Tom

CONTENTS

FOREWORD: THE DECLINE OF SEX

People can be classified in all sorts of ways. The easiest and the oldest way is to divide the human race into male and female. But people can also be classified according to the way *they* classify people.

Some views of life are founded on the difference between the sexes. The worlds of Sigmund Freud, Sir Lancelot, Tarzan, Richard Rodgers, Scheherazade, and the Lone Ranger elaborate the celebrated difference.

Other symbolic figures aren't "sexist" in this way. Benjamin Franklin, the Beatles, Eleanor Roosevelt, Shakespeare, Svetlana Alliluyeva are not sexless individuals, but they have made a great many statements about people which apply to men as well as to women. In their worlds, people have been and are classified on the basis of insight, politics, skills, and interests, and their pigeonholes are coeducational. Their ideal person combines characteristics usually attributed to men with characteristics usually attributed to women; he is, as the Greek word goes, "androgynous."

After a long period of celebrating the differences between men and women, we are heading into an androgynous world in which the most important thing about a person will no longer be his or her sex. The notion sounds unbearably dull and even blasphemous to everyone over thirty, the age at which, according to the new young, adults become untrustworthy. But how many culture heroes of the young now parade or exploit their masculinity or femininity? Teen-agers have abandoned

Richard Rodgers for the socially-conscious songs of Joan
Baez, and Sophia Loren does not excite the young admirers of
Twiggy.

Twiggy closely resembles her "companion," not husband,
beau or boyfriend. Both wear their hair much the same
way—except that his is longer. Both take an equal interest in
decorating their persons. And they are companions because
they are usually doing the same thing—riding a motorcycle or
rocking to the beat of music which provides a climate for a
mob rather than the key to a private world for two. The
hippies and the psychedelic experimenters call the old-
fashioned kind of sexual love egotistical. They want to break
out of the small-family grouping. In the Haight-Ashbury
section of San Francisco and in the East Village of New
York their open communes are dedicated to a more general-
ized kind of love than is celebrated by Rodgers and Hammer-
stein.

Androgyny is not confined to the hippies. In the jungles of
Asia and Africa, in our own primitive Kentucky mountains,
boys and girls go out to help the disadvantaged, wearing
identical clothes, living in tents or huts, or with the people
they have come to aid. Newlyweds from privileged families
often choose this conspicuously un-private trip as a honey-
moon. The style is everything young intellectuals admire:
humanitarian, austere, dangerous, uncomfortable—and androgynous. Arm-in-arm, they seem to be saying that they
enjoy the similarity of their experience as much as the possi-
bilities for pleasure in their anatomical difference.

In 1967, a Radcliffe girl and a Harvard boy took an
apartment together and allowed a magazine to print their
pictures and their names. The rebellion against marriage is
familiar, but past rebels have lived together as man and wife.
The youngsters pictured are living together as roommates.
"He cooks," the caption on their picture read. "She irons.
They do the laundry together."

These responsible young students are not revolting against
the responsibilities of marriage so much as against the premise
of the institution. What the long-haired boys and the shiny-
nosed girls seem to be telegraphing is a declaration of independence from sex roles. "We don't think men should be
shackled to desks and machines in order to prove that they
are men," they seem to be saying. "We don't think girls should

have to limit their interests in order to prove that they are women. As a matter of fact, we happen to think that traditional marriage is as corrupt as prostitution. It's based on economics, not love."

The contraceptive pill may reduce the importance of sex not only as a basis for the division of labor, but as a guideline in developing talents and interests. "It is most doubtful, in the new age, that the rigidly 'male' qualities will be of much use," Marshall McLuhan wrote in 1967. "In fact, there may well be little need for standardized males or females. . . . The whole business of sex may become again, as in the tribal state, play—freer, but less important."

Margaret Mead, the most reliable bellwether for changes in man-woman relationships over the past thirty years, now suggests that the family of the future won't even be based on sex or a sexual relationship. Many people will get the emotional reassurance now provided by marriage from individuals of the same or opposite sex who are *simpatico* rather than sexually compelling. Housemates may or may not be sex mates. This is the far-out thinking of 1968.

David Riesman, the Harvard sociologist, puts the new ideal in sociological language. "I think what I would ideally like to see in our society is that sex become an ascribed rather than an achieved status," he told an audience of college girls. "That one is simply born a girl or a boy and that's it. And no worry about an activity's de-feminizing or emasculating one." In this brave new world, babies would not be committed to a specific adult role because they happened to be *born female*. Sex would be a personal characteristic of only slightly more consequence than the color of one's hair, eyes—or skin.

Sex is here to stay, but its future is in private life, not in the office. Sex is becoming a less useful way to classify workers and organize work, yet the sex lines are still maintained in offices and plants and women are still penalized on the job by unexamined assumptions about their family roles.

This is a frankly feminist book. It counts the social, moral, and personal costs of keeping women down on the job and finds them high:

We are destroying talent. The price of occupational success is made so high for women that barring exceptional luck only the unusually talented or frankly neurotic can afford to succeed. Girls size up the bargain early and turn it down.

We are wasting talent. The able workers that employers say they can't find are all too often in their own back rooms or lofts doing jobs that use only a fraction of their ability.

We are hiding talent. Some of our brightest citizens are quietly tucked away at home, their aptitudes concealed by the label "Housewife."

The young see these costs, and some are refusing to pay them. Men and women of the future will share the work of home and shop on the basis of individual abilities and convenience. The discriminations *for and against* women in general are fading, but they are not fading fast enough to keep up with the changing conditions of home and work.

Change always hurts, but change in sex roles hurts women more than men. This book contends that women should not have to suffer all the pain and do all of the adjusting.

We are all in this life together.

BORN FEMALE

1

LADIES' DAY IN THE HOUSE

On the day the U.S. House of Representatives was supposed
to vote on the Civil Rights Bill of 1964, 81-year-old Howard
W. Smith of Virginia, Chairman of the Rules Committee,
proposed an amendment that sounded like a joke even while
the clerk was reading it aloud.

The proposal consisted of the addition of a single word,
"sex." Wherever Title VII of the bill on employment prohibited discrimination on the basis of "race, color, religion, or
national origin," the Smith amendment prohibited discrimination on the basis of sex, too.

Smith was no feminist. He was a Virginia gentleman who
had been defending the Southern Way of Life in Congress for
nearly a third of a century. Now that battle was finally lost.
Under pressure from President Johnson, Northern Democrats
and Republicans had formed a coalition with enough votes to
pass the bill giving Negroes really equal access to the polls,
schools, public accommodations, and above all, jobs.

Title VII was the most controversial part of the bill. Even
people who supported Negro rights were not sure that
discrimination in employment could be abolished by law.
Midwest and mountain state Republicans were as firmly
convinced as Southern Democrats that employers should be
allowed to choose their employees on any basis they saw fit.
Many feared that Title VII would destroy a man's right to run
his own business as he pleased. Many did not like the idea that

1

the law proposed a new Federal agency, the Equal Employment Opportunity Commission, to dig into individual complaints.

The Southerners knew they were beaten, but they kept chipping away at the bill with amendments that were designed to weaken or ridicule the coalition. Some amendments dramatized "race mixing," as the Southerners called integration, in an effort to break Southern Democrats away from the party line. One of these, for instance, proposed that the law should not be interpreted as forcing a person to render services against his will. To Southerners, this amendment meant that a white barber could not be forced to cut the hair of a Negro. Other amendments stipulated that the law could not be used to force an employer to hire an atheist or a Communist. One amendment appropriated $100 million to enforce the law, a device which called attention to the difficulty that was anticipated in legislating a change in popular custom. Another amendment stipulated that the law should not take effect until ratified by a popular referendum, the assumption being that most people would vote against integration if given a chance.

To minimize their impact, the managers of the Civil Rights coalition had saved debate on Title VII for Saturday, February 8, the day set for the final vote. Lincoln's birthday, February 12, was the following Wednesday, and Republicans were eager to adjourn for the holiday, traditionally a day of Republican drumbeating. Passage of the first truly effective Civil Rights Bill would make a splendid peg for their speeches in honor of the Great Emancipator. As Saturday wore on without progress toward a vote, Republicans became edgy.

Smith's sense of timing was practiced. He dropped his sex amendment into the hopper just at the moment when it could exasperate his opponents the most, then leaned back, with octogenarian patience, to hear the clerk read out the pages and lines of the bill where the word "sex" was to be inserted.

"This amendment is offered to prevent discrimination against another minority group, the women, but a very essential minority group, in the absence of which the majority group would not be here today," he explained. "Now I am very serious about this amendment. . . . I do not think it can do any harm to this legislation; maybe it can do some good. I think it will do some good for the minority sex. I think we all recognize and it is indisputable fact that all throughout industry women are discriminated against in that just generally speaking they do not get as high compensation for their work as do the majority sex."

What Smith called "my little amendment" extended the promise of equal opportunity from the seven million Negro men and women workers that Title VII was drafted to protect, to 21 million white women who did not get as high compensation for their work as the Negro members of "the majority sex." White men who worked full time the year round in 1964 earned a median income of $6,497; Negro men, $4,285; white women, $3,859; and Negro women, $2,674. There were more white women working full time the year round than all Negro men and women working full and part time combined. White women outnumbered Negroes of both sexes in the lowest income brackets: five million white women worked full time for less than $3,859 in 1964. Two million Negro males had median earnings below the $4,285 that was the average for full-time Negro men workers. One point four million Negro women averaged less than the median earnings of $2,674 for full-time Negro women workers. The Negro women earned the least, but they were the smallest of the four groups.

These figures would not have shocked Smith. He had voted against bills guaranteeing equal pay for equal work regardless of sex. His apparent conversion to the cause of "the minority sex" had occurred two weeks previously when he was on the NBC television show, "Meet the Press," with May Craig, the official feminist of the White House Press Corps who provided comic relief at Presidential press conferences by jumping up and asking the President what he had done for women lately. Mrs. Craig saw in the controversy over legislating Negro rights still another opportunity to win attention for women's rights. When her turn came to question Smith on the show, she asked him if he would put equal rights for women into Title VII.

"Well, maybe I would," Smith said with Southern gallantry. "I'm all strong for the women, you know."

"Amendment on the floor?" Mrs. Craig pursued.

"I might do that," Smith allowed. Discrimination against Negroes aroused indignation, but discrimination against women struck most people as funny. If Title VII could not be beaten, perhaps it could be laughed off the floor.

Addressing the House, Smith kept a straight face and played the concept of women's rights for all the laughs he could get. He began by reading a letter from a lady urging him to introduce a bill to remedy the "imbalance" between the sexes in the United States. She complained that there were 2,661,000 extra females at the 1960 Census:

> Just why the Creator would set up such an imbalance of spinsters, shutting off the "right" of every female to have a husband of her own, is, of course, known only to nature. But I am sure you will agree that this is a grave injustice to womankind and something the Congress and President Johnson should take immediate steps to correct, especially in this election year.
>
> Up until now, instead of assisting these poor unfortunate females in obtaining their "right" to happiness, the Government has on several occasions engaged in wars which killed off a large number of eligible males, creating an "imbalance" in our male and female population that was even worse than before.
>
> Would you have any suggestions as to what course our Government might pursue to protect our spinster friends in their "right" to a nice husband and family?

The letter brought down the house. Smith had to stop many times to beg for quiet. Once he reminded the Congressmen that he was discussing a serious subject—half the voters in the country.

"I read that letter just to illustrate that women have some real grievances," he finished. "I am serious about this thing. . . . What harm can you do this bill that was so perfect yesterday?"

Emanuel Celler, liberal Congressman from New York, was the Democratic leader of the bipartisan coalition that President Johnson expected to pass the bill. As floor manager he had to oppose the sex amendment before it sank the bill under gales of laughter.

The uproar was so loud that Celler did not attempt to be serious when he rose to speak. "I can say as a result of forty-nine years of experience—and I celebrate my fiftieth wedding anniversary next year—that women, indeed, are not in the minority in my house. . . . I usually have the last two words, and those words are, 'Yes, dear.' " He then quoted Esther Peterson, Director of the Women's Bureau of the Department of Labor, who insisted that the addition of sex to the Civil Rights Bill would "not be to the best advantage of women at this time."

Liberals and most of the women's organizations in 1964 opposed adding sex to the Civil Rights Bill, primarily because they did not want to endanger protection for Negroes, but also because absolute equality between the sexes before the law might endanger rights and immunities favoring women. Women might lose more than they gained. Men and women are different, Celler went on, and as the French say, *"Vive la différence"*:

> Imagine the upheaval that would result from adoption of blanket language requiring total equality. Would male citizens be justified in insisting that women share with them the burdens of compulsory military service? What would become of traditional family relationships? What about alimony? Who would have the obligation of supporting whom? Would fathers rank equally with mothers in the right of custody to children? What would become of the crimes of rape and statutory rape? Would the Mann Act be invalidated? Would the many State and local provisions regulating working conditions and hours of employment for women be struck down?
>
> You know the biological differences between the sexes. In many States we have laws favorable to women. Are you going to strike these laws down?

Although, as we shall see, responsible women did not later flinch from these difficulties, Congressman Celler assumed he could get rid of the sex amendment merely by raising them.

John Dowdy, Texan ally of Smith, kept the play on "rights" going. "Even the Department set up by the U.S. Government for the benefit of women is opposed to equal rights in employment for women," he said in mock sorrow.

The uproar has gone down in House history as "Ladies' Day" but it did not seem funny to the women of the House. Many of them had deferred asking for a sex amendment, but as Smith had foreseen, the ridicule began to get under their skins. Frances P. Bolton of Ohio tried to save the Negro bill by transferring the sex provision to Title X, Miscellaneous, where it could be voted down later without hurting Title VII.

"I do not like the idea here of it going in under 'miscellaneous,'" objected Smith. "I think women are entitled to more dignity than that."

"My colleague," retorted Mrs. Bolton, "may I suggest to you, that we are so used to being just 'miscellaneous.'"

Martha Griffiths, Democratic Congresswoman from Michigan, did not quibble. "I support the amendment because when this bill has passed, white women will be last at the hiring gate," she announced. She took the facetious analogy seriously and constructed hypothetical cases to show that it would be awkward to abolish race discrimination without abolishing sex discrimination, too. Without the sex amendment, for example, a white woman would have no case against a restaurant which denied her a job, while a Negro woman would be able to demand proof that she was rejected on the basis of her sex rather than her race.

Mrs. Griffiths says that she had intended to offer a sex amendment to Title VII herself. But she held off when she realized that Smith was going to do it, because she thought that his sponsorship of the amendment would insure the votes of at least a hundred Southern Congressmen who otherwise would never have voted for a feminist measure.

Mrs. Griffiths insists that she revolted against party discipline because she was sure that the Civil Rights Bill would pass and she honestly did not think it would work without sex in it. Other women eagerly followed her. Katharine St. George of New York got up to say that yes, indeed, she would be glad to abolish laws regulating working conditions and hours of employment for women:

> Women are protected—they cannot run an elevator late at night and that is when the pay is higher.
> They cannot serve in restaurants and cabarets late at night—when the tips are higher—and the load, if you please, is lighter.
> So it is not exactly helping them—oh, no, you have taken beautiful care of the women.

But what about the offices, gentlemen, that are cleaned every morning about 2 or 3 o'clock in the city of New York, and the offices that are cleaned quite early here in Washington, D.C.? Does anybody worry about those women? I have never heard of anybody worrying about the women who do that work.

The addition of that little, terrifying word "s-e-x" will not hurt this legislation in any way.

Edith Green was the only woman in the House who stood firm in opposing the amendment. She reminded the House that the gentlemen who were strongest in their support of women's rights when it came to Title VII had been the most opposed to the Equal Pay Act of 1963 outlawing discrimination in pay on the basis of sex, which was to go into effect June 11, 1964. "As the author of the Equal Pay Bill, I believe I have demonstrated my concern and my determination to advance women's opportunities." She said, "But—I do not believe this is the time or place for this amendment. At the risk of being called an Aunt Jane, if not an Uncle Tom, let us not add any amendment that would get in the way of our primary objective. . . . For every discrimination that I have suffered, the Negro woman has suffered ten times that amount of discrimination."

The Southerners kept the joke going as long as they could. "Since I am a man, which places me in the minority and makes me a second-class citizen," Congressman J. Russell Tuten, of Georgia, contributed, "and the fact that I am white and from the South—I look forward to claiming my rights under the terms of this legislation."

Liberals tried in vain to stem the tide of angry Congresswomen. John Lindsay, Emanuel Celler, James Roosevelt, and Edith Green could not rally the coalition to undo Smith's amendment. In vain did they point out that the American Association of University Women and other thoughtful organizations opposed cluttering up the bill and legislating equal rights for women across the board. Late in the afternoon of February 8, the sex amendment was put to a vote. When the tellers announced 168 for the amendment, 133 opposed, a feminine voice from the House gallery cried, "We made it! God Bless America!" She was promptly removed by guards.

Attempts to change the traditional sex roles have always

been countered with laughter. Suffragettes learned to endure ridicule. Sam Johnson likened an educated woman to a dog walking on its hind legs. They even made fun of Plato when he advocated military service for women as well as men in *The Republic*. Plato, however, stood firm. "In his laughter," he wrote sternly of an opponent, "he himself is plucking the fruit of unripe wisdom, and he himself is ignorant of what he is laughing at."

The real joke about the sex amendment was that it was taken seriously. Its implications are so revolutionary that it is worth a moment's analysis. Title VII was disturbing because it questioned the private decisions people make about the worth of other individuals. Employers, insurance underwriters, engaged couples, college admissions authorities, all are involved in pre-judging someone else's performance. They all have to rely primarily on past experience as a guide. Most of these decisions about individuals are beyond the scope of law, even when they hurt. Until recently, employer decisions to hire and fire have been held equally private. Champions of minority groups have by and large accepted this assumption and urged employers to make exceptions to the general rule in favor of specially qualified Negroes or women. You can succeed, as the cliché goes, if you're "twice as good" and prove it.

The purpose of Title VII was to require employers to disregard all the probabilities of good or bad performance associated with minority origin, including real and proven disabilities. The analogy with women was useful in Smith's case because women's disabilities were widely accepted (whether real or not) and accepted, furthermore, as "only natural."

Equal opportunity in employment for women was not a well-publicized cause in the beginning of 1964. Women workers were not complaining openly. They did not want to appear discontented, no matter how they sometimes felt. They wanted—or thought they wanted—the dream of domesticity relentlessly presented to them as their real happiness. And as long as women did not seem to feel strongly about working, employers felt justified in taking their overt lack of commitment into consideration when hiring, firing, and promoting. Employers and women shrugged off the issue.

"Women can get ahead here if they want to," employers

said, and most women believed them. Enough women had risen to prove that the dedicated could succeed.

"Women quit to have babies and follow husbands, so you can't promote them," employers said. Women agreed they were handicapped.

Of course some discontent over these inequities was inevitable. Friends of women and advocates of "womanpower" tried to show employers that they were missing a good bet. Campaigns to utilize women were mounted in much the same spirit as campaigns to employ the handicapped and save money. Psychologists pointed out that many women would be happier if they directed more energy into working and less into trying to live vicariously through their families. But again, no general public action seemed indicated. Individuals were expected to find their own remedies.

This also happened to be exactly the way most Southerners felt about hiring Negroes. They contended that Negroes by and large were not as competent as whites, and, in making personnel decisions, an employer could not ignore the probability that a Negro would not perform as well as a white, all other things being equal. Courts were expected to be color-blind, but a man had a right to choose an employee or a wife on whatever basis he pleased. This was not to defend unfair private decisions. Southerners like Smith sometimes deplored inequities in the employment of Negroes and urged employers to recognize Negroes who had demonstrated exceptional ability. But, argued these Southerners, individual Negroes would be happier if they tried harder to become exceptions and directed more energy into working and less to the repression or expression of hostility. Old-fashioned as this program seems in 1968, it probably still represents the majority view in the North as well as in the South.

Title VII rejected the analogy Smith made between the choice of an employee and the choice of a wife. The bill seemed to be saying to employers, "You have to consider what you know about the potential of an individual you hire. We expect you to weigh the probabilities. If you've found in the past that men who collect stamps make better bank officials, then we expect you to favor your stamp-collecting employees in the future. If you are wrong, you suffer, and so do your non-stamp-collecting employees, but these are the risks of business, and in any event, mistakes of this kind do not snowball into big social problems.

"Some mistakes, though, and some generalizations *do* become social problems. Even if you believe that Negroes (or women) really don't care about working and don't try hard enough to do a good job, even if you believe that they are content to do the dirty work at low pay, even if you believe that they are handicapped by poor training or by their home life, we ask you to ignore these feelings when you make a decision about an individual worker.

"We are stating here the ultimate case so there will be no mistake. Actually, we do not admit that Negroes (or women) are all that handicapped or that you will lose out in hiring them on the basis of their individual qualifications in competition with other applicants. But we are being this blunt because the intent of the law is that you must ignore these factors even if you do lose out."

Put this way, of course, the bill might never have passed. But decision-makers are often asked to close their eyes to preconceptions. Gypsies have admitted that they prefer to steal from non-Gypsies, but juries are charged to forget this cultural characteristic when an individual Gypsy is on trial.

Smith's analogy with sex was particularly adroit because people who attack discrimination on the basis of race often see nothing wrong with discriminating the same way on the basis of sex. Life insurance provides an interesting example. It is, of course, an economic device for protecting individuals against risks, but some high-risk groups are recognized and others are not. Because men die younger than women, they are charged higher premiums. But even though a Negro's life expectancy is statistically shorter than a white's, the rates are the same for both races. Insurance companies say, "White, black, it's all the same, we'll throw them in together and spread the risk just the way we spread the risk between those who die early and those who die late. That's the way life insurance works."

In other words, the racial differences are ignored, while the sexual ones are recognized.

It's the same way in employment. Most employers conceal discriminatory practices against Negroes, but they don't hesitate to discriminate openly against women. The risks of childbearing are charged against her as an individual and against her as a sex, even if she is beyond childbearing age and has only herself to support. In order to dramatize this countries recognized a social obligation to help a woman undergo a hysterectomy so that he could then not discount her value as an employee.

The point is that while we consider it "only natural" for employees to consider the possibility that a woman worker might have a baby, many foreign countries, including Sweden and the Soviet Union, won't let an employer fire a woman for pregnancy or even turn her down for a job solely because she is pregnant. These countries make employers take women back after they have had their babies just as we make employers take women back after military service. Some 70 countries recognized a social obligation to help a woman worker financially when she loses income due to maternity, but we expect the individuals involved to assume all the costs of childbirth and child care.

The implications of Title VII reached deep into social policy—so deep that it seemed easier to laugh than to think. Little of it was reported in the newspapers. The sex amendment itself was almost pointedly ignored. The morning after Ladies' Day in the House, *The New York Times* dismissed the fracas in an aside: "The civil rights forces had to accept some unexpected amendments." But they gave top billing, that same Sunday, February 9, 1964, to an item that seemed at the time to be more newsworthy: Senator Margaret Chase Smith opened her campaign for the Republican nomination for the Presidency from Plymouth, New Hampshire.

The newspapers did not follow the progress of the sex amendment through the Senate, in part because it seemed likely to be dropped along with many other obstructionist amendments. In April 1964, Senator Everett Dirksen, the Republican majority leader, favored dropping it, along with the amendment denying the protection of Title VII to atheists. But by this time a number of women were on the job defending the amendment. At one point, the sex provision was left out of the enforcement section of Title VII, leaving equal opportunity for both sexes a policy in name only.

Pauli Murray, a Negro woman lawyer and old friend of Eleanor Roosevelt, wrote a "Memorandum in Support of Retaining the Sex Amendment," which women active in the Business and Professional Women's Clubs circulated to Senators, Vice President Hubert Humphrey, and Lady Bird Johnson. A discreet acknowledgment from Bess Furman, Mrs. Johnson's social secretary, implied that the Administration wanted the Civil Rights Bill of 1964 to go through the Senate as "presently phrased"—with the sex amendment in it.

In June 1964, President Johnson boosted the cause of equal opportunity for women by officially celebrating the effective date of the Equal Pay Act of 1963. This act backed up the poorly enforced state laws prohibiting employers from paying men and women different wages for the same work. Johnson made news—and gallantly created headlines for candidate Margaret Chase Smith—by advising the Republicans to nominate a woman, because he believed "there are women today with the capacity to be President."

On July 2, 1964, the Civil Rights Act of 1964—Title VII, sex amendment and all—became law. Little was heard about Title VII until July 2, 1965, the date it went into force. On that day the Equal Employment Opportunity Commission, set up under the Act, opened shop in Washington under the chairmanship of Franklin D. Roosevelt, Jr. Under the law, the Equal Employment Opportunity Commission is charged with investigating complaints of discrimination and seeking to conciliate them. The Commission may ask the Attorney General of the United States to sue on the victim's behalf, but it has no power to order discrimination stopped.

"This woman business" embarrassed all hands at EEOC, as the Commission came to be known. Negroes feared that complaints of sex discrimination would take up all the time of the small EEOC staff so that it would not be able to get on with the job of investigating discrimination on the basis of race. The Commission's Executive Director, Herman Edelsberg, did not seem to be enthusiastic about equal rights for women. He told reporters at his first press conference that he and the other men at EEOC thought men were "entitled" to have female secretaries. Mr. Roosevelt was more genteel. He merely murmured that the whole sex question was "terribly complicated."

Discrimination against women was, as one EEOC member put it, "an uncharted sea." It was easy to ignore. Complaints from women were turned over to Mrs. Alfred W. Blumrosen, the lawyer wife of a member of the staff hired temporarily to deal with complaints from women. She told *The New York*

Times that there had been a burst of complaints from factory workers who claimed they had been laid off before men, but none from women who had been denied executive jobs. She hadn't realized, either, she said, that some employers still refused to hire married women.

In August 1965, members of EEOC attending a White House Conference on Equal Opportunity continued to treat the sex amendment as a joke. It was unclear, someone quipped, whether the law would require Playboy Clubs to hire male "bunnies." The press took it up, but far-fetched as the complaint was, the law provided a remedy. A provision exempting jobs for which sex is a bona-fide qualification permitted employers to specify sex where "authenticity" of one sex or the other is required, as in the case of actors and actresses and models.

In November 1965, EEOC issued guidelines for employers which took a narrow view of "bona-fide sex qualifications." An employer could not prefer a candidate of one sex or another to please customers, co-workers, or clients, or on the basis of generalizations about the ability of women in general or men in general. Women couldn't be preferred, for instance, because they were supposedly good at "detail," or denied because they were supposedly incapable of aggressive salesmanship. Separate seniority lists were barred; factories had to lay off men and women strictly on the basis of their length of service. Company policies forbidding the employment of married women would be permissible, the guidelines said, only if they forbid the employment of married men, too.

These important changes were generally unnoticed. Newspapers seldom reported them, and women tended to ignore the whole issue. The smirking nickname "bunny law" remained, suggesting that the law was not serious and would embarrass any women who invoked it. To the outrage of Martha Griffiths, EEOC Director Edelsberg publicly labeled the sex provision a "fluke . . . conceived out of wedlock."

In the same vein *The New York Times* headed its report of the August 1965 White House Conference: "For Instance, Can She Pitch for the Mets?" and went on to quote Richard K. Berg, EEOC's "Deputy Counsel on Bunnies," on the problem of whether sex was a bona-fide qualification for a job where a pretty girl is used to attract customers. "Better if Congress had just abolished sex itself," a *Times* editorial said.

"A maid can now be a man. Girl Friday is an intolerable offense. The classic beginning of many wondrous careers in the Horatio Alger fashion—Boy Wanted—has reached its last chapter."

Newspapers elsewhere joined in the fun, and not all of the fun was innocent. Some publishers opposed any attempt to banish the traditional division of "Help Wanted" advertisements into "Help Wanted Male" and "Help Wanted Female." They claimed that removing the sex labels from help-wanted columns would discourage job seekers from applying. The Commission listened and the August 1965 ruling of the Commission forbidding racial segregation in help-wanted advertisements said nothing about sex. The Toledo *Blade* and the Toledo *Times,* of Ohio, however, stopped printing job ads for men and women in separate columns before Title VII went into effect, and the Phoenix, Arizona, *Gazette* and the *Honolulu Star-Bulletin* integrated their help-wanted ads when state fair employment laws first outlawed sex discrimination. Other papers, including *The New York Times,* protected themselves by printing disclaimers in the smallest possible type. These state that "Help Wanted" and "Situation Wanted" advertisements are arranged in columns captioned "Male" and "Female" for the "convenience of readers and are not intended as an unlawful limitation or discrimination based on sex."

In April 1966, EEOC advised that the Commission would judge only the advertising of the employer and not headings selected by publishers. "We didn't feel in a position to try to make newspapers comply with this kind of request," a Commission spokesman said, "so we just gave up." The Commission reported that papers which had listed jobs for men and women together complained that replies to the want ads declined. Mrs. Griffiths challenged this contention.

"It is the Congress, not the classified ad managers of the newspapers, that writes our nation's laws," she insisted.

"Column headings do not prevent persons of either sex from scanning the area of the jobs available page," Luther Holcomb, acting chairman of EEOC, pointed out in the course of a warm exchange of letters with Mrs. Griffiths.

"My answer is: I have never entered a door labeled 'men,' and I doubt that Mr. Holcomb has frequently entered the women's room," Mrs. Griffiths retorted.

In her speech to the House of June 20, 1966, she charged that women were being deprived of their legal rights by the EEOC, which was charged with protecting them. She maintained that listings by sex discourage applicants of the other sex in exactly the same way that listings by race discourage applicants of the other race. "Help Wanted White" and "Help Wanted Negro" ads were outlawed by EEOC with little fuss because few papers used this form.

The battle for taking the words "male" and "female" out of help-wanted listings raged well into 1967. In May of that year, for instance, Will Muller of *The Detroit News* wrote a humorous column headed "Martha Griffiths Is Reading Wrong Ads." According to him she should have been scanning the display advertisements depicting the luxurious life of American women. In July, Muller continued the vendetta with an article headed "Sex Discrimination Protest Bears Fruit—in Kremlin." This one argued that Mrs. Griffiths was giving comfort to the enemy by the complaints.

But from the very beginning, the women who had kept the sex amendment in Title VII through the Congressional debate fought for serious press attention to the law. On September 3, 1965, *The New York Times* printed a letter from Esther Peterson, Assistant Secretary of Labor, listing the many serious issues discussed at the August White House Conference. "*The Times* saw only the 'funny bunny,'" she concluded. "Fearing neuterization is an old and illogical defense against seeing the discrimination that really exists." A few weeks later, Pauli Murray won more newspaper attention by charging that women were kept down by the same techniques used against Negroes. "If it becomes necessary to march on Washington to assure equal job opportunity for all, I hope women will not flinch from the thought."

Most people did not share her sense of grievance. Hadn't women supposedly overcome all the barriers once raised against them?

2

UP FROM SLAVERY

"I'm a *person,* not just a wife and mother."

Although few people are aware of it, this common complaint actually has a legal origin. Until fairly recently, the law treated a corporation as a person but did not recognize a woman except in specified circumstances.

When the grandmothers of middle-aged American women were married, they ceased to exist in the eyes of the law and became, in the memorable phrase of Blackstone's *Commentaries,* "incorporated and consolidated" with their husbands. Legally speaking, they died on their wedding day. "A man cannot grant anything to his wife," decreed Blackstone, "for the grant would be to suppose her separate existence."

Under the common-law doctrine of *"femme couverte,"* a married woman was "covered" or veiled by the name and authority of her husband. She could not own property in her own right or sign a contract. She could not sue or testify against her husband any more than she could sue or be made to testify against herself. He had a right to her property, earned or inherited. He supposedly "represented" her at the polls, and he could even be made responsible for criminal acts committed by her in his presence.

Under the common law, a husband came close to owning the body of his wife. He had the right to "restrain her, by domestic chastisement." If she left him, she lost all right to her children. He could—and sometimes still can—legally require her to submit to sexual relations against her will and reside at a place of his choosing.

Marriage traditionally was such a cut-and-dried exchange of domestic service and sexual availability for financial support that in nineteenth-century England some men sold their wives for these services, just as if they were indentured servants. In Smithfield, England, there actually was a market for women. *The Times* of London reported in 1797 that women were selling there for three and a half guineas. Women were not, of course, as helpless as slaves but they had no voice in the government. Local authorities sometimes didn't even bother to record female births and deaths.

In the colonies women enjoyed a scarcity value. The children they bore were badly needed, and labor was so short that they worked alongside the men, even shooting down Indians. If there was a schoolmaster, there were so few pupils that he could teach the girls along with the boys. In any case, most education was given at home, where girls were exposed to it.

In colonial America women became butchers, silversmiths, gunsmiths, upholsterers, jailkeepers, printers, apothecaries, and doctors (or "doctoresses," as they were then called). Women helped their men, and when they became widows, which happened frequently, they had no choice but to go on running the farm, store, mill, newspaper, shipyard, and even the ship. Nantucket Quaker wives managed substantial enterprises for years while their husbands went on whaling trips. Colonial and frontier courts, recognizing these realities, stretched the common law to protect widows and single women.

Conditions favoring women's independence moved west with the frontier. Western states led the East in letting women vote and hold office, and women have always had an easier time getting elected in the West than in the East. Female suffrage began quietly in 1838, when widows rearing children in the backwoods of Kentucky were allowed to vote in school elections. In 1869 they began voting on an equal basis with men in the Territory of Wyoming. Except for Sweden, which gave women local suffrage in 1869, too, the only places in the world where women could vote in regular elections in the nineteenth century were the frontier American states of Wyoming, Colorado, Utah, and Idaho, and similar frontier communities in Australia and New Zealand.

But even in the wilderness, American women had more power in practice than in principle. Although the masculinist theory that women derive their identity and status from men was challenged by feminist demands that women be treated as persons "in their own right," the old attitudes were hard to change. As new ways of making a living shifted the division of labor between the sexes, new arguments were developed to keep women in their old roles. Generally speaking, frontier conditions—wars, revolutions, and feverish boom times which provide urgent work for all hands—have motivated men and women to similar or androgynous goals. By contrast, periods of slow or orderly economic growth such as the first and fifth decades of this century have cultivated masculinity or femininity as goals in themselves. In these periods, men are encouraged to submit to industrial discipline in order to make money as the primary way to prove their "manliness," while women are encouraged to stay at home and be "feminine."

Androgynous periods are often marked by feminist movements which assert the right of women to independent action. Male-dominated or masculinist periods, on the other hand, encourage women to define themselves in terms of their relationship to men. The two philosophies have alternated just frequently enough to keep every generation of American women from using their mothers as models.

The Industrial Revolution emphasized the difference between men and women. The new machinery reserved some jobs for men and others for women, and it set up a "capitalist" class and a "labor" class and made it profitable to exploit poor women by employing them in factories to do the kind of chores they had always done at home, while freeing rich women from making clothes, growing food, and the other household tasks that had made them equal partners with their husbands.

In some ways, the Industrial Revolution can be said to have created the feminine mystique. It began by commercializing the spinning and weaving of cloth that women had always done for their own families. The first textile entrepreneurs hired women to spin and weave in their own homes at piece rates, but in the early nineteenth century, power equipment took the work to mills where it could be done with fewer hands. Women followed the work out of their homes, and they worked for less than men because there was less work open to them.

The consequences of their move out of the home were far-reaching. When women worked at home, even at piece rates, their subordinate role was dictated by family convenience. Men and women could help each other, if need be. But in the impersonal mill, where tasks carried wage rates, it was profitable for the owner to hire women over men, since he could pay them less. Yankee invention was stimulated to invent machines which allowed women to handle masculine jobs at a lower cost.

Tasks changed sex. By the mid-nineteeth century, Canadian and Irish immigrants were beginning to replace native white women in the New England mills, but factory operations were still minutely divided into "men's jobs" and "women's jobs," and there was considerable resistance to any attempt to get men and women to perform the same job in each other's presence. Barnard Professor Elizabeth Baker provides an excellent example with her detailed breakdown of the way men's socks were made toward the end of the nineteenth century: women turned down the tops of the hose and hemmed them; men dyed and pressed them; women next paired, stamped, stacked, and boxed them; men packed the boxes and prepared them for shipping.

Skill, strength, and particularly prestige determined whether a job was to be done by a man or a woman. The nature of the product did not matter so much. When butter was made by hand, women made butter; when mechanical churns were developed, butter-making became man's work. When the invention of canning made food preservation a paying business, men took it over, and although canning factories employ women, they are run by men. Like the Indian tribes which exclude women from sacred "secrets," our own culture has kept women from understanding sophisticated machinery and the tricks of a trade that businessmen like to call "unpatentable knowhow."

An early and striking illustration involves the most feminine of all functions, childbirth. When babies were born at home and without instruments, midwiving was a woman's job. In 1646 a man was actually prosecuted in Maine for practicing as a midwife. Male interference was regarded as indecent and the first male midwives were ridiculed as effeminate.

Then in sixteenth-century England, the Chamberlain family invented a mysterious device which miraculously rescued women in difficult labor. For three generations, the Chamberlains were called in, often when hope seemed gone, to practice their magic. The birth room was cleared so that no one could see exactly what Dr. Chamberlain did, but anxious families had reported hearing the clink of something metallic concealed under the doctor's frock coat as he passed. It was, of course, the obstetrical forceps.

The secret was too important to keep, and in the seventeenth century Hugh Chamberlain sold it to the Medical College of Amsterdam. Only men were admitted to medical school, so the forceps, as well as the developing body of scientific medical knowledge, was confined to male physicians. Royalty and discriminating families recognized the value of this training and led the way in demanding licensed physicians. By the end of the nineteenth century, only poor and rural babies were delivered by midwives, and even now when women are licensed to practice medicine they have not been especially attracted to obstetrics. The male domination of obstetrics remains.

By 1830, it was not as easy as it had been in colonial times for women to become doctors, lawyers, storekeepers, innkeepers, or women of affairs. Young people were now educated outside the home in formal schools and impersonal places of business from which women were excluded as a matter of course. Like the new wage workers, the new capitalists went out to work, but they left their wives behind them. The Industrial Revolution which created the working woman also created her more influential mirror image, the lady of leisure.

The role was embarrassing in an egalitarian, work-oriented society. The millowner's wife couldn't help her husband or even understand what he was doing in the shop or mill. She was not allowed to get the education that would have fitted her for a satisfying profession, and she did not need money badly enough to work at anything else. In fact, she had so much money that in the eastern cities where there were so many immigrant girls looking for domestic work, it would have been downright unfair for her to do her own housework and deprive them of jobs.

The Victorian ideal of a lady was a masculine concept in

the sense that it highlighted those female characteristics designed to attract and flatter a husband of "substance" or capital. Girls whose mothers had chopped wood and hauled water in the wilderness now swooned to advertise their appealing frailty and need for protection. A proper, genteel, and conspicuously idle wife was herself a consumer good, the crowning ornament of the impressive town houses and ornate furniture built by men born in log cabins.

The role of "lady" quickly became the model for all women, and in egalitarian America every girl could hope marriage would bring her this status. Only those few who lived the ideal could see that the home in which they were enthroned was no longer the center of all activity, but a monument to the success of a husband or father who lived his real life outside. Most Victorian ladies happily spent their new leisure on competitive display, but a few looked longingly at the great world outside their gilded cages.

Sarah Hale, editor of *Godey's Lady's Book*, the pioneer woman's magazine, understood these exceptions well. Although she persuaded Matthew Vassar to drop the adjective "Female" from the name of the college he was founding ("What female do you mean?" she wrote him tartly. "Not a female donkey?"), she did not advocate androgyny. Women were different but equal, she preached, and femininity could be used for more than catching a husband. She urged women to undertake the work men were neglecting in their eagerness to make money. In 1852 she wrote:

Women are the teachers—they should be qualified for this great department . . . in a tenfold proportion to men.

Women are the preservers—they should be instructed in medical science.

Women are the helpers—they should be intrusted with the management of charities. . . . They might manage savings banks and they would do this to better advantage for the poor depositors than is now in fashion.

To these ends, women needed a better education than was offered by the 200 finishing schools founded between 1820 and the Civil War. Pioneer feminists, like Elizabeth Blackwell, the first woman medical school graduate, pushed their way into colleges, but higher coeducation was generally opposed, even though girls were being admitted to the public high schools springing up to prepare boys for college.

Opponents argued that women were mentally weaker than men: the Bible said so, and anthropologists had reported that the brain cases of women were smaller. It was feared that higher studies would endanger women's health and injure their delicate childbearing apparatus. The presence of women in classrooms would not only lower academic standards, but would also distract men in class. Most important, women would lose the "femininity" a girl needed to attract a husband. When the first coeds were admitted to Oberlin College in 1837, they were given a watered-down literary course and expected to serve the men students at table and remain silent in mixed classes. A segregated literature arose for literate but uneducated "ladies." "Women's fiction" became an industry, and 64 magazines for women were launched between 1830 and 1860.

Protected from the rigors of study, business, and politics, the more serious new ladies saw the defects of the society their menfolk were creating. From the sanctuary of a privileged position, they protested against slavery, drink, corruption, and the prevailing barbarous treatment of the poor, the sick, and the insane. Men who treated women as their mental and physical inferiors were quite willing to regard them as moral superiors, and women reformers put this new formulation of masculinism to good social use.

But if some women used their cages as fortresses from which to reform society, there were women less cunning and more angry who forthrightly rattled the bars and demanded out.

In 1848 at Seneca Falls, N.Y., Elizabeth Cady Stanton, the plump daughter of a judge, stood up in public for the first time in her life and persuaded a churchful of people to endorse a "Declaration of Principles." The language was familiar:

> We hold these truths to be self-evident; that all men and women are created equal; that they are endowed by their Creator with certain inalienable rights; that among these are life, liberty and the pursuit of happiness.

The parallel with the Declaration of Independence continued:

> The history of mankind is a history of repeated injuries and usurpations on the part of man toward woman, having in direct object the establishment of an absolute tyranny over her. To prove this, let facts be submitted to a candid world.

It was the first public demand for woman suffrage in America, but Mrs. Stanton's primary goal was to secure for women the right to own and control their property and earnings, serve as guardians of their children, get a divorce, sue and bear witness in court, go to college, and earn a living. Mrs. Stanton was especially outraged at the Biblical assumption of female inferiority.

The Seneca Falls Convention of 1848 is considered the beginning of the Suffragette movement in America. As a world movement, feminism is usually dated from 1792, when Mary Wollstonecraft followed her *Vindication of the Rights of Man,* a tract written under the inspiration of the French Revolution, with a companion piece entitled *A Vindication of the Rights of Woman.* Mrs. Wollstonecraft attacked the notion that women existed only to please men and asserted that they, like men, must "bow to the authority of reason, instead of being the *modest* slaves of opinion."

In America, as early as the Revolution some women were so carried away by the injustice of taxation without representation that they thought the new Constitution should logically ensure equal rights for women.

"Do not put such unlimited power into the hands of the husbands," Abigail Adams wrote her husband John, the future second President of the United States. "Remember, all men would be tyrants if they could. If particular care is not paid to the ladies, we are determined to foment a rebellion, and will not hold ourselves bound by any laws in which we have no voice or representation."

Tom Paine, champion of all aspects of liberty, pursued the comparison in dead earnest. "Robbed of freedom and will by the laws, surrounded by judges who are at once tyrants and their seducers," he thundered, "who does not feel for the tender sex?"

Ten years later, during the French Revolution, *Citoyennes*

manned the barricades and stormed the Bastille, but failed to get the vote. Edith Thomas, a French historian active in the underground during World War II, investigated the French revolutionary movements of 1848 and 1871 and discovered that women who had fought alongside men had not been given the equal political status their service deserved.

In fact, during most revolutions and guerrilla wars, women have fought, agitated, done the same kind of work, and worn the same kind of clothes as men. Women have served in the armed forces during the Russian, Chinese, Spanish, Cuban, Algerian, Israeli, and Vietnamese revolutions. Following the Israeli victory over the Arabs in 1967, Syria organized uniformed women's units for guerrilla service against Israel, to prove that "Israeli women are no better than Arab women." In this century, women have won the right to vote following revolution or independence in Algeria, Byelorussia, Cambodia, China, Germany, India, Ireland, Israel, Laos, Malaya, Poland, Uganda, Ukraine, U.S.S.R., and Vietnam.

In America the pioneer feminists cast men in the role of oppressors. Although Mrs. Stanton married and bore seven children, her colleague, Susan B. Anthony, remained single. Before birth control, it was the only way a woman could control her own fate. Although the early feminists did not necessarily want to change their sex, they envied men their freedom. Before the Civil War, some of them tried wearing loose, Turkish-style pantaloons or bloomers, named for Amelia Bloomer, a feminist who wore them all the time.

Queen Victoria thought the feminists were wicked. She appealed to women of good will "to join in checking this mad, wicked folly of Women's Rights, with all its attendant horrors, on which my poor feeble sex is bent, forgetting every sense of womanly feeling and propriety."

In general, feminists remained a small minority. In 1854 most women simply said, "Thank God I have a husband to look after me," when they were asked to sign Susan B. Anthony's petition to the New York State legislature. This petition asked the state to give women the vote, custody of children in divorce, and control over their own earnings, then a burning issue for women married to alcoholics. When Miss Anthony presented her petition with 6,000 signatures, the Judiciary Committee reported to the New York State Assembly that it had canvassed the married men on the committee and determined that "ladies always have the best seat in the cars, carriages, and sleighs . . . their choice on which side of the bed they will lie, front or back." The report suggested that married couples who had signed the petition together be permitted to exchange clothing.

One of the commonest arguments against women's rights was that women were so weak that they needed special protection. A stock joke was the possibility of a woman doctor, lawyer, or voter being seized with labor pains in public. The overprotected lady feminists were unable to combat this kind of heckling, but on at least one occasion their tormentors were dramatically silenced. In 1851, a remarkable Negro freedwoman by the name of Sojourner Truth intervened at a woman's rights convention in Akron, Ohio.

"The man over there says women need to be helped into carriages and lifted over ditches," she began slowly. "Nobody ever helps me into carriages or over puddles, or gives me the best place—and ain't I a woman?" Raising a great black arm, Sojourner Truth went on:

> Look at my arm! I have ploughed and planted and gathered into barns, and no man could head me—and ain't I a woman? I could work as much and eat as much as a man—when I could get it—and bear the lash as well! And ain't I a woman? I have borne thirteen children, and seen most of 'em sold into slavery, and when I cried out with my mother's grief none but Jesus heard me—and ain't I a woman?

Most of the pre-Civil War feminists were also Abolitionists, and when they thought they needed the help of a man they sometimes enlisted a Negro freedman. They spoke of marriage as a form of slavery. Anti-Abolitionists reversed the analogy, pointing out that everyone didn't have to vote: if women didn't need a voice in Government, Negroes didn't, either.

But Abolition attracted many more women than Feminism. Most women Abolitionists championed Negroes in the same womanly spirit that they cared for the sick and the helpless. No less a figure than the New England poet, John Greenleaf Whittier, urged the militant Southern feminists, Sarah and Angelina Grimke, to drop women's rights for fear it would undermine their crusade against slavery. The Grimke sisters refused. "What then can woman do for the slave," remonstrated Angelina Grimke, "when she herself is under the feet of man and shamed into silence?"

But other feminists were willing to shelve their cause all through the Civil War. Then at its end, their Abolitionist friends betrayed them. As finally adopted, the Fourteenth Amendment deliberately excluded female suffrage by guaranteeing the vote to "male" citizens, introducing the word "male" into the Constitution for the first time. "This is the Negro's Hour," a politician explained. "Do not embarrass the Republican Party with any new issue."

But postwar conservatism could not erase the gains the Civil War itself brought women. Four hundred had fought as uniformed soldiers of the Union Army, and Dr. Mary Walker, a woman physician, who wore a man's swallow-tail coat, had won the Congressional Medal of Honor. Women had provided food and clothing for the soldiers on a mass basis. They had kept farms and business organizations going while the men were away. They had flocked into Government service and into factories. Storekeepers found that women sales clerks were not only cheaper than men, but easier to control and more courteous to customers.

The most propitious gains were in the professions. The Civil War made nursing an educated, respectable occupation rather than an unskilled domestic service. Before the Civil War, men teachers outnumbered women. After the war, women predominated, and thanks to the dual pay scale, they quickly increased their hold on the school system.

The feminization of teaching had far-reaching consequences. Women were so cheap to hire that public education in the United States quickly became universal. And since girls could get work as teachers, they had more incentive to stay in school than boys, who tended to drift away to physical work. More girls than boys have been graduated from high school every year since the Civil War. The unheralded result has been that some American women have always had to marry men with less formal schooling than themselves. This education gap set up hostility on both sides, and it may be the reason why American women seem bossier and more demanding of their men than women in countries where men are generally better schooled than their wives.

None of this, of course, was intended, but the demand for education feeds on itself. Girls educated in college-oriented high schools wanted to go to college themselves. A few decades after the Civil War, the major Ivy League women's colleges were founded by men and women who believed that women would be so intimidated by the presence of men that they could only get an education if they had their own schools.

The industrial expansion following the Civil War opened up new kinds of work which had not been preempted by men. Although the first telephone operators in the 1880s were boys, they did not do well and were soon replaced by girls. Confined, disciplined, personal services did not attract American men long used to outdoor work.

The invention of the typewriter in 1867 favored women in much the same way. The old system of handwritten accounts could not handle the rising volume of office work, but male clerks were more interested in moving up and out of clerical work than in doing it better. Then in 1881, the Central YWCA in New York City offered women a course in typing. As a promotion device, the Remington Company stationed some of the prettier graduates in hotel lobbies. Visiting businessmen were enchanted with the first public stenographers. They bought the newfangled machines and hired the "typewriters," as the girls who demonstrated them were called. The new vocation enchanted girl high-school graduates, too. It offered them a respectable, light, clean way to earn money and to meet prospective husbands. "Business schools" for girls sprang up all over the country.

When labor unions were first organized, they didn't know whether to exclude women from desirable jobs, insist that they be paid less, or eliminate wage competition between the sexes by insisting on equal pay. In some trades, like printing, all three tactics were tried at various times during the nineteenth century. Although the American Federation of Labor passed general resolutions favoring equal pay for women beginning with its convention of 1898, American craft unions downgraded women in the same way they opposed labor-saving machinery. European immigrants succeeded in organizing women needle-trades workers in part because their socialist tradition had asserted equal rights for women. To this day, women commonly take tickets on European railroads unionized by socialists, but they are conspicuously absent from American railroads organized by the craft brotherhoods.

Native "bread and butter" craft unions promoted the notion that women were too weak and incompetent to do all but the most undesirable work. This was just as well, one antifeminist declared in the 1890s, because "no working girl does or can, or ought to enter any field of occupation on the same level as a working-man, . . . a permanent worker from the very beginning."

This prejudice allowed employers in 1890 to pay women about half the wages of men doing the same work and to require women to end the working day by getting down on their hands and knees and scrubbing the factory floor while the men went home. It did not, however, prevent the employment of women in foundries so hot that they ended by stripping to the waist, side by side with the half-naked men. Women social workers, graduated from the new woman's colleges, were appalled by such sights. Since they often knew more about the human cost of working conditions than their employer husbands, and since the "lady" tradition allowed them to protest the exploitation of the weak, they were able to crusade effectively.

Working with labor reformers and unions, upper-class women secured passage of state laws improving women's working conditions and restricting their hours. As the early reformers hoped, the conditions prescribed by these laws were gradually extended to all workers.

Unfortunately, the argument many reformers used emphasized the idea that women were weak. In *Muller v. Oregon,* the Supreme Court declared that "women are fundamentally weaker than men in all that makes for endurance; in muscular strength, in nervous energy, in the power of persistent application and attention."

By 1890, the suffragette movement was well organized, well heeled, and politically sophisticated. A new generation of women argued that women should vote not because they deserved equal rights but because they were morally better than men and would reform society. The suffragettes had learned to play politics. They enlisted conservatives on the ground that since middle- and upper-class women outnumbered the new immigrants and Negroes, they would keep

Government in the "right" hands. They enlisted liberals on the ground that women would vote for Prohibition and other humanitarian causes.

By this time the opposition to the movement was organized, too, largely with money supplied by the brewers, who shrewdly foresaw that women would vote for Prohibition. They said that women didn't have the wit to judge public affairs, shouldn't be burdened with the responsibility, and anyway, ought to stay at home. Women didn't want the vote. They didn't need it because they were represented by their menfolk. If they voted with their husbands, their vote was not needed; if they voted against their husbands, they would be disrupting family unity; and if they didn't have menfolk, they were just out of luck. But the argument which kept most women silent was the inference, usually conveyed by ridicule, that a suffragette was unable to attract a man.

Carrie Chapman Catt was interested in rousing the majority of women from their apathy. Under her leadership the National American Woman Suffrage Association enlisted millions of members. Her state-by-state "winning plan" was finally able to secure the vote for women before women had any votes of their own to lay on the line.

But like the Negroes in the 1960s, the suffragettes could not win power without defying the laws of the Establishment which excluded them. In the closing days of World War I, the Congressional Union for Woman Suffrage, a militant group that shocked most women, picketed the White House with signs protesting that "Democracy Should Begin at Home." Jittery authorities claimed the women were unpatriotic, jailed them, and when they refused to eat, force-fed them. But they made their point. In the hot summer of 1919, the woman suffrage amendment was ratified by the last state, Tennessee.

The end was dramatic. The suffragettes believed they had enough votes to carry the Tennessee legislature, but when the amendment came up for action, railroad, liquor, and business interests plied the legislators with so much liquor that a number of members wavered and reduced the women's margin to a tie. After several wild scenes, the tie was broken by a man who confessed that he was changing his vote because his mother wished him to support ratification.

In the postwar years, other countries all over the world

were recognizing the fact that women had performed traditionally masculine tasks during the war years, and performed them well. Austria, Belgium, Canada, Czechoslovakia, the Federal Republic of Germany, Hungary, Luxembourg, the Netherlands, Poland, Sweden, and the United Kingdom all gave or widened woman suffrage. In addition, of course, the Soviet governments enfranchised women as part of their Marxist program. French and Japanese women didn't get the vote until World War II overturned their governments.

The wartime service of American women was prodigious. More than a fifth of all American women over ten years old were working in 1910, and there were at least some women working in all but a handful of the hundreds of occupations recognized by the Census. When war broke out, women were flatly told that their place was in the munitions factories, and they went where they were told to go. General "Black Jack" Pershing, no feminist, called for women telephone operators to run the exchange for the American Expeditionary Force in France, and women who were not nurses joined the uniformed army. There was so big a demand for women war workers that the Ordnance Department set up a Women's Division. In 1918 the National War Labor Board directed Government contractors to pay women men's wages when they did men's work. The next year Michigan and Montana passed equal pay laws supposedly applying to all employment, and in 1920 Congress created the present Women's Bureau of the Department of Labor. Asked to set working standards for women, the Bureau advocated regulating working conditions rather than the sex of the worker. Finally in 1923, the Civil Service Reclassification Act barred discrimination on the basis of sex from Government service.

After the war, employers avoided equal pay laws by simply refusing to give women men's jobs, but they could no longer say that women belonged at home because of weaknesses and incompetence. In 1919, only one of thirty-five industrial plants queried by the New York State Labor Department admitted that it was firing women who had replaced men during the war because they were slow to pick up mechanical knowledge, and the foreman of that plant ascribed the difficulty he had with women to their lack of training rather than their lack of innate mechanical ability.

The war, the vote, and the heady "New Freedom" of the

jazz age ushered in an age of achievement for educated women. They founded banks and businesses. They flocked to colleges and invaded professional and graduate schools. They went into politics and became full professors at universities. Women's fashions became more masculine. Gone were the corsets and trailing skirts and time-consuming frills that had formerly hobbled women in the name of femininity. Flappers bobbed their hair and ran around in handy, flat-chested sacks that would have delighted Lucy Bloomer. And for a few there was the thrilling notion that sex could be for pleasure and even "free" of marriage.

Single girls got jobs right after high school as a matter of course. There was more paperwork than ever, and big organizations like the life insurance companies hired girls as young as possible so that they would not leave to get married right after they were trained. Business also depended on them, not only as cheap, dispensable employees, but as a market for products they would not be able to afford if they stayed at home, such as silk stockings, ready-to-wear fashions, cosmetics, and women's magazines.

Before World War I, immigrants from Europe and from the farms, and teen-age boys, had provided the cheap, dispensable labor factories needed; after the war, Negroes migrating from the South supplied the factories; and girls waiting to marry were available, cheap, to do the rising office work.

The Depression kept the relatively low-paid single woman working longer, and because her work was more apt to be in an office, she often held her job after the mill laid off her boy-friend. Equal-pay laws were simply ignored, and dual-pay scales were posted at the factory gates.

One of the achievements of the new Women's Bureau was to get equal pay for men and women written into most of the National Recovery Administration industry codes set up during the black year 1933. The precedent secured the same minimum wages and maximum hours for men and women in the Walsh-Healy Act of 1936, setting standards for employees on Government contracts, and later in the Fair Labor Standards Act of 1938. But the laws were not enforced. And many organizations forced women to quit when they married, on the theory that they didn't need to work. Most people felt that a woman worker was taking a job away from a man.

Women tried so hard not to compete with men in that

period that there is even a case on record of a single girl giving up her job to her father. Femininity was in fashion. Bosoms and waists reappeared, and partly to stimulate the textile industry, skirts dropped below the knee. Equality was no longer the ideal it had been back when the flippant flappers proclaimed their emancipation. However, women were less tied to the home. Newly married couples adopted birth control to postpone babies and learned to be companions instead of complementing each other's differences as parents.

"Career women" dotted the landscape during the New Deal. Women social workers and journalists shared President Roosevelt's humanitarian concerns. But career women like Secretary of Labor Frances Perkins were conscious of choosing a public life at the expense of a private life, and unlike "Madam Perkins," few were married.

As long as marriage and employment were considered incompatible, there was a natural limit to the proportion of women who could be expected to work. In 1920, 20 percent of the adult female population worked. In 1940 the figure had only risen to 25 percent.

Then came World War II. The U.S. Department of Labor looked back to World War I and reported that "it can hardly be said that *any* occupation is absolutely unsuitable for the employment of women." Women became crane operators, riveters, tractor operators, truck drivers. When all the single girls were hired, employers hired married women and even mothers. Women were welcomed in law schools and medical schools, in the professions, and in the armed forces.

Girls who started working during World War II never learned that some jobs supposedly "belong" to men and some to women. So many women were doing the work of men that equal-pay laws and policies again became applicable. The shortage of candidates narrowed the differentials between the pay of men and women in practice, and as in World War I, the equal-pay principle was written into defense contracts. This time, the War Labor Board tried to enforce the rule. When the telephone company argued that women operators didn't need as much money as men because "most of these girls lived at home where they got their room and board," Senator Wayne Morse said he saw no reason why girls should subsidize the cost of service to subscribers by taking lower pay. Another employer tried to argue that women workers should be paid less because their facilities cost more. The "facilities" turned out, on inspection, to be a hot plate, a cot, some old rocking chairs, and a mirror in the women's toilet.

Government studies of defense contracts established that women workers were often a bargain even when paid the same rates as men. To the surprise of some old soldiers, including General Eisenhower, the Army found that one woman in uniform frequently replaced two draftees assigned to clerical work. Service studies showed, too, that women soldiers cost less to keep. Their clothes cost more than men's, but the women had fewer dependents and were easier on the furniture.

Rosie the Riveter was married, and increasingly she was a mother, too. But whether her menfolk were at war or simply working overtime, Rosie's daily life was much more like a man's than it had been in peacetime. Feminine fashions became an unimportant part of most women's lives, because of wartime fabric restrictions, the absence of men for whom to dress, and all the masculine chores that women left alone had to do. Women could wear pants in public without apology. Many were, of course, heartily sick of it. They were working for money to buy a house and waiting for the end of the war to marry and have babies. At the beginning of the war, 95 percent of women war workers said they would quit when victory was won. Victory came in 1945, and 300,000 women war workers were fired.

To everyone's dismay, they didn't like it. You would never have learned as much from the newspapers. The patriotic reporters who had lured Rosie into riveting for victory now pictured her yearning for a cozy cottage, a kitchen apron, and a baby. The picture was not wrong but late. As victory approached, more of the women found reasons why they should keep on working. At war's end, two out of three women war workers queried by Elmo Roper wanted permanent jobs.

Led by liberal Congresswoman Helen Gahagan Douglas, feminists made a gallant fight to get a Federal Equal Pay Act in 1945 and again in 1948. Unions and employers opposed the law as an unworkable invasion of free enterprise which might bring on a postwar depression. Mrs. Douglas argued that equal pay would protect men's wages. She reported that men had struck a propeller plant in Lansing, Michigan, which had tried to fire men and keep women paid ten cents an hour less.

Women *should* get less, one employer testified, because of "the additional facilities and expense required, greatly increased absenteeism, larger turnover, and other sociological factors."

The "sociological factors" turned out to be the likelihood that a woman would quit to marry and raise a family. Congressmen drew on their own experience with women secretaries. Girls did leave, they admitted, but they weren't sure that a man wouldn't leave for a better job just as quickly. Was it fair to discount the pay of a worker because he or she might not stay? And if so, how much was permanency worth?

"What do you think?" a member of the Committee asked Elizabeth Christman, an English-born glove-maker testifying for the National Women's Trade Union League. "Do you think permanency is of any value in some industries?"

"Oh, sir," the factory girl replied, "I think permanency would be wonderful. Where is it?" Miss Christman reminded the gentlemen of the Committee that there was another world, a blue-collar world, in which the impermanence which supposedly made women workers worth less than men was initiated by employers for their own convenience.

Congress was in no mood for reforms. The Women's Bureau, official spokesman for working women, barely saved its budget from a postwar Congressional economy drive. The WASPs (Women's Airforce Service Pilots) were permanently grounded. And although military manpower planners figured that in a pinch women could have replaced nearly half the men in the armed forces, in 1948 Congress arbitrarily limited women to 2 percent of uniformed military personnel.

Everyone wanted to get back to "normal" life. Men took back their jobs in oil refineries, metalworking shops, and railroads. Boys replaced the girls who had worked as pages on the floor of the New York Stock Exchange. Women were told to go home, whether they wanted to or not. They went.

The 1950s saw an unprecedented return to family life. Never had husband, home, and children been more sentimentalized. Never had so many girls married so young. Not for fifty years had American women been so fertile. Never had so many women defined themselves so exclusively as "mother."

Never, said the press, had women been so well off. Never, they were constantly told, had they been so happy. Businessmen delighted in pointing out how women "owned the country"—without working for it, just by being women. Magazines kept printing figures proving it didn't pay a wife to work. Aggressive women were losers, they said, because the only right that mattered was the right to be loved.

Women had not, as promised, purified politics after winning the vote, but they had made a start in public life. After World War II, this progress stopped. In 1968, Margaret Chase Smith was the only woman in the United States Senate, and there weren't enough women Representatives to justify putting a ladies' locker room in the House gym. "There are more whooping cranes in all North America than lady legislators," mourned Illinois Republican Charlotte Reid in May 1967. Women did not even go into local government, where their community service made them natural public administrators. Lady mayors, even of small cities, remained rare enough to be worth featuring as oddities in newspapers.

Instead of preparing themselves for professional careers after World War II, girls were marrying young and working at any job that would bring in money. In 1950 a record 11 percent of the students graduated from medical school were women, but by 1960 this figure dropped to 7 percent. The same thing happened in other professions, with the result that women lost ground or barely held their own in law, pharmacy, science, engineering, and journalism.

Men edged out women at the top levels on editorial staffs of women's magazines and faculties of women's colleges. Men entered hospital administration, nursing, and even nursery-school teaching. Between 1950 and 1960, the proportion of men among secondary-school teachers increased from 43 percent to more than half; men elementary-school teachers increased from 9 to 14 percent; men social workers from 31 to 37 percent; men librarians from 11 to 14 percent.

Nobody seemed to care. Instead of the expected postwar depression, times kept getting better and better. Increasingly, girls married right out of high school and started having babies. More people were well-off, and the new rich began to have as many babies as the poor. Houses sprang up like dragon's teeth around the outskirts of cities, and home became the center of life for men as well as women.

In this new climate, young women felt no sense of exclusion from the great world "outside." Assertion of women's "rights" seemed old-fashioned and irrelevant. Feminism as a movement was forgotten, and girls could go through high school and even college without learning the name of Carrie Chapman Catt or Susan B. Anthony. By 1960, feminism was all but dead.

A Woman's Party lived on, remnant of the powerful old Congressional Union for Woman Suffrage which had picketed the White House. It continued to demand a sweeping Constitutional amendment guaranteeing women equal rights across the board. The political connections of some of the rich old suffragettes were still good enough for them to get their cherished amendment introduced into most Congresses. But these militant, "rightsy" women did not attract young followers. Indeed, few young women knew anything about them.

When President John F. Kennedy was elected in 1960, he found no organization representing all American women to work for his New Frontier. The old network of dedicated women around Eleanor Roosevelt had disbanded during the Eisenhower years. Although Eleanor Roosevelt's spirit remained unquenchable, she was frailer than most people realized, and Kennedy had not been her first choice. But her deep sense of service to her country and her President overcame her personal feelings about him when he asked for her help.

In 1961 Esther Peterson, Kennedy's Director of the Women's Bureau and a long-time friend of Eleanor Roosevelt, proposed that the President set up a Commission on the Status of Women which would explore the opinion of contemporary women on laws and practices affecting them. The results of the study would then be made the basis of national policy. Mrs. Roosevelt was ailing, but she accepted the job of chairman. President Kennedy honored her willingness to serve by effecting a reform she had never succeeded in getting when her husband was President.

Although the U.S. Civil Service had long declared the policy of equal opportunity for men and women, women were still arbitrarily passed over for many promotions. This was because of an old rule permitting officials to request a candidate of one sex or the other without giving any reason for the preference. Ever since 1941 Mrs. Roosevelt had been asking the Civil Service Commission why they permitted a discretion that violated the principle of promotion by demonstrable merit.

In April 1962, she asked again. In June, Deputy Attorney General Nicholas Katzenbach interrupted a meeting of the President's Committee on the Status of Women that was conferring outdoors, in the Rose Garden at Hyde Park, where President Roosevelt lay buried.

"Madam," he said, "I have the honor to present a letter from the President of the United States." President Kennedy had personally written to tell her that his Attorney General, Robert Kennedy, had ruled that the President now had the power to direct Civil Service officers to consider women on an equal basis with men in requesting candidates for promotion. In July, President Kennedy so directed.

When we went into World War II, only one out of every three women wage earners was married. At the end of the war, a woman on her way to work in the morning was as likely to be married as not. Between 1950 and 1960 more girls under twenty found husbands than ever before in our history. Employers hired more and more married women because there simply were no single ones left to hire.

The married women expected—and their employers expected—that they would retire when they had children. During the 1950s, American girls had more babies than Japanese girls, and our teen-agers proved as fertile as those in India. According to the Conventional Wisdom, the new young mothers should have stopped working during the affluent 1950s with sighs of relief. Instead, the proportion of mothers of preschool children who were employed outside their homes kept rising as inexorably as the national debt. In 1950, 14 percent of mothers of preschoolers worked, double the rate of 1940; in 1960, 20 percent worked; in 1964, 25 percent; in 1966, 26 percent. And for every young mother who went to work, some older woman was likely to find at least part-time employment caring for the babies left at home. Most of the mothers found ways of caring for their families without help from employers, government, or outside organizations.

If all the married women who supposedly "don't have to work" should quit, business would be paralyzed. The crisis would be as serious as the sex strike Aristophanes dramatized in *Lysistrata*.

Not, of course, without comic touches. Trucks would roll, but without the paperwork guiding their cargo, drivers wouldn't know where to drop their loads or what was in them. Bills would be so mixed up that deadbeats would go free. Men would root helplessly in files, and with no cleaning women to haul out each day's paper snowstorm, they'd soon be sloshing knee-deep in waste, and begging postmen not to stop.

Men would learn to cope. But just about the time they'd licked the work, they'd find that there was less of it to do. The $90 billion women earn and freely spend would evaporate. Sales would slip and layoffs would follow.

Without quite realizing it, we have come to depend on a work force of married women who do not think of themselves as workers and are not treated seriously on the job. Only when we look back into history do we see how they have been pulled into wage work and pushed back home at the convenience of the changing economy. Women make no noisome ghettos, join no unions, organize no demonstrations, come when they are called, and go quietly when bidden.

America has always had a labor reserve. We have been ingenious in finding cheap, docile labor. First, we captured primitive Africans and made them slaves. Then, when the sight appalled us, we freed them but kept them segregated so that we could use them when, as, and if industry needed extra hands. We attracted landless European peasants and did the same with them when we saw them huddled in ghettos, exploitable and tractable.

We used children until reformers—and the angry men that the children had displaced—shamed us into outlawing child labor. In booms, our factories have recruited teen-agers; when times were slack, we sent them back to school. We lured farm boys to work in town and sent them back to live off the land when the work ran out. We used single girls, too, but until recently housework was so inescapable that mothers had to stay at home, and before birth control became common, most wives had to count on being pregnant and hand-rearing their children for many of the best years of their lives.

Now all these labor reserves are gone or going. The children and the boys are in school. Negro men are further along the road to job equality than white women, and their claim to equal opportunity is more urgently pressed and widely recognized.

We do not like to admit it, but in 1968 our prosperity depends on the labor and earnings of women.

3

THE INVISIBLE BAR

A young wife carrying her first unborn child may privately hope for a boy, since traditionally the world has honored the mothers of men. But if her baby turns out to be a girl, she adjusts very fast. An infant girl can be a lot of fun. You tie a pink bow in her hair—if she has anything more than a fuzz to tie it on—and ruffle and beribbon her pretty bassinet. When she starts to toddle, you put her in filmy dresses and flowery aprons. You brush her hair until it gleams like silk and buy her soft dolls so that she can play Mother. When she grows up, she will marry and have babies of her own to cherish, perhaps more pleasures and happinesses than you, and more luxuries, too, because the man she marries will . . .

But our girl baby must first grow up. Despite her mother's leanings to frills and ruffles, the toddler packs mud pies side-by-side with boys, and pumps on swings as zestfully as boys, and fights boys stubbornly for the vacant swing when she must. She pedals her tricycle as fast as she can, just like the boys, and she may organize the neighborhood group that includes both boys and girls. She wears shorts, like boys, although more brightly colored, and snowsuits and jeans, like boys. She climbs trees and bruises her knees, like boys.

A small girl learns by the time she is two or three that she is a girl. The nursery books that mother reads her tell what girls are like and what they do. Girls are mommies. Girls are nurses. Mommies care for children. Nurses are helpers. They help men, and doctors are men. The books do not show girl scientists. They don't show sisters leading brothers. They don't show girls making discoveries, creating inventions, making important decisions that others of both sexes follow. Experts tell us children live up to the unspoken expectations of parents. Girls are encouraged to be clean, neat, tender little charmers, while boys are expected to be physically active, exploratory, rebellious, and noisy. Boys must be physically competent. They don't have to be talkers.

But from nursery school on up, we educate girls equally with boys. Girls sit in the same classes and learn the same subjects at the same time from the same teachers. And until almost the end of high school, girls make better grades than boys and respond at least as enthusiastically to challenges. At ten a girl may outswim a boy her age and dream of scuba-diving to the bottom of the sea, paradiving through space, and penetrating the heavens as an astronomer.

Sometime in high school a girl learns, often poignantly, that class honors are fine, but attracting the boys is what counts with her peers. The message comes over from other girls even more loudly and clearly than it does from boys. Many girls read it and cash in their aspirations. They may go on to college for more education "for oneself," but the real business of life is attracting a desirable husband. "I've never talked vocation to Mary," the mother of a pretty high-school senior said. "Her father wants a four-year education for her, not an eight- or twelve-year one he'll have to pay for. And as a mother," she added feelingly, "I believe the real vocation for a woman is marriage."

Even if a girl tries for a professional career she may be actively discouraged. Educators hold vocational guidance counselors responsible for the scandalous waste of talent, and they indignantly circulate anecdotes to prove it. One story alleges that the first woman engineering student to enroll at Detroit's Institute of Technology in ten years arrived because of a clerical error. When Thelma Lowe, an attractive Negro, was in eighth grade she was assigned to a drafting class by mistake. She did so well at it, however, that her guidance counselor then guided her into a pre-engineering course. Later, her younger sister studied mechanical engineering at Wayne State University.

In the 1960s guidance counselors were urged to encourage adolescent girls toward careers. The counselors were told to be positive. Instead of saying, "Have you thought how you would manage to do that if you had children?" they were instructed to say, "Veterinary practice is a good field for a woman, because she can carry it on near her home." A girl who had a reasonably enlightened high-school counselor might not even realize that she had to get much higher marks than a boy to get into a coed college. But the closer she approached paying work, the more she was slowed by the unspoken assumption that a woman really could not be serious about a vocation but must be working to mark time, earn a little money, or if she were obviously gifted, "just for fun." This is the Invisible Bar that keeps women down.

The Invisible Bar is unofficial. It is effective because almost everyone accepts it. Officially, graduate and professional schools invite women to apply. In private, their administrators deplore wasting facilities on women who marry and do not use their educations, but "throw it away to get married and have babies." Dr. Milton Eisenhower, President of Johns Hopkins University, once figured that it cost $200,000 to train every practicing woman biologist. He arrived at this high figure by charging the cost of educating all female biologists against those few who went on to lifetime careers.

In 1966, the dean of a leading Eastern law school confided to a nationally known woman leader that his school would admit more women if the big law firms would hire them. The story puzzled Seth Taft, who recruits law school graduates for the leading law firm in Cleveland. "I don't think we're biased against women," he said. "It's just that we don't see very many who come even close to our standards."

Girls who go to women's colleges sometimes crash unexpectedly on the Invisible Bar when they look for their first jobs. "Men don't have to type and take dictation to earn a chance to begin learning!" a Vassar graduate wrote her English professor after making the rounds of employment offices in New York. Employers seem equally dismayed. They don't always know what to do with college girls. Big companies give a Princeton senior who has majored in English an aptitude test to see where he might fit, but give a Vassar senior who has majored in English a typing test. If she demurs, they complain that liberal arts colleges simply don't prepare girls for business. "Show me the girl with a bachelor's degree in engineering from M.I.T. and a master's in business administration from Harvard, and I'll show you how much discrimination there is against women!" Bennett Kline, a management consultant, challenged a 1966 symposium, sponsored by Teachers College, Columbia, on opportunities for women executives.

Pursuing Mr. Kline's suggestion, we talked with a half-dozen women Harvard MBAs. None of them wished to be quoted. "The company recruiters were as surprised to see us as your Mr. Kline," one of them said. In 1963, women were admitted directly to the Harvard Business School in equal competition with men applicants for the first time. Before that, a few had been allowed to take the second year of the course at Harvard after completing a Radcliffe course especially designed for women. When the company recruiters came shopping for talent in 1965, they found eleven women among the hardy survivors of the two-year "B School" obstacle course.

The B School makes no compromises. It proudly avoids teaching students how to do any job below that of president of a big company. And like such a president, the students learn the hard way. They are given long, noncommittal fact-packed accounts of real companies. With no clue from the teacher, they diagnose the problems they see and recommend action. They dig for answers in books, talk out ideas with each other, and work at devising solutions until the small hours of the morning. In class, each student tries to sell his recommendation in a two-minute talk to a hundred fellow students.

"At Wellesley, the pressure came from the teachers," one of the pioneer women MBAs said. "At Harvard, it came from your fellow students." The girls reported that classroom discussions were conducted with the sharp, impersonal, but courteous manners of the best big-business executives. All the women said that they were scrupulously treated as equals in the nonstop "bull" sessions which are a B School tradition. They got their trial by fire from the company recruiters. But they gave as good as they got.

"Harvard makes the recruiters see any member of the graduating class who requests an interview," one of the pioneer women MBAs of 1965 pointed out. "We took the chance to probe the policies of companies which notoriously don't hire women who can't type. No one could say we were not prepared. No one could say we were not serious about business. Some of us had borrowed to meet the $8,000 cost of the course. So we were a perfect test case for sex discrimination. One recruiter finally broke down and blurted out that his company did not have any woman higher than a secretary, and furthermore his management didn't *want* any woman higher than a secretary."

The girls compared notes on their interviews in order to rate companies on their attitudes toward women executives. They were offered jobs, but they did not average as many offers as the men in the class, and they had trouble getting the jobs they wanted. Marketing majors wanted to be product managers, the executives who have responsibility for the success of a product. Some recruiters frankly told them to forget it.

"You'd have to get out in the field to become a product manager," one of them objected.

The girl he was interviewing said she was willing to travel.

"But you'd have to lug heavy cartons around!" the recruiter argued. She reluctantly settled for the only job he offered—research.

Another girl took a job market-testing brassieres and quickly moved up to brassiere product manager. "The idea was that I would have a big advantage because I could march into a fitting room with a tape measure over my shoulder," she said. "But when you get into management, you sort of lose the consumer point of view."

When a representative from an advertising agency tried to sell one of the girls on a job in market research, she coolly asked him why the job was open. "The woman we had in it left," the recruiter told her. "She wanted to do account work and we don't feel our clients will accept a woman account executive." The girl didn't take the job.

Recruiters wanted to know whether the girls planned to marry. "They'd never have believed me if I had said 'No,'" one attractive young graduate told us. "So I always told them 'Of course,' even though I had no plans at the time. Then they'd want to know if I was planning to have children, and I'd say, 'Not immediately.'" Several of the girls married fellow B School graduates. Most of them got to do "men's jobs" in leading companies, and their record of return to work after babies has been good. These girls demonstrated that a well-prepared, self-confident young woman didn't really have to start out in business as a secretary.

Jane Johnson, Director of Vassar's Vocational Bureau, advises girls not to learn shorthand. She warns that a bright girl who can take dictation is such a rare treasure that she may never get to do anything else. In order to get a start in merchandising, for instance, Mildred Custin, President of Bonwit Teller, ran a Christmas gift department while continuing to do the secretarial work of an officer of the store.

Other successful women have taken equally heroic measures to get out of the secretarial rut. Some of them have quietly taken on extra work until they have created a job that obviously required a title. Twenty years ago Virginia Culver was a secretary helping her boss keep tabs on the credit cards Signal Oil and Gas Company sometimes issued. Now that credit has become a way of life, the Credit Card Department of the company is a sizable outfit, and she's its Collection Manager. Jan Knoop, Director of Research at the Colorado Association of Commerce and Industry in Denver, made her present job by digging out information to help her boss answer complicated questions from association members when she was his secretary.

Women assistants often get valuable professional experience. The first magazine article the author ever wrote for print appeared in *Fortune* magazine where she was an editorial researcher. When the writer for whom she was researching a story quit in the middle of it, the editor of the issue asked her to try her hand at writing it. She did, and it ran. The editor happened to be John Kenneth Galbraith. Years later, she wrote an unashamedly adoring profile of him for *Esquire*.

But hard work and real contribution haven't always been enough. The moment comes when a woman has to refuse a dead-end job. Kay Moore, a successful stockbroker in Cleveland, once bargained with a boss who wanted her to learn how to run a Teletype machine. "I'll learn to run that machine," she offered, "provided you let me hire all the people who will ever use it." The deal gave her experience in personnel work and left her free to advance.

In order to get ahead women have frequently had to quit secretarial jobs, conceal their talent for shorthand, and start out all over again, often at lower pay. Roberta J. Berkel, one of the first women branch managers of a major New York City bank, took a cut in salary to become a platform assistant at Chemical Bank New York Trust in 1959. Mary Stewart of San Francisco stuck it out as a secretary for twelve years. Then she took the examination for Certified Professional Secretary given by the National Secretaries Association. Notification that she had passed was sent to her boss, Chief Estimator in a construction company. "I suppose this means you want more money," he said.

"No, I've never asked for a raise and I'm not going to start now," she said. She was already getting top pay for a secretary and knew she could not do any other job in that organization. But she was able to use her "CPS" (Certified Professional Secretary) in lieu of a master's degree in business education to get a job with International Business Machines helping set up customer-training programs.

Women in high-level jobs advertise their lack of secretarial skills to avoid being pressed into secretarial service. The fear is not groundless. Once a woman is cornered, heroic defense measures may be needed. "They tried it only once," a fiery Irish woman engineer in a West Coast space research company told us. "They asked me to take notes at a conference—and I did!" Instead of transcribing the long-winded and inconclusive discussion, she wrote an analysis of the meeting with critical comments of her own, such as "Target Date: None" and "Action Required: Policy Definition." None of the men involved was willing ever to risk letting her take the minutes of a meeting again. A gentler woman, now vice president of a Los Angeles bank, confided that the president sometimes forgot her present title and asked her to do the little chores she used to do in the days when she was a secretary. She does them, but she sometimes signs her covering notes, "Your Slave."

Many high career hopes are shot down by a dead-end first job, but women encounter far more frustration of this sort than men. "If we had wanted a woman, we would have advertised for a woman," a girl was told when she tried to apply for a job listed in the Help Wanted, Male column of the newspaper. She explained she had applied under the impression that Title VII required employers to consider applicants of either sex. But even women who have managed to get jobs leading to promotion find that it is hard to realize the potential.

It takes training and experience to move out of the bull pen, and big companies have just begun to open these essential areas to women. After Title VII, some management training squads accepted women, but they were still rare enough to warrant newspaper attention. Women were more likely to teach trainees than to be trainees. We found women who were skilled in processing claims against insurance companies forced to train young men for the management jobs they should have had. Some of these teachers had "brought up" several of their own bosses. In one telephone company, customer service representatives drew an extra fifty cents a day for "having a student," but none could recall a management trainee "student" who was born female.

Ambitious men get experience and a chance to show what they can do by taking on extra work, but if it requires a trip outside the office or staying after hours, an employer often hesitates to ask a young woman to do it. In 1966, a 25-year-old customer service representative charged the Southern Bell Telephone Company with discrimination for refusing to let her sell coin-operated phones in commercial locations even though she had come out first on the tests for the job. The company contended that the work wasn't suitable for a woman because it required going into "all kinds of places." The EEOC disagreed. "The respondent's arguments sound like those used by Arabs to keep their women indoors or behind veils," the investigator snapped.

But the principal reason women aren't considered for promotion is that managers assume they aren't serious about working. If a woman wants to advance, she has to ask for a better job, and she has to ask in a way that won't arouse antagonism—or ridicule. There is something irresistibly funny to men about a woman doing a "man's job." Newspapers endlessly feature women in unexpected jobs under cute headlines:

YOUNG WOMAN FINDS HER PLACE IN BARBER SHOP.

PHONE GIRL SUITS UP FOR A MAN'S JOB.

SHE'S ALL ALONE IN MAN'S WORLD OF TOOLS AND DIES.

A girl who asks for a "man's job" can expect ribbing along this line in her office. During World War II, a woman who was actually supervising a bull pen of layout artists asked for the title of Director. Her boss just laughed. "We can't have a lady pitcher on the ball team," he told her.

Women aren't brought up to assert themselves, but a man expects to fight his way to the top. The system is designed to fit his reproductive cycle, not hers. During his career-building twenties and thirties a man's career and sex drive reinforce each other, but a career-committed woman has to be aggressive in her work just at the time of her life when she is engaged in finding a mate and bearing and raising young children. Moreover, everywhere she turns she sees sex portrayed as a woman's only value. The questions raised are how much she wants it, whether she looks as if she enjoys it. Career ambitions figure as a side issue, an extra: some men like the idea that the girl of their dreams is smart "too."

In 1967, newspaper columnist Flora Lewis got a man to define "femininity." "It's looking pretty and elegant," he began. "And it's being nice, not arguing with men or nagging or complaining, or having different opinions. Not pushing them, or interfering or anything, not wanting to get their own way instead of doing what they're told. I would say it's wanting to please a man all the time." A girl who wants to get out of the bull pen has to be assertive in the office and seductively submissive when husband-hunting after five. It can be done, but it isn't as easy as television, films, advertising, and women's magazines airily pretend.

When a girl marries, the problem simply takes another form. The energy that used to go into dating now goes into building a marriage around two careers, while back at the office it is necessary to convince the boss that her husband isn't going to move her out of town. Will she have a baby? The office waits to see before giving her more responsibility, even though she is ready for it. The women Harvard MBAs reported that their employers stopped worrying once they had had a baby and come back. Some didn't think a girl should wait too long. Others said it depended on the boss and the job.

In the past, women who had their babies and their jobs too were resented with special vehemence by spinsters who grew up at a time when marriage and career were mutually exclusive. Young women sometimes return to work after having a baby only to find that their employers don't treat them seriously as career workers any more.

A career woman who has survived the hurdle of marriage and maternity encounters a new obstacle: the hostility of men. When she was younger, men in the office liked to help her: a bright girl is usually attractive and fun to have around. But as she grows older, and particularly as she begins to exercise authority, she mobilizes the resentment men harbor against the women who disciplined them when they were boys. Sometimes they strike out against a woman colleague on the basis of her sex. Some men claim that they can tell when a woman colleague is having a menstrual period. One actually boasted that he kept a calendar to avoid riling a key woman "on those days." And if a woman is beyond "those days," she can be accused of causing trouble because she is "going through the change."

A woman who presses her case for promotion risks reprisal. "She's an aggressive woman, and I don't like to deal with aggressive women," an executive told an EEOC investigator in 1966. A secretary who wanted a chance at a technical writing job had filed a charge of discrimination under Title VII when she wasn't considered for it.

"How do you feel about aggressive men?" the mediator asked the company executive.

"That's okay," he answered. In his book, men could be aggressive but women couldn't.

When Garda Bowman, now a personnel consultant, was interviewing executives for her doctoral dissertation on the business image of a promotable person, she uncovered a great deal of hostility against women in business. "Some women are married to their jobs instead of their husbands," a bank officer told her.

"A woman's emotions take over," another man said, adding that when responsibilities pile up, the most ferocious "female kitten of management" reverts to the role of "purring, whimpering kitten, who seeks the protection of her male master." Most of the male executives Dr. Bowman queried told her that women were "temperamentally unfit for management," but three-quarters of the women in executive positions whom she interviewed disagreed.

The criticism troubles women executives. "You have to

walk on eggs," one of them told us. Some of them deliberately throttle their emotions. "When I started working on a newspaper, we had a man who used to get so mad at people he was interviewing that he once tore the telephone right out of the wall and threw it across the room," said Llewellyn Miller, a magazine writer, recalling the time when she was a drama critic for a Los Angeles newspaper. "Everybody admired his manly anger. But I used to wonder what would happen if I had tried anything like that. In order to avoid criticism, I was careful never to raise my voice."

Fear of looking aggressive deters many women from seeking promotions due them. "I suppose I could be a branch manager if I really wanted the job," Kay Lewis, assistant vice president for personnel at the Crocker National Bank in San Francisco, told us. "But then I would have to call up perfectly strange men and invite them to lunch." Women in public relations in New York City, where expense accounts are common, have no such inhibitions, but in other fields and other cities it is not so easy for a woman to do. Some arrange with the headwaiter to hold the bill, or use credit cards. But even where women are accustomed to taking the initiative, they are not expected to run up the expense accounts permitted men in the same jobs. It is notoriously cheaper to maintain a woman on the road than a man, and economy is one reason why women have an easier time getting jobs requiring travel in small and marginal enterprises.

Women in executive positions try to ward off hostility by phrasing their orders as suggestions and "planting" ideas in the heads of associates in the hope that they will accept them as their own. They talk a great deal about maintaining their "femininity" and never forgetting that they are women. Many women sign their business letters with initials to avoid calling attention to their sex.

A retiring manner may disarm hostility, but it does not always ward off criticism. A woman who deliberately cultivated a quiet style complained to us that a man who was assigned to her department assured associates that she was "too reticent to toot her own horn." He made it sound like loyal defense, but the president of the company got the message: "This woman is too reticent to toot the company's horn in public."

Really successful women say that it doesn't always pay to

pussyfoot—at least all the time. Women bank officers, stock-brokers, lawyers, doctors, engineers, and executives all recall confrontations with men bosses or associates. Men test each other's intentions all the time. It is the "game." If a woman shows she is willing to play it, they accept her. Bea Hicks, president of her own Newark Controls Company, realized this when she went to work, during World War II, as an engineer at Western Electric, an organization which had not theretofore employed women in that capacity. An associate was frankly skeptical. He gave her an electronic part with which they were having difficulty, and asked her to redesign it.

"The design's no good," he grunted when she brought him her solution to the problem.

"Try it," she challenged. He did, and it worked. "That broke the ice," she recalls. "From then on out, I think he actually thought I was better than I was."

Women who survive the competition for positions of authority face new problems. Every responsible manager, man or woman, needs support from above and below, access to information, broad experience outside the immediate organization, and the self-confidence to make decisions. Leaders must be recognized as leaders so that others will follow them. To that end, the Army puts bars on a lieutenant's shoulders. Civilian organizations label leaders by giving them titles, decorated offices, secretarial help, pay, and above all, authentic information. All organizations resist giving these perquisites to women. Almost every sizable organization has some women exercising authority on an informal and undefined basis.

It is much harder for a woman to get the title than the work. When women were promoted during World War II, they were generally called "acting manager" or "acting head." This form is still used to identify a woman's role for a specific occasion without conferring a permanent rank. Secretaries who take on projects of their own are sometimes allowed to sign as "assistants," so that they can engage in direct correspondence with outsiders. A woman who has written many letters to collect past-due accounts was allowed to sign as "collection manager" for years on an unofficial basis. She was given the title formally only when an outside job evaluation of the entire organization disclosed that she was, in fact, carrying the responsibility that warranted the title.

"When I applied for my present job, I was told that I would be an assistant bookkeeper," a California woman told us. "I didn't want to work directly under anyone, so I asked whom I would assist. The man interviewing me couldn't think who it would be. He just looked embarrassed. I took the job, managed the books, and got raises, but it would have been easier to deal with outsiders if I had been able to identify myself as the bookkeeper in charge, which of course I really was."

Because most women work in subordinate positions, those who have responsibility need status symbols to mark their authority more urgently than men. If a woman is at all young and unassuming, she runs the risk of being taken for an assistant with no authority of her own. "Most people around here are used to me by now," Anita Best, personnel services representative of Chrysler Corporation, Chemical Division, told *The Detroit News* in 1967, "but there are still times when an employee I approach thinks I'm a secretary and wants to talk to my boss."

In retailing, where there are many women at all levels, executives sometimes signal their status by wearing hats. In journalism it sometimes works the other way: when *Fortune* magazine formally requested women researchers to wear hats when interviewing business leaders, the order was quietly defied. "If you wear a hat, they'll think you are somebody's secretary," one of the researchers complained.

Women sometimes find it hard to get their names on company letterheads, or to obtain business cards of their own. In some big companies with several lunchrooms, women promoted to executive rank are discouraged from using the executive dining room unless they have visitors to entertain. At one automobile company, the first woman engineer was asked not to have herself paged over the public address system because secretaries hearing a woman's name might think that a secretary had been granted this privilege and demand it for themselves. In another company, women were not allowed to park as near the building as the men.

Women are not assigned secretaries as readily as men doing the same work, and for the sake of appearances some fake secretarial initials on the lower left margin of the letters they type themselves. "They think that because you are a woman, of course you can type," one woman told us. More than status is at stake when a professional woman is expected to serve as her own secretary. She loses time, as well as prestige.

Women notoriously resent working for women, but even when the relationship is pleasant, a woman seldom gets as much help from her secretary as a man gets from his. She isn't as willing to do personal errands for a woman boss as for a supposedly helpless man. Older women sometimes think that girls prefer to work for men because they have more chance to meet eligible bachelors, but the situation is more involved. Girls resent the discipline of their mothers even more than boys, and perhaps are less willing than men to accept women supervisors. Young secretaries sometimes think their women bosses are jealous of their youth and looks, but the problem often stems from the older woman's sense of sex betrayal: "I suffer because you are flighty," she thinks to herself. The office politics of women working for women is further complicated by the attitude of the men. Many of them expect women to bicker with each other.

Hostility and denial of status are trying to an ambitious woman, but denial of office information is fatal. In our culture, men come to women for personal sympathy, but they do not talk shop with them because they think women "would not understand." Men flout rules of the organization chart and bypass women bosses as a matter of natural right. Sometimes a woman boss is frankly told that it would be humiliating for a man to report to her. Usually she isn't told. Some time ago a woman public relations director was authorized to hire a man to assist her. When she resigned from her job to start her own business, her male assistant took her out to lunch to celebrate. After a few drinks he became confidential. "Now that you are leaving, I am going to tell you something that I know but that you don't," he said. "I know your salary, but you don't know mine." When he correctly quoted hers at $10,000 a year and claimed his own was $12,000, she realized that he was right. Although she knew the salaries of all the women working for her she had never been told his.

Home economists in business complain that the men in their companies expect them to promote products to women by implying that women have had a hand in developing them, when in fact they often have not been told about them in time to influence their design.

In some companies, women vice presidents are either not

invited to meetings attended by all the men vice presidents, or they are expected to confine their advice to issues affecting women customers or employees. "They go to lunch to tell the men about a change in policy," a woman promotion director complained, "but they send me memos. When you get a memo, you can't answer back. And you don't like to run in to someone else's office to ask questions, so if you don't understand it, you just sit and wonder what it means." A highly placed woman executive in a nonprofit organization, who should have been in on board meetings, confessed that she was forced to listen through a ventilator to find out what was being planned at these sessions from which she was excluded only "because women had never attended."

Some men hate to fire a woman, so they freeze her out with silence. An art director once sat without work for months. Finally she was told there was no room for her and she was moved with her drawing board to the accounting department. All this time the other artists in the bull pen were working day and night. Every once in a while she would tiptoe in and ask them if there wasn't something she could do to help. They would always say, "No, nothing." She stuck it out until a change in the organization put her in charge of the young men who had tried to scare her into quitting.

The technique was used with more success on a woman who worked for a travel agency. She discovered, by accident, that her reports to headquarters were being thrown in the wastebasket, unread, by a man who had been told that she would soon be replaced. Her letters were not answered. She was not invited to meetings. She was given no assignments. After sticking it out for a few months, she quit and started a travel agency of her own.

These are, of course, exceptional cases. Most men have been taught as boys that it is wrong to take advantage of the weakness of a rival, particularly if the rival is a woman. The silent treatment is one of the few weapons most men feel comfortable using against her. More commonly, men simply leave out the women in the organization as a matter of course. Like waiters in a restaurant, they are present but not recognized. "I might as well be a walnut desk," a woman invited to committee meetings in a civic organization complained. "They don't want to hear what I say, so I don't speak."

Women so rarely attend some meetings that their presence is often ignored both socially and physically. Some have been roomed in with men or mistaken for wives. Virginia Sink, an engineer at Chrysler, had to ask men colleagues to stand watch at the men's room that was provided for engineering meetings, while she used it, because there was no ladies' room.

Policy is literally made in rooms officially closed to women. In law and brokerage firms, important decisions such as bonus allocations may be made at lunch in a men's club to which a woman with the rank to attend has to be admitted by a side door or up a back stairway.

Women may even be separated from their work. Before 1965, women reporters who had to cover press conferences at the stag National Press Club in Washington were seated in the balcony, where it was harder to hear and ask questions than on the floor where the men sat. The Economic Club of Detroit has barred women from high-level conferences at which national figures have made important policy announcements. The presumption that anyone important enough to attend must be a man hurts policy-making women more than missing the event itself.

Women who pioneered in certain high positions agree that the men who put them there have been nervous about the impression they would create. "My boss went to great lengths to introduce me to everyone I would need to know," one of the young Harvard women recalled. "He was particularly careful to introduce me to the secretaries as 'Mrs.' because they call the men 'Mr.', but I told them later to call me by my first name." She was, of course, a very smart girl.

Extra solicitude does not always make a woman's job easier. "They expect you to fail," an unusually well-qualified and attractive woman told us, describing her induction into a high-level job in a Detroit automobile company. "Everyone around here smokes, drinks, and swears, but they must have figured that a woman lush would have been intolerable. I told them I didn't drink, but even so, they hired a private detective to check on it." She is now one of a handful of women in the company who rank high enough to buy and run a car on favorable terms, charge gas, park in the executive lot, eat in the executive dining room, and get her hair cut (if she wishes) in the executive barbershop.

The first day on the job, her boss hovered over her. "Let me know right away if you have any trouble," he told her. Men colleagues got the idea. "During the first month I went ahead and ordered some booklets reprinted without realizing that I should have taken bids on the printing work. We needed them, and I didn't mind sticking my neck out. The man next to me asked if he could help by explaining my mistake to our boss. I told him not to bother, I'd simply cut the order to the number of booklets we needed on an emergency basis and take bids on the rest. So what did he do? He ran to the head of the department anyway and told him that *he* had thought of this way to help me out of my embarrassment. With friends like that you don't need enemies!"

Work went well, but the tension did not abate. When it came time for personnel reviews, her boss called her in, closed the door, brewed a cup of coffee, and started telling her how hard it was for him to rate people. "I thought at first he was leading up to firing me, and I couldn't imagine why," she told us. "But the trouble was the other way around. I deserved a rating of excellent, but, according to company rules, that rating would entitle me to consideration for the next opening above me. Rather than take the responsibility for forcing a woman on upper management, he had taken the unusual step of asking a vice president whether company policy on equal opportunity for Negroes also applied to women. He had been told to stick to the rules, whatever that meant. So he was going to give me the rating, but he wanted me to know that if I failed on the job in the future, he'd be ruined! Frankly, I hadn't expected such male insecurity in the rough-and-tough automobile industry. But then, I'm not bucking for vice president."

Women who get high enough to buck for vice president of a major organization face so many problems that they frequently decline to run. They know that they will be resented much more deeply than before, and they often have less to gain. The title may not mean as much to a woman as to a man. Then, too, women are more likely than men to be gifted people who are working for the stimulation of the work itself. Whatever the explanation, the fact is that many professional women really prefer writing advertising copy to running an advertising agency or working on a research project to the game of grantsmanship that wins the funds for it. Many women would rather teach children than direct other teachers. Many would rather research legal briefs than drum up law business. "We don't want the top," eight well-known journalists and business women chorused cheerfully on the "Today" show of January 10, 1967. "We just want to be near the top and have the fun."

Society doesn't push a woman to succeed as hard as it pushes a man, so it is only natural that women drop out of the rat race more frequently. But even if a woman doesn't try as hard as a man to be a vice president, the fact remains that she encounters a new handicap attributable to her sex if she does try. She has no bargaining power. Unlike the promising men, it isn't as easy for her to back a demand for promotion by threatening to get a job elsewhere. Maude Lennox, one of the most-respected executive recruiters, said that there isn't enough call for women executives to warrant setting up a "Women's Department" in her service. William A. Hertan, President of Executive Manpower Corporation, told a 1966 meeting of American Women in Radio & Television that he had not been asked to fill a single executive job for a woman in ten years. He warned his audience that a woman has to rely on personal friends when she changes jobs, and that most moves by women are lateral, to similar jobs in other organizations, rather than better ones.

Sex prejudice alone does not fully account for the absence of a market for women executives. Women are older than men when they are ready for high-level jobs, simply because their promotions come more slowly. They have fewer years before retirement during which they are eligible for important positions. And while a few gray hairs might enhance the prestige of an impressive man, they seldom improve the business image of a woman. Most women in high-level jobs color their gray.

An equally important handicap is that the experience of most successful women is not transferable because they have so often risen as a result of circumstances peculiar to one organization. A woman lawyer in a city that shall remain nameless rose in her firm as an assistant to a senior partner who had become mentally ill. Although her unusual duties were extremely valuable to this particular firm, her relatively small compensation undoubtedly reflected the narrow market for lawyers who are also psychiatric nurses. The point of this story is that most women are much more valuable to the organizations in which they have risen than they could be anywhere else, so that they find it unprofitable to move even when their employers underpay them.

Successful women have fewer jobs than men who stay in the same field, but in his study of the careers of educated women, Dr. Eli Ginzberg, Hepburn Professor of Economics at the Graduate School of Business, Columbia University, found that women were more apt to change their fields than men. Teachers have done very well in business. Business machine companies hire them for their training programs, and schools are increasingly important to big companies because they are a public relations "audience" which has to be kept informed. Dr. Dorothy Gregg went from the Economics Department of Columbia University to a job promoting "economic education" in the public relations department of U.S. Steel, where she was one of the nine or ten highest-ranking women in the company. Marion Corwell, formerly Associate Director of School Relations in the Dearborn Public Schools, became Educational Affairs Representative on the Public Relations Staff of the Ford Motor Company.

In academic life as elsewhere, rules against nepotism limit professional women and sometimes deprive them of the opportunity to work at all. Men and women meet at work and marry. For a while, both may continue to work on the newspaper or in the same department of a university or on the same hospital staff. But as they rise to positions of power the situation becomes uncomfortable, even if it does not violate specific rules, and it is always the wife who withdraws. Dr. Ginzberg points out that anti-nepotism rules prevent husbands and wives working together as a team. They also work grievous injustice on talented women. Dr. Maria Goeppert Mayer, the only woman since Dr. Marie Curie to win the Nobel Prize in Physics, once worked as a "volunteer associate" at Johns Hopkins in order to keep on doing physics. She could not be paid, because her husband was on the faculty, but the University didn't object to getting her free. "I sensed the resentment of the role of women in American academic life," she says, "so I learned to be inconspicuous."

Women have less bargaining power for top management for another reason, too. They are less secure than men in the jobs they hold. A New York radio station revamping its program schedule started cutting down by firing a woman commentator. "You're the first to go because it's easier to fire a woman than a man," the manager of the station told her pleasantly. They thought they were right to protect the jobs of men. Employers are proud of this policy. In one communications company, every woman above the secretarial level was fired in a general budget cut while men were dropped or retained on the basis of their individual records.

Close to the top, the nature of the competition for advancement changes. No longer can a woman rise on competence alone. A woman can't expect to be "twice as good" as the superior men who are also competing for the top spot, because they're all good. And mere competence is less important. "Face validity"—looking the part of boss—counts more than it does at lower levels. Credibility—the ability to persuade outsiders—counts for more. Self-confidence is more important and much harder to fake. The captain dines alone. Emotional support can no longer come from within the organization. If it is needed, it has to come from home.

All these requirements for a chief executive are harder for women to fulfill than men. Take credibility, for example; it has been proved that most people simply don't believe a woman knows what she is talking about. Jessie Bernard set up an experiment in the Speech Department of Penn State University, where she was teaching sociology, to test it. A man and a woman who were equally good speakers memorized the same lectures and delivered them to different sections of the same course. One of the lectures was on politics, a "masculine" subject, the other on sex differences, a supposedly "feminine" subject. Then students were tested on the contents of the lectures. Both teachers got the information across. Students reproduced the facts equally well. But analysis of semantic clues in the examination papers of the two sections disclosed that the students believed the man more than the woman on both subjects. Student papers contained more "she saids" than "he saids," indicating that they did not necessarily accept the woman's statement. And in class discussions the students indicated that they were more aroused by the man's comments and ideas.

Finally, women are disqualified for many top jobs because they don't have wives. David Riesman, the Harvard sociologist, has said that it is hard to find a woman who can take on the presidency of a college because a president needs a wife to help him. This is true of elective office, most visibly the office of the President of the United States. Professional men, ministers, and ambassadors require home settings that need the services of wives, and they are judged in part on the performance of their wives.

More important even than the services wives render is the climate of acceptance they provide for their husbands. Women need approval as much as men. Those who have real careers are apt to be either single or married to men who are proud of them. But very few men can make a career out of providing an encouraging climate for a woman, and very few women will admit they want such a man. As Riesman has complained, "Our society really isn't set up to be very helpful to women who want to pursue careers rather than jobs."

4

THE SEX MAP
OF THE WORK WORLD

It isn't polite to admit it, but money is one of the reasons why sex is important. The fact is that women simply do not get hold of as much money that they can legally call their own as do the men in their lives. Very rich widows sometimes do, and so do very poor Negro women, who can get work when their husbands can't, but they are treated as exceptional cases.

Everyone seems to think that this country is full of idle rich women living on money inherited from a husband or father. Such women are highly visible on Caribbean cruises or at resorts, and stockbrokers and other salesmen often cite the vast assets that idle rich women are supposed to control.

The sad fact of the matter is that idle rich women are very rare. Census breakdowns prove this. If you modestly define as idle rich any person with an independent income of $10,000 a year or more for which he did not work, there were only 87,269 idle rich women in the United States in 1966, or one-tenth of one percent of all the women 14 years old and older. That same year there were 96,252 idle rich men in the same situation lolling around the United States, and since there were seven million fewer men than women 14 years old and older in the population, your chances of being idly rich were a shade better if you were male. In 1966, most people in the upper income brackets worked for at least part of their money.

However women come by money—whether by inheritance, by earnings, or as dependents—they simply don't get as much money or as unequivocal control of it as men. This isn't supposed to matter, but in an increasingly money-driven society, it *does* matter. If it really didn't matter, no one would giggle when saying that women "really own" the country (they don't, of course, not even if you count property nominally owned by women but controlled by men), or that "women are the reason why men want money," or that "Mrs. Consumer makes or breaks business" because she is the family purchasing agent.

Money is divided along sex lines so sharply that the statistics are worth a close look. In 1966, the most recent year for which census breakdowns are available, nearly 40 percent of adult women had no independent income at all. Most of them, of course, were supported by husbands who handed them money to spend or bought them what they needed without legally transferring funds to them. The other 60 percent had incomes of their own, from investments, earnings, welfare payments, alimony, or some other source, but half of these received less than $1,638 during the year. Adult men did much better: 92 percent had income from some source, and their median income—half above, half below—was $5,306.

Many conditions contribute to this gap. First of all, most income is earned, and men are the earners. Many more men than women earn money, and men spend more of their time earning than women. Most of the women who earn work only part time, or part of the year. In 1966, 60 percent of all the men reporting income from any source were full-time, year-round workers, compared with only 30 percent of all the women with income of their own. What's more, the men earned almost twice as much money for the same effort. In 1966, half the women working full time earned only $4,000 or less, compared with $7,000 for men. This difference reflects the fact that women are often limited to work that pays less than the work done by men, and also that women are not paid as much as men even if they are doing the same work.

Many employers see nothing wrong in a dual pay scale. In 1961, for instance, one third of 1,900 employers queried by the National Office Managers Association frankly admitted that they systematically paid men more than women. That year, the Women's Bureau reported sizable differentials between the wages paid men and women for jobs carrying identical titles. Male bank tellers, for instance, earned from $5 a week more in Atlanta to $31 a week more in Milwaukee.

The gap widens at the upper brackets. Women scientists and engineers are paid $2,500 to $3,000 less a year than men in the same positions, according to an article in the Winter 1965 issue of the *Harvard Medical Alumni Bulletin*, by Ruth Kundsin, a bacteriologist. An executive recruiter reports that the managers of a manufacturer in northern New Jersey saved money by hiring a woman to serve as their chief financial officer at $9,000 a year. When she left, they had to pay $20,000 to get a man to do her job. When *he* left, they went back to a woman at $9,000 and they then replaced *her* with a man at $18,000. According to the recruiter, all four employees were good at the job.

Employers have long assumed that there is a ceiling on the financial "worth" of a woman. When President Grover Cleveland was pioneering the nonpolitical Civil Service in the 1880s, the first administrators were quoted as saying that no woman appointee could be paid more than $1,200 a year. In 1919, Senator Reed Smoot established a salary ceiling for the staff of the Women's Bureau. "No woman on earth is worth more than $2,000 a year," he told Mary Anderson, the first director.

The dollar figures have inflated, of course, but the notion of a ceiling persists to this day. In 1967, for instance, the leading public relations placement agency told a woman looking for a job that $12,000 was the most any employer in this field would pay to hire a woman from the outside, while salaries for men were negotiated on an individual basis. Many women who have founded businesses of their own say they did so to get out from under an arbitrary salary ceiling, and the census figures bear them out. Women earning top incomes are slightly more apt to be self-employed than men making the same money.

Wherever distinctions of pay can be drawn, women draw the lower-rated job. A study reported by the Women's Bureau shows that in 1964 women sales workers earned 60 percent less than men sales workers; women managers, officials, and proprietors earned 45 percent less than men in those classifications, and women clerks earned 44 percent less than men clerks. Unions are quite candid. Women earn less, they report, because they are assigned to jobs that pay less.

Men and women often do exactly the same thing in all but name and pay. In some organizations, for instance, both men and women process applications for employment. Both have the same authority, but the men are called "interviewers" and are paid more than the women, who are merely "clerks." A woman lawyer who worked for the Government during the war recalls with amusement that men who adjusted minor differences with war contractors called themselves "expediters" "negotiating" contracts, while women who did the same thing, at lower pay, said they were "writing a change order." Management consultants frequently turn up men and women doing the same job under differing titles when they analyze what each employee really does.

"Women's jobs" pay less than "men's jobs" of comparable education. A college education has been a reliable economic elevator for all minority groups, but according to a calculation for a recent year, California women with four or more years of education beyond high school averaged $4,151, only $300 more than California men who had left school at the end of the eighth grade. At the same time, California men with four or more years of college averaged $8,108. In California, as in the nation, teaching is the most popular vocation for educated women. Teaching is defined as a "woman's job," and like nursing, another woman's profession, it pays less than other occupations requiring comparable education.

"Women's work" pays less than "men's work" of comparable skill and steadiness. A taxi driver has to be about as skillful as a cleaning woman who can run the machinery of a mechanized home. Moving up the skill ladder, a trained nurse has invested more time and money in her education, and her responsibility is at the very least as great as that of an electrician—but the electrician earns more money per hour. Part of the reason for the gap is that transport workers and electricians are more apt to be unionized.

The gap between the pay of men and women is wider than it seems on the basis of take-home pay. Half of all the people who work in offices, factories, or establishments of any kind except farms are now covered by a pension or retirement plan other than Social Security, but few of these plans protect the families of women employees as well as they protect the families of men. The plan may force a woman to retire earlier, even though a woman can expect to live longer and in better health than a man.

During her 1967 investigation of pension plans, Congresswoman Martha Griffiths dramatized the inequity by asking Government men who testified before her pension committee, "Why should I be paying to support your widow, when you aren't paying to support my husband?"

The Social Security system favors widows over widowers of workers in a similar way. If a working woman elects to take benefits as a widow rather than as a worker—and she often comes out better that way—she doesn't get any benefits for Social Security payments that have been deducted from her earnings. But when she dies, her husband does not benefit from her payments in the same way she benefits from his. Unless he can prove that he is indigent, he gets nothing at all from her Social Security account. But why shouldn't her heirs benefit from all that that she has paid in—just as a man's heirs do, whether indigent or not?

Pension plans entirely paid by the company discriminate against women workers in a more subtle but nonetheless effective way, Mrs. Griffiths charged. A typical "noncontributory plan" will vest, or set aside, funds for an employee only after he or she has worked for ten years and reached age 40. This sounds fair enough. If a woman stays ten years and is 40 years old, she gets the pension the same as a man. The fact is, of course, that a woman usually doesn't stay long enough to get the pension. When she leaves, the company hires another woman, and uses the money that would have gone to fund a pension for her job to finance bigger pensions for the men.

Employers see nothing wrong with this arrangement. Their position is that pensions reward long service and protect a man's dependent wife and children. If this is so, Mrs. Griffiths contends, then the pay gap between long-service and short-service employees (in practice, men workers and women workers) is wider than their paychecks indicate. If, on the contrary, the pension is really deferred salary, then the girls who leave are literally cheated out of part of their pay.

Women workers lose out in much the same way on group life insurance, available now to 90 percent of all clerical and production workers. Many of these policies provide larger benefits for men than for women workers and pay less to widowers than widows. And insurance plans that give higher-salaried employees more coverage often allot them additional insurance on the basis of long service, a proviso that discriminates against women workers who have lost their seniority during child-rearing years or even for taking a few weeks off to have a baby.

At the 1967 Congressional hearings on pension plans, a spokesman for American Telephone and Telegraph testified that differentials were adopted "in recognition of different needs and roles of men and women in society." But whatever the intent, the effect is to cut women's pay.

When unions bargain with employers, they add to the dollars in a worker's paycheck all the various fringe benefits— vacations, holidays, sick leave, bonus rights, rights to overtime and premium pay, stock options, savings plans, health and life insurance, rights to buy meals, products, or services at a discount, allowances for uniforms or expenses.

In 1963 a government estimate put employer expenditures on supplementary compensation for nonfactory workers at 24 percent of the payroll. This invisible pay has been rising faster than the dollars workers take home, so those who don't get the "fringes" lag farther and farther behind those who do.

This lag increasingly divides the working world into two groups: first-class workers who have rights to their jobs and the benefits that go with them, and intermittent, second-class workers who, like the poor, are out of the system and entitled only to be paid for the work actually performed. What seems to be growing is a sharp class distinction between work that is less skilled, less responsible, less permanent, and so carries lower pay and fewer fringe benefits, and the more skilled, more responsible, permanent work that carries high pay and a stake in the future of the enterprise.

This cleavage between the ins and the outs worries idealists. It is often used to condone riots in city ghettos. But the fact is that most of these "workers anonymous" without job protection are not Negro men primed for revolution. Most of them are docile wives and mothers. White and Negro women outnumber men in restaurants, hotels, stores, and many other fields where the work is not steady.

Whatever the field, whatever the function, whatever the training, however contribution is measured—by piece rate or time rate or commission—women wind up with less money than men doing the same work. According to the Department of Labor, only 14 percent of the women receiving unemployment compensation earned enough to qualify for the maximum benefit allowed by the various states in 1965, while 59 percent of the men did. Although one out of ten families is headed by a woman, and the Women's Bureau says that nearly half the women working really need the money, a woman worker is nearly twice as likely to be unemployed as a man, and she gets second-class treatment even then. In 37 states, for instance, she cannot draw unemployment insurance if she is fired for pregnancy.

Women are supposed to be worth less pay because they aren't as steady workers as men, but continuing U.S. Public Health Service studies of time lost from work because of illness or injury show that age, occupation, and salary make more difference than sex. Women seem to be out sick more than men because they hold the dull, ill-paid jobs that invite "sickness." Some studies show that men in clerical jobs are actually out sick more than women and that women over 45 years old were out sick substantially less frequently than men their age.

It's the same way with turnover. Women quit because they are confined to jobs that anyone would readily quit. Employers can't expect to reduce the turnover of any particular job by hiring men instead of women. Men will resign to get another job almost as often as women will leave for family reasons. The Bureau of Labor Statistics concludes that absenteeism and turnover rates depend much more on the nature of the job than on the sex of the job-holder.

The uncertainty women feel about their job futures handicaps them in another way. Rather than take a lower-paid job that permits them to earn while learning, as career-oriented men often do, they choose dead-end jobs that pay well right from the start, such as stenographic work. Professor Jacob Mincer, of Columbia University, who has calculated the money investment in "human capital," found that women invested only one-tenth as much as men in on-the-job training defined this way. When women do train on the job, they are more likely than men to bear the costs themselves, rather than have them financed by employers. Thus a typist pays a business school to learn how to operate a typewriter, but the man who repairs it is usually trained at the expense of a manufacturer. Hairdressers, nurses, teachers, and many other skilled women are in fields which are entered from vocational schools that charge tuition. Men, on the other hand, may qualify as skilled craftsmen by serving as apprentices on the job.

William H. Miller, marketing vice president of American Oil Company, believes that this "statistical discrimination" is unfair:

> So some women do take time out from the jobs to have children. Some men leave one company to go to another or to start a business of their own; some men crack up on a job and must be replaced; some men become seriously ill or die before they reach the normal age of retirement. Some become alcoholic. But management doesn't refuse to hire or promote men just because these things happen.

Reasons for dividing jobs on a sexual basis can be pretty far-fetched. Years ago, when girls unexpectedly turned out to be good at typing, people said, "Of course! Girls can type because they are good at playing the piano!" Women themselves claim they are better at paperwork because of a feminine "instinct" for order in the home.

Women's "knack for detail" has been cited as the reason why they should do everything from the filing to computer programming. Fannie Klein, a woman member of the New York City bar, once declared that if a woman were appointed to the Supreme Court, she would be able to handle the "painful and minute details under judicial consideration that men ordinarily leave to their assistants and secretaries." But there is neither agreement on exactly what this knack is, nor evidence that men do not possess it, too.

Very little scientific work has been done on differences between the productivity of men and women in specific jobs. Personnel directors are more apt to go by characteristics such as finger dexterity, strength, speed, coordination, language, and other skills for which sex differences have been established by academic psychologists. But sex-based differences are seldom the critical factor in on-the-job performance.

People have fixed ideas about whether a job should be done by a man or a woman, but their reasons are as arbitrary as a Frenchman's attempt to explain what's so feminine about *la table*. In 1962, a Presidential order requesting all Federal appointing officers to give reasons for requesting a man or a woman for a job opening cut down requests for candidates of a certain sex to one percent of their former volume. Apparently many of the reasons looked lame in writing. Reasons for preferring a man given by the one percent included travel, arduous duty, geographical location, exposure to weather, and lack of facilities for mixed groups.

Explanations for sex-typing are often given in the tone of voice a teller of fairy tales uses to warn his audience that what he says is not to be taken literally: women cannot be railroad yardmasters because they might have to "work at night." Everyone knows, of course, that women telephone operators and trained nurses have always taken night shifts.

A British firm explained to a United Press reporter that it did not hire women executives because all its executives had to make "frequent visits to extreme tropical climates, for which women would not be suitable." No one offered evidence that women suffer more than men in the tropics, nor did anyone mention that wives frequently follow their husbands to jobs in the tropics.

A foreign visitor noticed that workers on electronic circuits in a factory were all women. "It's close work, and women have the finger dexterity for it," the visitor was told. Later on in her tour she visited a medical school class in brain surgery and remarked that the students were all men. "But they've got to be men," the answer came. "Brain surgery takes a steady hand!"

Women are seldom accountants, it is often said, because they have "no head for figures"—a failing which does not prevent them from doing the less prestigious bookkeeping work which really does require a head for figures.

Women practically never manage supermarkets or grocery stores, because "they couldn't move those heavy boxes around in the back room," but except in the smallest stores or in emergencies, the manager doesn't tote boxes himself.

In 1956, a *Fortune* reporter found that corn-husking was a woman's job in Eureka, Illinois, but a man's job in Jackson, Wisconsin, while textile spinning was done by women in Chattanooga mills and by men in North Carolina. Women pharmacists and dentists are common in many European countries, but they are rare in the United States.

The most general explanation of the division of labor between men and women in all societies has been advanced by Talcott Parsons, of Harvard, a leader in sociological theory. Parsons believes that every culture, including the primitive tribes observed by Margaret Mead, assigns men what he calls "instrumental-adaptive" roles and women what he calls "expressive-integrative" roles. Men are "instrumental" or active in doing things to the physical environment and "adaptive" in making policy for the family, the firm, the nation, or the group. By contrast, women are "expressive"—or concerned with registering emotions and "integrating the group." According to Parsons, women generally manage "the internal motivational tensions of the members of a group and their solidarity with each other."

These terms translate quite easily into the popular masculinist stereotypes which have been advanced to keep women "privatized" or unrecognized in law or public affairs. According to Jessie Bernard in *Academic Women,* women are in charge of "domestic relations." They help the insiders get along with each other and keep the place organized. Men are in charge of "foreign relations." They negotiate with the outsiders, the customers, the suppliers, the government, the adversaries, or the allies. The inside-outside principle holds up when it is tested on existing occupational sex labels.

The occupations most completely monopolized by women are the personal services where women do for pay exactly what they would do for their own families. Not unexpectedly, more than 90 percent of all nurses, baby-sitters, household workers, hotel maids, dressmakers, milliners, and dietitians are women.

Women also tend to monopolize those jobs of limited responsibility which involve greeting and serving outsiders in much the same way that a wife welcomes visiting acquaintances of her husband. More than 90 percent of receptionists, attendants in doctors' and dentists' offices, airline flight attendants, and demonstrators, more than 80 percent of persons employed to wait on tables, more than 75 percent of cashiers are women.

Like the 100-percent female "bunnies" who wait on table in Playboy clubs, these women hold their jobs in part because they help to bring in and please customers. The mild titillation of a feminine presence is an admitted factor in offices where the men to be pleased are not paying customers. In 1961, more than a quarter of the 1,900 employers queried told the National Office Management Association that sex appeal figured in some jobs in their offices.

The public image of the millions of women who work in offices is the private secretary or office wife to a policy-making male boss. No clearer definition of the "integrative" function Parsons ascribes to women could be stated than W. M. Kiplinger's "Salute to Secretaries" at the National Secretaries Association meeting of February 1967:

> Secretaries are marvelous people. They are ornamental and they are useful. They take down what you say and improve upon it. They know where to put in the double l's, the commas and the paragraphs. They hold the mad letters until tomorrow. They answer the telephone, sidetrack the bores and put through those on the important list. They remember the birthdays and anniversaries. They remind you that it's time to get going for the lunch date. They see when you need a haircut.

Secretaries may be specially prized, and the top secretaries exceptionally well paid, because they give men who can afford to pay well the subservient, watchful, and admiring attention that Victorian wives used to give their husbands. But increasingly, office wives are rebelling, too. According to an anecdote printed in *Reader's Digest,* one secretary had long resented her boss's boast that he hired girls for their looks and then taught them to type. One day when he was interviewing a particularly handsome male job-seeker, she slipped a note on his desk which read, "Hire him, we'll teach him engineering."

A few brilliant managements have systematically exploited the man-woman relationship. Henry Luce tapped the talents of women with journalistic ability by creating a new wifely role for them. Under Time, Inc.'s system of "group journal-

ism," work was divided along sex lines: men developed ideas
and did the writing, and to keep their minds free and untrammeled by details, each was supplied with a girl researcher to
take notes on interviews, set up appointments, look up facts,
and ultimately check the writer's statements against available
evidence. Experience as a researcher has developed some
competent women writers, but most of them became writers
only after leaving Time, Inc.

The writer-researcher team is powerful because it mirrors
the contemporary ideal of American marriage. Researchers
are not mere handmaidens. They have their own area of
authority, and writers are not allowed to forget it. If a writer
insists on using a fact his researcher cannot substantiate, she
may keep the story out of the magazine by refusing to put a
red dot over the disputed word on her "checking copy" of the
manuscript.

This complementary relationship of "separate but equal" is
not universal. In his comparative study of the occupational
roles of women in three cultures, Chester L. Hunt, of West
Michigan University, found that American women supplemented men, while Japanese women served them as subordinates, and Filipino women were their occupational equals.
Americans may be especially self-conscious about the role of
women in part because it is so much harder to supplement
another person than to serve, direct, or even treat him as an
autonomous equal.

Journalism is one of the few occupations which has a
woman for every two men, roughly the ratio of women to
men in the labor force generally, yet particular jobs can be
rigidly sex-typed within the field. Personnel and labor relations workers, managers in apparel and accessory stores,
personal service workers, and foremen in textile and apparel
manufacturing have this average sex ratio, too. Yet women in
these occupations are sometimes more aware of the limitations of their sex than women in fields where women either
predominate or are so rare that like women engineers, they
can be taken as exceptions to every rule.

Are there any principles that explain the meanderings of
the sex boundaries? One is the idea that women should work
inside and men outside. Another earmarks service work for
women and profit-making for men. Other rules reserve work
with machinery, work carrying prestige, and the top job to

men. Most sex boundaries can be explained on the basis of one or another of these three rules.

Take the inside-outside concept. It divides the work of women and men along many axes: cooperation-competition; helping-fighting; welfare-profit; and hence, in our time, public sector-private sector. Let's see how it works.

Competitive private enterprises are apt to be dominated by men, especially if the risk is high and there is a big profit to be made. The automobile and appliance industries fall into this category, and they are frankly hostile to women above the rank of secretary. Investment banking, canning, and large-scale real estate speculation are other highly competitive, profit-oriented businesses where the pace is regarded as "too fast" and the going "too rough" for women in policy-making spots. Retailing and garment-making are high-risk, fast-paced, profit-oriented industries which do promote women, but it must be added that the women buyers or designers who share in the rewards are deprecated as "hard" and "masculine."

Cooperative, helping, welfare work is dominated by women, especially when it is done for little or no money. This idea even carries over into the field of medicine.

In the United States, medicine is still largely private enterprise, and nowhere else do physicians make so much money. At the 1960 Census, for instance, physicians and surgeons led all other occupations in earnings: their median income was nearly $15,000 a year, compared with less than $10,000 for dentists, the next highest-paid occupation. Unlike physicians in some countries, our doctors have to invest their own money in their education and make it "pay out" in private practice. Those who don't have the capital themselves are usually financed through their training and internship by the "sweat capital" of working wives. Nowhere else in the world is medical training so long, so expensive, and so little supported by public funds. And few countries make it quite so hard as we do for women to become doctors.

One reason, of course, is that women are reluctant to invest as much in their own professional training as men. Russia has a high proportion of women doctors partly because since Czarist days the Russian medical system has had a second grade of physician for routine illnesses whose training is shorter, partly because under Communism the Government bears the total cost of medical education for women doctors as well as men. But an additional and significant reason is the strong welfare orientation of Russian medicine. Medical care is a free service that cannot be considered a business. Britain, Yugoslavia, and other countries with socialized medicine also have a higher percentage of women doctors than we.

The welfare-profit boundary is convincing because it exists even in American medicine and law. The few women we do attract to medicine tend to enter Government service or teaching rather than private practice. It's the same way with our women lawyers. They are more apt to work for the Government, nonprofit organizations, or on salary than in what lawyers call the law "business" of serving clients on a fee basis.

The welfare-profit boundary exists within business organizations as well as in broad industry categories. In selling, men are more apt to be compensated by commission than women. The line is dramatic in department stores. Men manage high-priced, high-margin merchandise such as appliances and furniture, while women buyers usually manage departments where the margin is lower.

We had a bit of fun asking our friends why it was that men usually sell women's shoes, while women may sell men's underwear. One acquaintance surmised that there was probably "something masculine about leather." Another thought that women especially valued the attention of men to their legs and the opinion of men on the sexiness of their shoes. The fact is that women's shoes carry a high enough margin to be worth selling on a commission basis, while men's underwear is sold by a salaried clerk.

Organizations which distinguish between "sales" and "service" often assign sales to men and service to women. Office machine manufacturers, among many others, send men out on the road as "salesmen," but follow up with women "service representatives," who teach customer employees how to use the products. Another nonprofit service that women dominate is the adjustment of complaints. They have an easier time holding customers to the rules because a woman isn't expected to have the authority to break regulations.

The service-profit boundary divides personnel work. In business concerns, women hire the routine workers, but men recruit the executives. Women run employment agencies serving job-seekers, but most executive recruiters paid by employers are men. In labor unions or in management departments set up to deal with labor relations, women watch out for employee health, education, and welfare of various kinds, but seldom appear on either side of the bargaining table when contracts are being negotiated and substantial money is at stake.

The service-profit boundary works in banks. Able women sometimes get good jobs in escrow and trust work where the funds of women and children must be protected against risks. They have less chance in the loan department, where profit for the bank can be made and the bank's resources must be risked. The Invisible Bar even separates receiving money from paying money. Banks employed women as receiving tellers before they were allowed to be paying tellers. As late as 1942, the U.S. Department of Labor classified the job of "paying teller" as only "apparently" suitable for women. Everywhere, it seems, "mamma can take the money in, but only papa can pay it out." The town clerk who receives taxes is often a woman, but the clerk who pays the town bills is usually a man. And it's the same way with cashiers and paymasters.

The inside-outside boundary between "domestic" and "foreign" relations runs along the same lines as the service-profit boundary. Men compensated on commission are the "outside" purchasing agents and salesmen who visit vendors and customers to make the deals that result in profit or loss; women on straight salary buy and sell routine, fixed-price items over the phone. It works the same way in newspaper advertising departments: want ads for the classified section are solicited and filled by women telephone workers; display ads are solicited by men on commission who travel and entertain prospects.

Everywhere the women stay inside, "at home" in the office, the organization, the profession, the country, while men work "outside." Advertising agencies employ both men and women to check television commercials, but the men in the bull pens check out-of-town shows that require travel to cover and, say the girls, have to spend fewer hours glued to the screen. Factories don't like to hire women as expediters because this liaison job requires a lot of "running around" from department to department. And it took a major labor shortage as well as equal opportunity laws to convert the Fuller Brush man into a Fullerette and to create jobs for girl letter carriers and gas station attendants.

Women stay "inside" their occupational groups in a figurative way as well as inside the office physically. In organizations, they hold the office of secretary, which deals with the membership. They sometimes become presidents of professional societies which exist to assert the solidarity of an occupational group; in the past few years, women have headed the Society of Magazine Writers and the New York Society of Security Analysts. By contrast, trade associations representing whole industries with Government or the public "outside" the industry seldom, if ever, have a woman chief. When Jessie Bernard compared the publications of male and female college professors, she discovered that more men published in journals "outside" their fields than women. She found that the men were more apt to interpret their specialties to the lay public as "men of knowledge," while women were more apt to teach it to students.

Men are "instrumental" in a literal sense. They will do anything that can be done by *machinery,* including, as we have seen, attending the birth of babies by "instrument." Engineering is the American profession with the fewest women, and the heavy, highly mechanized industries are the ones most opposed to women policy-makers. In railroads, steel, shipping, aviation, space, automobiles, and metal-working the opposition to women above the secretarial or pretty-girl level is categorical. One president of a metal-working company shrugged women off as "totally unsuited to most manufacturing operations." The bad language of men in machine shops is so frequently and seriously cited as a bar to women that it sometimes looks as if men cuss deliberately to prove that no women are present.

The male affinity for machinery is a mystique accepted by both sexes. Women sometimes don't realize that they can change a tire until they have to do it because there is no man around to do it for them. "Women drivers" are a staple joke even for those who know that the most sophisticated studies seldom disclose a significant difference between the accident rate of men and that of women. American women have to drive cars because American life would come to a halt if they didn't, but the notion that a man ought to do it is so strong that a wife usually slides over and gives the wheel to her husband when she picks him up in the car.

As machines have been invented to do women's work, men have taken it over. In 1968, the most sophisticated machine of all, the computer, was bringing men back into clerical work. "You always see *men* sitting at the consoles in the ads for computers," an office manager explained. Ida Hoos, a social scientist who has analyzed the impact of automation on employment, foresees fewer office *girls* but more work for the repair*man*.

It's interesting to see what happens when, as has frequently been the case in America, a job changes sex. "I wonder what's going on in banks," a woman telephone company supervisor said to us. "A bank teller used to be important, but now women do it. They must have changed the teller's job."

"Not really," George Ward of the American Bankers Association replied when we put the question to him. "The teller has always really had a contact job. What's changed is public acceptance of women."

A woman bank teller, accosted on the floor of the bank, disagreed with this view. "It's just money," she said. "Bank salaries haven't risen as fast as salaries in other fields. They can get women cheaper."

A woman personnel officer of a Newark bank told us she didn't discriminate. In her bank all tellers, men and women both, started at $68 a week and advanced regardless of sex to a ceiling of $140. Most of the tellers were women, she said, only because there weren't enough men to go around.

It was not always so. In 1940, women tellers were few and far between. When World War II came, some banks tried to get draft deferment for their tellers on the ground that they were essential. But by the end of the war, women bank tellers were common and everybody liked them. A lot of women stayed on.

What happened next resembled nothing so much as the stampedes that used to occur when a neighborhood shifted from white to Negro. In 1950, bank tellers were almost evenly divided between the sexes. In the next ten years—a decade not marked by gains for women in employment—the job of bank teller passed from men to women. By 1960, 70 percent of the bank tellers in the country were women. In

1966, the First National City Bank of New York was buying
display advertising in the help-wanted column:

HOUSEWIVES

TIME ON YOUR HANDS?

CHILDREN GROWN?

TRAIN TO BE A TELLER

Pleasant and interesting work meeting the public
No experience necessary—We will train you

The solidly masculine "important job" had become not only
"just a high-grade clerk's job," but a job suitable for bored or
rusty housewives.

What has changed? The clue is in Mr. Ward's definition of
the job of the teller as the bank's contact with the customer.
The old teller was a gatekeeper to money, protected by a
literal cage. The bank he guarded financed production. Now it
finances consumption and sells bookkeeping services to house-
holders.

By the end of the 1960s, banks have become as friendly,
noisy, and informal as supermarkets. Money is just another
item on a shopping list. Today everyone has a checking account. Everyone borrows money. Paying the bills has become
a housekeeping chore for wives instead of a ritual symbolizing
the husband's leadership of the house. The bank is a service
station, not a temple. You have a friend at the Chase Manhattan who knows how to fix it so you can fly now and pay later.
The banker is no longer a glassy-eyed father judging your
character and intentions. He is a kicky playmate.

Or a permissive mother. Banks don't exploit the sex appeal
of their tellers as blatantly as airlines exploit the sex appeal of
stewardesses, but tellers are supposed to sell, and it helps if
they are attractive. In 1966, *The New York Times* business
section reported that The Meadow Brook National Bank, "in
accord with a theme of peppy conservatism," had retained a
fashion consultant to restyle the hair and makeup of the
bank's tellers at its Manhasset and Great Neck, Long Island,
branches.

Although the lady bank tellers seem to indicate that there
are a rising number of women in men's jobs, this is not the

case. Women have flocked into the labor market to fill the demand for women's jobs like teaching and nursing or to fill jobs which were too new to be assigned to either sex, as was once the case with typewriting. In his statistical study of the sex ratios of Census occupations from 1900 to 1960, Dr. Edward Gross, Professor of Sociology at the University of Washington, found that men have invaded women's working territory more often than the other way around, while maintaining their monopoly on traditionally male occupations, with the exception of a few odd and unlamented jobs like running elevators.

And so it is today. Men are now invading nursing, secretarial work, teaching, and library work. Teaching is an important example, but library work is closely allied and a more compact field to study. What's been happening in these decorous institutions is more dramatic than meets the casual eye.

In 1940, more than 90 percent of the American librarians were women. At the end of the war, library schools eager to get their share of the tuition money provided under the GI Bill of Rights went out to recruit veterans. The graduate course was only a year, there were plenty of jobs and, since former soldiers couldn't be called sissies, veterans charged unembarrassed into library work. Sometimes they chafed under the direction of elderly female librarians, but more often they by-passed them by getting newly created library jobs at higher pay.

Why the change? Libraries had become important. The war had raised the prestige of knowledge. Government and business were investing in research. Instead of offering genteel entertainment to individuals, librarians had become, in the public mind, the gatekeepers of that knowledge that is power. The change in role unlocked a great deal of money. Federal funds were lavished on library building. Universities with Government research contracts and private companies investing in scientific research were expanding library services. Big "Librarian Wanted" ads appeared in *The New York Times.*

The machine mystique changed libraries, too. When knowledge became a competitive weapon, it was slated for mechanization. Now specialists called Information Technologists talk of putting knowledge into giant computers from which any fact can be extracted without the trouble of shuffling index cards. They are, of course, men who regard cataloguing as dull, "detail" work suitable only for women. The cataloguers who have been coping with the avalanche of printed material say that the Information Technologists are going through all the stages of trial and error which went into present indexing systems. The dialogue has a homely ring. It is repeated every time a husband refuses to take his wife's warning against a short cut that she has already tried and found wanting.

"Young man, be a librarian," Arnold Gingrich advised *Esquire* readers in a 1964 publisher's editorial. "Most of the top jobs in the profession want male librarians to fill them." Young men took the advice. By 1967 men headed 39 of the 46 biggest public libraries and all 74 of the members of the elite Association of Research Libraries. Administrators said they were hiring men because there were not enough trained women librarians to go around. At the same time, bankers were saying they had to hire women bank tellers because there weren't enough *men* to go around. And while Mr. Ward's cheery explanation that "women are better accepted in jobs" could conceivably account for the increase in women tellers, it couldn't account for the increase in male librarians.

In banks the changeover was good-humored, but a sex war rages in the library field.

"I say, kick the women out!" a state librarian wrote candidly to a colleague. "How are you going to get any worthwhile man to go into a field dominated by old women? We need more men in the library game." Whether he's right or not, the sex ratio in the library "game" has become a topic for survey, comment, and acrimonious debate. The same hostility shows up in public school systems and women's colleges. The young men seethe under petticoat rule, while the older women complain, with some justification, that the young men aren't as loyal, dedicated, competent, or manageable as the old maids they replaced.

Money makes a difference, of course. The men women replaced in banks went on to better jobs. The women that men replace in libraries and schools have nowhere better to go, and remain as obstacles to higher pay schedules for the men. But prestige is involved as well as money. Anthropologists find that women's work in one part of the world may be men's work in another, but whatever men do is regarded as more important than what their womenfolk do. In many

Oriental cultures, including the Japanese, for instance, women make decisions about family spending because handling money is undignified in these societies. In some primitive tribes economic activity of any kind is held in such low esteem that women do all the productive work. In his study of women's work in three cultures, Chester Hunt found that Filipino women are more apt than ours to be doctors, lawyers, storekeepers, merchants, bankers, and pharmacists, and he thought the reason was that Filipinos do not value professional achievement as much as we do. They are agricultural, not industrial. In England, learning was long believed to be an aristocratic privilege, rather than a common right; consequently its high status has drawn a larger percentage of men into teaching than we have here.

The Invisible Bar has sometimes liberated women from the shackles of prestige. A thousand years ago, Lady Murasaki, a Japanese noblewoman, wrote *The Tale of Genji,* one of the world's greatest novels. She was freed to write as creatively as she pleased because it didn't matter what she set down in the "woman's language," vernacular Japanese. If she had been a man, she would have had to write in the much more limiting court Chinese.

In general, institutions don't like to get the reputation for "having a lot of women." Critics of the Federal Civil Service warn that the best men may not consider careers in Government if "too many women" advance in it. For more than a century, opponents of coeducation argued that the admission of women would drive the best men out of a college or a field of study. In 1968, admissions officers of coeducational schools continue to watch their sex ratio out of an uneasy feeling that "too many women" may lower standards. The standards involved are not academic ones, because women generally average better grades than men.

A bird's-eye view of the sex map of occupations shows how outmoded home roles limit women at work. Women are least accepted in work involving machinery, negotiation, travel, risk, profit, and substantial sums of money. But the most striking boundary of all is occupational *status.* In a field as masculine as railroading, women are employed to clean the railway cars. In fields as feminine as cosmetics, a man is usually found in the president's chair.

Men dominate the top of the professions of cooking,

dressmaking, and child study. During the 1960s school
home economics and social work sought men deans in c
to "improve the status of the professions." Women wor
commercial artists, but seldom rise to become art direc
They write advertising copy, but they seldom become par
in advertising agencies. The managing editors even of w
en's magazines are often men. Successful actors grad
from the screen to directing, but the only actress-direc
who come easily to mind are Ida Lupino, who was bor
Britain, and Mai Zetterling, who is Swedish.

If you rank the number of individuals in any occupatio
the basis of income, they fall into a pyramid, with lot
people at the ₁owest bracket on the bottom and fewer at e
rise until you reach, theoretically at least, the one indivi
who exceeds all others at the top. The higher you go
course, the thinner the ranks. That is the iron law of suc
But as you go up the ladder you find a lower percentag
women on every rung.

A handy example is the Federal service, which emp
650,000 women, promotes them according to explicit r
and grades the many different occupations in the Governi
by income brackets. In 1966, women dominated the lo
grades, but they thinned out at every rise in grade until
were only 1½ percent of those earning $20,000 or n
Students of the Federal service say that conditions are sin
to those in private employment.

The bigger the job, the less likely it is to be filled t
woman. This means that women at the top are excepti
among women. It also means that the elite of any group
assume that it is stag; the few women at the top can
ignored or treated as exceptions. Yet there are always s
women up there. The fascinating thing about it is that wh
er the measure is money, power, prestige, or achievem
and whatever the field, the proportion of women at the to
remarkably constant and low. In the mid-1960s, wor
were:

—Less than 10 percent of all the professional or "kno
edge" elites except classroom teachers, nurses, librari
social workers, and journalists; 9 percent of all full profess
8 percent of all scientists; 6 percent of all physicians
percent of all lawyers; 1 percent of all engineers.

—Five percent of the income elite of the individuals v

incomes of $10,000 or more, including all the rich widows and the five former wives of Jean Paul Getty, the oil man who has not disclaimed the title of richest man in the world.

—Five percent of the *prestige elite* listed in *Who's Who in America* for 1967, down from 6 percent in 1930.

—Two percent of the *power elite* of business executives listed in Standard & Poor's Directory of leading American corporations; less than 4 percent of all Federal civil servants in the six highest grades; 1 percent of Federal judges; 1 percent of the United States Senate.

These women at the top look as if they are exceptions to all the rules of the map. A closer look at who and where they are and how they got there discloses that they are all of them exceptions that prove the rule.

5

THE LOOPHOLE WOMEN

What about these women at the top? They can be found in every field. Katharine Meyer Graham, working publisher of *Newsweek* and *The Washington Post*. Anna Rosenberg Hoffman, crack labor negotiator and public relations consultant. Helen Meyer, president of Dell Publishing Co., Inc. Dr. Maria G. Mayer, winner of the Nobel Prize for physics. Mildred Custin, chairman of the board and chief executive officer of Bonwit Teller. Mary Wells, president of Wells, Rich, Greene, reputed in 1967 to be the fastest-growing advertising agency in New York City. How did they make it? What do spectacularly successful women have to say about the Invisible Bar against women?

Topflight women don't say much about the obstacles. A surprising number of them don't think there are any barriers that a determined woman cannot overcome. If more women don't get to the top, the reason, they say, is that women simply don't try hard enough. Some of them talk as if an admission of barriers might weaken their resolve.

"I've never encountered anything I could call discrimination," Marian E. Trembley, manager of Macy's San Francisco, says. A forthright athletic-looking woman, Miss Trembley was a schoolteacher who got a chance to learn administration as a WAVE officer during World War II and did such a good job that her superior officer offered her a job in Macy's when he went back to the store after the war. The number of women managers of stores the size of hers would not exhaust the fingers of one hand.

"It's a lot easier for women to blame discrimination than to face up to their own inadequacies," she told us. "Many women think that because they have done a good job at the middle level they deserve promotion to the top. They don't realize that the top takes a different kind of talent. I hate to say it, but generally speaking, men are more dedicated, more willing to stay late and get work done, and more willing to put the job first. Career women are going to have to pay the cost of women who are not dedicated for a long time to come."

Some high-ranking women are privately bitter about instances in which young women quit their jobs in a pinch and so confirm the suspicion that women really aren't interested in working. More constructive women in top positions hope to educate girls to greater responsibility. "I think it's wonderful that women now have so many choices," wrote Geraldine Rhoads, Editor of *Woman's Day* magazine. "But unless a woman uses her choice responsibly—whether at home or at work—she hurts the chances of women everywhere."

Some of the most influential women in the country turn their backs on the whole subject. "I am so involved in the problems of news that I don't think very much about problems concerning women either in connection with my own job or with their progress in general," Katharine Meyer Graham wrote us. "My situation is so individual that it has very little relevance for other people."

Katharine Meyer Graham grew up in Washington politics. She is the daughter of Eugene Meyer, formerly head of the World Bank, and Agnes Meyer, a writer who believed educated women should speak out on public issues. After working for a year as a reporter on her father's *Washington Post,* she married Phil Graham, a lawyer, and retired to have four children. Eugene Meyer sold *The Post* to his daughter and son-in-law, and Phil Graham expanded and strengthened the property. In 1963, Phil Graham committed suicide, leaving a profitable newspaper and newsmagazine, *Newsweek,* as well as interests in other publishing ventures. Katharine Graham took over active management. By 1967, she had built *The Washington Post* into the third biggest U.S. daily in advertising linage. In 1968, Donald Robinson was planning to include her in his forthcoming book on the 100 most important people in the world.

Women who have inherited or married positions of power may not like to talk about the barriers which prevent less fortunate women from rising to the very top, but privileged women are not alone in denying barriers. "I think women are given a fair chance to get ahead in business," a conspicuously successful professional woman wrote us. "Of course, there are isolated instances when women are discriminated against because of the personal prejudice of the discriminator. In my opinion, personal prejudices of this type are not exercised so generally that one could conclude that women do not have a fair chance to get ahead in business." The woman who wrote this letter is not rich or privileged. She is Judge Juanita Kidd Stout of Philadelphia, a Negro.

Statistically speaking, a Negro woman judge is an exquisite rarity. Less than 3 percent of American lawyers are women, and prejudice against women lawyers is outspoken. Nearly 1,000 recent women law school graduates queried by James J. White, Assistant Professor of Law at the University of Michigan, reported nearly 2,000 separate occasions on which prospective employers told them that it was against their policy to hire women lawyers. In his report, "Women in the Law," published in the April 1967 issue of the *Michigan Law Review,* he pointed out that these statements all violated the Civil Rights Act of 1964 forbidding discrimination on the ground of sex, and so enjoyed the special credibility lawyers ascribe to "admissions against interest."

Women judges are even rarer than women lawyers, and Negroes are notoriously under-represented on the bar and the bench. Yet Judge Stout believes that she has encountered no discrimination. "As a law student, as a practicing attorney, as an assistant district attorney and as a judge for over eight years, I have enjoyed the greatest cooperation and respect of my colleagues and litigants as well. I neither rely on the fact that I am a woman nor recoil from it. As an assistant district attorney, I was Chief of the Appeals Division of the office and had seven assistants—all men—under my supervision. They did not mind, neither did I. The law is sexless. All that is required for success in this field is honesty, good preparation, hard work, love of fellow man and a cooperative spirit. Any woman possessing these qualities should enjoy the profession."

Judge Stout undoubtedly possesses all these qualities. And just because she does, she may not realize how exceptional they are. But can outstanding merit win out over the double barrier of sex and race? Whenever both sexes are asked whether merit can overcome prejudice, more women than men say yes. Men sometimes find such women irritatingly naive. Professor White comments that women lawyers have "a continuing, and perhaps irrational, belief that hard work, good grades, and perseverance will overcome the obstacles which they face." Judge Stout is no exception when she confesses that she is a "confirmed optimist" about barriers.

Her unique position and her optimism can both be used to political advantage. As a Negro woman, Judge Stout is a double minority, twice as visible as a white man running for office, and so twice as valuable in a political campaign. And although few Negro women can identify with her, her success in overcoming the double bar against her demonstrates that opportunity is not totally denied to those underprivileged by race and sex.

"The sex provision of Title VII of the Civil Rights Act of 1964 provides women with machinery by which charges of discrimination may be aired," she wrote us. "It will certainly be helpful in eliminating such discrimination as may exist. It will be helpful also as an educational tool for the public and the complainants alike. Employers will strive toward compliance. Women who have legitimate complaints will secure redress. Women whose complaints are not well founded will learn they cannot substitute femininity for competence."

Among the other successful women who share Judge Stout's reluctance to complain about barriers is Esther Raushenbush, former president of Sarah Lawrence College. "In my judgment, there has been too much defensive, complaining, 'how-women-are-kept-down' writing on the whole subject of women in this society." She doesn't think there is a yes or no answer to the question of whether women get a fair shake in business; she claims she really doesn't know whether she has suffered personally in her own career; and while she thinks that laws against discrimination in employment are a good thing "in principle," she points out that "legislation on equal pay rights has sometimes worked to the disadvantage of women in preventing their being hired." As is fitting for an educator of women, she is less interested in the treatment women get than in "positive concern, education, and activities directed toward the women."

Still other women frankly duck the issue for fear of reprisals. A nationally known woman whose record takes up three inches of fine print in *Who's Who in America* begged us to keep her name out of this book. "My work is almost exclusively with men," she wrote. "Almost anything I could say one way or the other might be misconstrued. You are writing on a subject close to the heart of almost all career and working women, but I prefer not to be quoted on it."

Like successful men, successful women are naturally optimistic people who avoid subjects that make them sound like soreheads or threaten their all-important morale. "I have a way of never making much of my difficulties," Dr. Rosa Lee Nemir, Professor of Pediatrics at New York University School of Medicine, says of herself. "My husband says that I just brush my difficulties under the rug."

Pediatrics is a natural field for women doctors. Twenty percent of all American pediatricians are women. But women heads of pediatric departments in medical schools are virtually nonexistent, and Dr. Nemir is one of the few women full professors of medicine in the country. The long list of blue-ribbon credentials behind her name shows that she has been accepted into the tight inner circle of the medical elite. She is a fellow of the American College of Chest Physicians and of the American Academy of Pediatrics, and a member of the American Pediatric Society, the American Thoracic Society, and many others. As an attending physician at New York University-Bellevue Medical Center and at the New York Infirmary, she cares for patients and teaches medical students and house officers. She goes out of her way to encourage girls to go into medicine, drawing freely on her own happy experiences, but she does not fall into the unconscious snobbery of saying, in effect, "There's really no discrimination against a woman as smart as I am." She admits barriers, but she thinks they can be overcome.

"I could never have done what the women pioneers in medicine did," she confessed. "I couldn't have stood the sneering deprecation that Dr. Elizabeth Blackwell, the first woman physician, had to endure. I gave up a fellowship to go to Johns Hopkins medical school because of its reputation for treating women medical students on an equal basis with men, and I was not disappointed. I couldn't do my internship in pediatrics at Johns Hopkins because the hospital had only two beds for women pediatricians and I was the third, but the head of the department placed me personally in a hospital in San Francisco with oh so much kindness and consideration! In San Francisco I lived in a private house across from the hospital. I am happy to say that housing is not a limitation on the number of women interns any hospital can now accept. Today interns of both sexes are apt to be married and live out of the hospital, and we no longer think that men and women doctors have to live on different corridors of a hospital."

Dr. Nemir works quietly behind the scenes to get medical schools and hospitals to adopt flexible schedules which will permit women to combine families with medical careers. She has vigorously supported programs under which two women interns share the work ordinarily done by one. "The number of hours a doctor works a week aren't important," she says. "What matters is keeping her hand in."

For a variety of reasons—and most simply, perhaps, because they have succeeded—women at the top play down the barriers they have overcome. Like Judge Stout, they frequently imply that their own success proves that any woman worth her salt can overcome them. But the situation is not so simple, and some candid women admit it.

The top of any heap has rules of its own. A woman who is twice as good as the men on her level can rise through the middle ranks by working twice as hard as they do, but the higher she gets, the less this competence and dedication will avail her. At the top, all the survivors are competent and dedicated. What counts is a nuance of personality, connections, a personal relationship, the "breaks" of politics, and blind, brute luck.

Both men and women play the cards that are dealt them. Many a man has used his sex to get control of a business owned by a widow, but there are so few women in controlling positions that men rarely can "use sex" to get the top spot. The case of women is the other way around. Because men control the top, it is hard to think of a really successful woman in business or professional life who has not found some way to make her sex work for her.

At the top, where merit alone no longer insures success, many women adopt the tactics of wrestlers who throw their opponents off guard by feigning weakness. A smart woman can take advantage of the fact that men do not regard her as a threat.

Take male pride. Men won't express their feelings to another man as readily as to an unassuming woman. Anna Rosenberg Hoffman has built an impressive career on this fact. She has served as the eyes and ears of two Presidents of the United States, improved the morale of the armed forces by relaying the gripes of soldiers to the high command as the only woman Assistant Secretary of Defense, settled bitter labor disputes, and furthered the careers of a half-dozen political and business leaders, including the Rockefeller brothers.

Anna Rosenberg Hoffman shares with her compatriots, Ferenc Molnar, the playwright, and the irrepressible Gabor sisters, a Hungarian flair for role-playing and enormous personal charm. She was born in Budapest. Her father fled to the United States when Emperor Franz Joseph refused to pay for furniture he had ordered Mr. Hoffman to buy for an imperial palace. In New York, Anna organized her high-school class for woman suffrage, managed the political campaign of a Tammany alderman before she was old enough to vote herself, and finally drifted into the unlikely career of helping management cope with labor disputes. This tiny bundle of feminine energy got her real start when her political skills came to the attention of Franklin Roosevelt, then Governor of New York State. According to one source, Mrs. Hoffman has always had a sure instinct for the role appropriate to the situation, acting with some men as a sympathetic mother, with others as a bright gamin, a brusque executive, or even "one of the boys." Her dramatic timing is legendary.

Shortly after World War II, a brewery hired her to talk to workers who had been out on strike for 65 days. She pulled out all her stops, watching their faces for signs of response. None came.

"You're wasting your time," the union lawyer finally told her. "I know these men. I've eaten with them, slept with them . . ." That gave little Anna an idea.

"You've got me there," she interrupted. As she had expected, a roar of laughter broke the ice. Several days later, the strike was settled.

Mrs. Hoffman was characteristically quick to size up the situation when we asked her whether she thought that women got a fair shake in business. "I know I'm supposed to say that there are no difficulties any more," she said with refreshing candor, "but I'm not going to say it. Of course there are barriers. I've always tried to move women into key spots, and I've always had trouble doing it. Many times I've had a man say 'But the job's too big for a woman.' They say it right to my face. If I remind them that they're talking to a woman, they say, 'Oh, but, Anna, you're different!' They don't accept other women when they accept you. That's why women have to keep on proving that they can do responsible jobs all over again. No, I don't think that the equal opportunity law will help. It may help for the lower jobs, but as long as women are willing to work for less to get a chance at a responsible job, the law can't help."

Mrs. Hoffman modestly credits her success in large part to sheer luck. "I'm not different. There are lots of women—I won't say as brilliant, because I don't think I'm brilliant—but there are lots of women who work as hard as I do and are much better educated—I have honorary degrees, but I never really went to college. I was lucky. Once you get in, one thing leads to another, and it's easy. It may be easier for a woman than a man because men go out of their way to help a woman once she is in."

Senator Maurine Neuberger says much the same thing. "A woman has no special difficulties *being* a United States Senator. The hard part is *getting* the job." When her husband, Senator Richard Neuberger, died in 1960, Governor Mark Hatfield offered to appoint her to fill his unexpired term if she agreed not to run for the seat when it became vacant in 1961. She refused, ran for the seat, and was elected Senator from Oregon in her own right. On her first day she gathered, with other freshmen, around the desk of Senator Everett Dirksen, then minority leader. Dirksen saw a woman approaching and started automatically to get to his feet. "Please sit down," she told him. "I want to be treated like a *Senator.*" He sat down, and she was treated like a Senator.

Some women have actually become successful because there is a prejudice against them at the top levels. A good example is Jane Trahey, who founded Trahey Advertising, Inc., in New York City in 1958.

Miss Trahey is one of the few top women who willingly admit there are barriers against career women in advertising. She has likened the advertising fraternity in New York to the mythical savages who greeted the arrival of a Piper Cub on their veldt by running out and getting under the plane to determine whether it was female or male. "I tried to get going in a couple of the big shops," she told students at the School of Visual Arts, "but the personnel directors were such discouraging and stupid people that I felt the only way to lick them was to join them. Therefore, I joined them. I started my own agency. If they won't let you in because you're female, simply buy the damned place. Today, our agency is small, but it's exciting. *I could not write the ads I write in most of New York's agencies.*" (Emphasis ours.)

The ads are, of course, marvelous. Jane Trahey was the creative spirit who invented much of the distinctive advertising for the Neiman-Marcus specialty store in Dallas. In 1967, she created a squiggly sound to sign off radio commercials for J. C. Penney's Treasure Island Stores in Wisconsin, all of which have roofs that look squiggly. But it is even harder to sell daring new advertising campaigns than it is to create them. "In this business, you've got to find a way to attract and hold attention," she told us. "My way of doing it is to write." Jane Trahey's books, columns, and articles project the image of an *enfant terrible* candor in constant rebellion against the status quo.

The image attracts talent-hunting clients, but it is founded on solid fact. Jane Trahey is a sharp, blonde Irish girl from Chicago with a mind like a burning glass and a restless imagination. She has chronicled her past escapades in *My Life with Mother Superior,* which millions have enjoyed in hard cover, soft cover, and *Reader's Digest,* or seen at the movies, starring Gypsy Rose Lee as the gym teacher and Rosalind Russell as the long-suffering Mother Superior. A sequel movie is appropriately titled *Where Angels Go . . . Trouble Follows.*

"In advertising, it's important to keep the feeling that you can tell the client to go to hell," she says of her own success. "I find that the men in the business have a harder time holding on to that feeling than I do. Most of them have hungry wives and children waiting for them at home. All I've got is my sheep dog, Clovis. She eats enough, but she doesn't talk back." Jane Trahey's talent and her independence are her trademarks.

Except for a few like Jane Trahey, who make candor work for them, leaders of both sexes maintain tight security over the real circumstances which carried them to the top.

Over a period of nearly two years, we talked with more than a hundred women from coast to coast earning more than $10,000 a year. We got the job histories of women doctors, lawyers, and personnel specialists; union executives; editors, writers, and professors; women in science, fashion, banking, insurance. We talked with several women brokers earning more than $50,000 a year; with engineers, the profession where men outnumber women 99 to one, and with leaders in retailing, where more than half the executives are women. We talked to management consultants, employment services, advertising executives, and one television producer.

We hunted for them in different ways. We asked friends. We wrote to leading companies. We went to club meetings. We saved news stories. For several weeks, we picked names at random from *Who's Who in American Women* and phoned them cold turkey. This was at the suggestion of Dr. Peter Rossi, Professor of Sociology at Johns Hopkins University and a specialist in survey techniques. "Executive women have so many defenses about being women that you won't get very far interviewing them face to face," he advised.

But many women we interviewed gave us information about their own careers which could have hurt or humiliated them. One woman doctor who insisted that she had always been treated with great consideration confided, at the end of the interview, that she would have been head of her department at the hospital if she had been a man. "I'm only telling you this because I trust you," she added. Many others said, "I am glad that you are doing a book about discrimination against women. It's badly needed. But please don't tell anyone that you talked with me."

Whenever we traveled, we continued interviewing. Starting with a college classmate, a friend of a friend, or the women's editor of the local newspaper, we would ask for the names of the most successful business and professional women in town. Then we would get them on the phone and ask for the names of other women like them. When the same names began to be repeated, we would close our list and try to set up appointments. In some cities, we got a half-dozen or more of them together in a hotel room at one time and encouraged them to talk to each other. The stories that were told in these "henfests" frequently surprised participants who had known each other, by reputation at least, for many years.

All of these women would have stood out in a crowd. Some were so strikingly attractive you could hardly pay attention to what they were saying, and others were as unvarnished plain as Eleanor Roosevelt, but all of them had energy to burn. The ones we saw confirmed the findings of a careful U.S. Civil Service Commission study of women in the Federal service which showed that women generally were older and better educated than the men in their grade.

We saw so many really tall women that we started keeping their actual heights and checked into the relationship between height and intelligence. We found that the psychologists suspect there is one. The gifted children Dr. Lewis M. Terman, Professor of Psychology at Leland Stanford University, began following forty years ago grew up to be taller, though not heavier than the national average. (Terman's gifted men average 5′11″ tall, an inch and a half taller than American men in general, and his gifted women averaged 5′5″, an inch more than the national average for women.)

We found few embattled feminists. Most of these women were busy doing their jobs and taking care of their families. Those who said that there were barriers had usually made their peace with them. But almost everyone we interviewed began by explaining that while she knew that "some women" had been badly treated, she herself was an exception. In a great many cases, women felt constrained to tell us the family circumstances which they felt had exempted them from reproach. "I lost my husband and just tried to hold on to our radio station for the children. . . . I couldn't have children. . . . I was left some money and my husband let me invest it. . . . I just had to make money to support my retarded sister and my mother, and the only way to do it was to keep the family business going. . . ." Others spoke glowingly of the men who had given them a chance.

Many ascribed their success to sheer good luck. United Press reporter Sandy McClure says that she was the only newsman in the Detroit office who was free to go out on the street and ask people how they felt the day President Kennedy was assassinated. She did such a good job that she was assigned important stories and is now on the Mayor's development team investigating the conditions which led to the Detroit riots of 1967.

We talked to women in New York, Washington, Pittsburgh, Cleveland, Detroit, Chicago, Los Angeles, San Francisco, and Denver. There were regional differences. New York, the "headquarters city," and Washington, where women have a chance to rise in the Federal service, showed the greatest number of women in high positions. Southern California seemed to have more women engineers and scientists than the East Coast.

Aspiring women in San Francisco and Denver complained that their cities were so attractive that women were willing to work for less to live in them, but the prosaic Bureau of Labor Statistics could not confirm the charge. According to their figures, office salaries in both cities merely reflected living costs. In 1966, Class A Secretaries—the appointment-making, dictation-taking kind—were getting $128.50 in San Francisco and $113 in Denver, compared with a high of $140 in New York and a low of $90 in Memphis. And EEOC found a higher percentage of women in white-collar jobs exclusive of retailing and clerical—the good jobs aspiring women want— in San Francisco than in any other city surveyed except New York and Washington.

Women in Cleveland and Pittsburgh were conscious that they lived in "men's towns" dominated by heavy industry, which did not create the jobs talented women held in New York in advertising, promotion, journalism, and Government services. Midwestern cities like Toledo, Ohio, and Southern cities like Nashville, Tennessee, are socially conservative and their economic structures lend themselves to domination by an establishment of aging, old-fashioned men. But the remarkable thing was that even in these unlikely places there were some women who earned $10,000 a year or more, if you knew where to look for them.

After an hour or so of telephoning around in a new city, we would find ourselves waiting for the counterparts of the women we had seen in other cities, and sooner or later they would appear. Someone always told us about a wizard woman advertising copywriter or department store buyer, or a woman doing a wonderful job in public relations for a store or utility or enterprise concerned with the "woman's point of view." There would often be a woman personnel director, either in the local telephone company or in a manufacturing enterprise which had brought a woman into personnel to hire women workers during World War II and kept her on afterwards. Usually we were told of a woman who was described as the "only" woman bank vice president, stockbroker, or insurance agent. And everywhere there were widows doing creditable jobs of managing businesses, and women without title but with more authority than secretaries who "really ran" local public or business leaders.

And each of these women sincerely believed that she was an "accident," that we couldn't "go by her." But these accidents fell into a predictable pattern. We studied lists of outstanding women named by various organizations and the titles of women in college class records of the past twenty years. Through the courtesy of William H. Booth, Chairman of the New York City Commission on Human Rights, we were able to examine the results of a survey that Commission conducted in 1966 to find out how many women the most important New York City corporations employed in job categories likely to command $10,000 a year or over. Little more than 2 percent of the 9,738 officers making $10,000 or over in the 69 companies which gave salary data were women. Their titles were significant: Home Economist, Administrative Assistant, Archivist, Manager, Employee Publication, Product Testing Manager, Consultant Women's Activities, Manager of Office Training, Stylist, Designer. There were also many women in newly created jobs that sounded like staff positions specially created for some outstanding woman: Supervisor, Personnel Action Center; Manager of Design Administration.

As we scanned lists of titles and talked with achieving women we found ourselves mentally classifying them according to the loophole they had used to slip through the Invisible Bar. We found:

Dynastic Women, who got a chance to show what they could do because they were wives, widows, or daughters of the owners, are common among nonprofessional women heading sizable commercial or industrial enterprises. The half-dozen women who classified themselves "business executives" in the first few hundred pages of *Who's Who in America* were all clearly related to the owners by blood or marriage. When Margaret Thompson of the University of California Business School at Los Angeles was looking for women executives to study for her doctoral dissertation, she found that 30 percent of the California women listed as executives in Dun & Bradstreet's Million Dollar Directory of 1961 were relatives of the president or owner.

Widows like Katharine Meyer Graham are active in every city, but many of them are publicity-shy. In Cleveland, Mrs. Nellie Knorr took over the operation of radio station WKNR after her husband died and built it from tenth to first place in listenership for many time periods of the broadcast day. She is a motherly, unpretentious woman who worked along with her husband and has carried on his ideas. In Denver, Mrs. Virginia B. Razee kept the title of treasurer when she inherited the Newstrom-Davis Construction Company from her uncle, who had been president. A quietly effective woman who had worked in the business from the beginning, she is not shy. She has settled building trades strikes. But the habit of staying in the background was so strong that she left the presidency vacant for three years before assuming it herself.

Women's Women exploit the male domination of business by interpreting business and women to each other. Store buyers, women's magazine editors, home economists in business, advertising copywriters sell to women. Personnel directors, office managers, training specialists supervise women employees. Even Margaret Mead, the great anthropologist, is a woman's woman in a way. She examined primitive cultures by talking to the women as a woman.

Women's women probably account for half of the women earning $10,000 a year or more through their own efforts, and their role is the best accepted and defined. "As head of our Betty Crocker Kitchens, Miss Mercedes Bates fills a most vital role in our company," the president of General Mills said in the announcement naming her the first woman officer in the company's history. "The Kitchens are one of our most important links with the nation's homemakers."

Sears Roebuck elected Claire Giannini Hoffman, daughter of the founder of the Bank of America, to its Board for what Board Chairman Austin Cushman called "some very selfish reasons. Seven out of ten Sears customers are women. We've got 124,000 female employees. The plain truth is that no one understands women like another woman."

Token Women are elevated for token representation. They perform the same function as the "token Negroes" that companies selling to the Negro market promote to important jobs to prove that they are not prejudiced. Since the passage of Title VII, national companies have been showing off their women executives in the same way that they used to show off their Negroes. "I'm the company woman," the editor of a magazine published by a leading corporation once answered when asked what role she played in its affairs. "Company women" aren't supposed to exercise the authority that their titles imply. Some women vice presidents are consulted only on women's affairs. In broadcasting they may be treated as talent rather than as management. But politicians and, increasingly, business executives feel that they should appoint at least one woman to every high-level group to "represent" the sex.

A surprising number of Negro women are serving as double tokens. Edith Austin, the relaxed Negro woman editor of the Berkeley *Post,* a Negro weekly newspaper in California, calls herself the "Mayor's Rent-a-Negro-Woman" because of the many committees on which she serves. "I'm two for the price of one," she says, "a Negro and a woman, too." Mrs. Patricia Roberts Harris, an attractive, poised young Negro lawyer, has served the United States as Ambassador to Luxembourg. As alternate delegate to the United Nations, she worked on the United Nations Commission on the Status of Women. When one of the smaller non-white nations cited the status of Negroes in the United States as proof that laws against discrimination don't work, she told of being served at a restaurant which only a few years before had turned her away because of her race.

Gimmick Women exploit the attention women attract when they turn up where they aren't expected. In 1967, Betty Skelton, the daredevil test-car driver, was listed as an account executive on the payroll of Campbell-Ewald, an advertising agency in Detroit. Her job was to generate publicity for Chevrolet cars. Lillie Lee was once hired to sell power plants on the theory that purchasing agents would want to see whether a cute little Korean girl really knew anything about them. She did, and her sales record was excellent, but she tired of life as a gimmick. In 1966, she was working as a senior research engineer on the Apollo project at North American Aviation in Downey, California.

Women in nonprofessional work are frequently dressed up to attract business. In 1967, Manhattan was brightened by the appearance of a Bunny Limousine Service featuring girl drivers in tight white tops, black pants, leather boots, and tiny tails. Airlines use their "hostesses" to attract and hold customers in a way that is only slightly more restrained.

Sex Women exploit their personal attraction to get in with the boss, the customer, or the client. This sounds more sinister than it is. Sometimes—and opinion differs on how often—the sex woman is actually sleeping with the boss, and not infrequently she marries him. More often she uses a seductive appearance and manner to win attention. One of the few women employed by a national management consulting firm is a striking blonde who came to one of our hen-fests in a pink suit topped by a matching tulle hat that looked as if it had been spun out of cotton candy. After officially inveighing against the use of sex to get ahead on the job, she conceded privately that it helped to make an indelible first impression on men clients. Attracting the boss or the client is, of course, as far as sex appeal can go. Like other loopholes, it merely gives a woman a chance to show what she can do on the job. The legendary dumb blonde is not maintained in a responsible job.

Office Wives and Housekeepers seldom become famous successful women because by definition their role is behind the scenes, but a surprising number of the women earning $10,000 a year or more are the backstops of top men in business and professional work. In many enterprises, the chief executive officer has an executive secretary to maintain the tone of his office, greet his callers as a wife would do, and monitor the subordinate "children." "Executives remark that they want their secretaries to be dignified and gracious, reflecting their surroundings," *The Wall Street Journal* reported in a feature article headed "Executive Secretaries Sometimes Wield Power in the Boss's Behalf." The reporters found one secretary with a salary of $25,000. Crackerjack secretaries sometimes wind up their careers with a title that rewards long and faithful service. Sometimes they are made treasurer, a job that can be limited to responsible but non-policy-making functions such as the handling of stock transfers and records.

Evelyn Borning was made vice president of the Union Bank of Los Angeles by the successor to the president whom she had served for nearly twenty years as "secretary with a small s." "Women are more patient, more understanding, more intuitive and sympathetic than men," she told an audience of women executives. "They succeed by having warmth and easy charm and by being good listeners. A conscientious, hard-working, cheerful distaff member can be an invaluable complement to anyone in high position." A relaxed, unpretentious, and pretty redhead, Miss Borning was unconsciously describing herself and her role.

The careers of successful women are uncharted. There is not, as there is for men, a clearly marked path, so success goes almost exclusively to individuals who can create their own opportunities. The adjectives "practical," "realistic," and "expediential" dotted our notes on interviews. Men sometimes become successful by cutting themselves off from whole areas of common experience, but there was not a single impractical dreamer among the successful women we saw.

When Julia Coburn, co-founder of the Tobé-Coburn School for Fashion Careers, graduated from Vassar, she wanted to be a creative writer, but everyone told her that there were no jobs for women in writing, so she accepted a job in the advertising department of LaSalle & Koch's, the leading department store in Toledo, Ohio. "I hadn't considered business, let alone a department store," she says. "My parents were shocked at the idea that their daughter was going to work in a shop. But a wise man I knew advised me to take it. He pointed out that if I had been a man I could have gone to work for a newspaper and learned about life on the police beat, but since I was a woman, the best place for me to meet types I had escaped at Vassar would be in a big department store which employed and served all kinds. If I was going to write, I'd have to learn about people."

Somewhat to her surprise, Miss Coburn discovered that business was fascinating. She bubbled with "crazy ideas," and the head of the store liked them. Six months later the advertising manager left and she got the job, becoming, at the age of 23, one of three women to hold the title in a big store at that time.

"No, I don't think I felt any barriers because I was a woman. I had succeeded a woman, so that battle had been won. But I did suffer because I was known as 'that college girl in the advertising department.' I discovered, too, that in a store I had to speak up and demand a raise. The head of the store told me I was going ahead faster than anyone had ever gone. I told him I wasn't comparing myself with anyone else. A girl can be much nervier than a man in business and get away with it."

Like Jane Trahey, Julia Coburn found that as a single woman without dependents she could take bigger risks than the men on her level. After eight years at LaSalle & Koch's, she decided she had learned as much as she could from the store, so she quit. "One advertising man I knew was scandalized. He wanted to know what I would do with myself. I told him I was going to go to Europe and just sit for a while. I'll never forget the expression on his face when he said, 'God, how I wish *I* could do that!' "

Back in New York, Miss Coburn moved through successively better jobs using her retail background to advise women's magazines. "There was only one job on which I ran into any barriers because I was a woman, and then I didn't realize it until it was too late. My contract wasn't renewed, and at first I couldn't understand why. Then something made me think of a group of men working at my level but in another department, and I asked the boss point-blank whether they knew my salary. He didn't reply directly, but he did say that salaries couldn't be kept secret. I had succeeded a man and by that time I had worked up in my own field to the point where I could get a man's salary. I was no longer a 'bargain,' so they let me go."

Miss Coburn (she is Mrs. Dante Antolini at her weekend house in Poughkeepsie) avoided all problems of female prejudice by literally creating her own occupation. The Tobé-Coburn School was one of the first in its field.

Like many Women's Women who have escaped direct competition with men, Julia Coburn is friendly, spontaneous, and remarkably relaxed for a leader in the notoriously tense fashion field. As an educator, she is under considerably less pressure than Mildred Custin, who as chief executive officer of the Bonwit Teller chain of speciality stores is holding down the kind of job that usually goes to men. Some big stores, like

Macy's San Francisco, have women managers, but Mildred Custin and Gerry Stutz of Henri Bendel are rare as women store presidents, and they owe their jobs to Maxey Jarman of Genesco, Inc., which owns both stores. "When I was made president of Bonwit Teller, the newspapers wrote about how I wore iron-gray tweeds that matched my silver-gray hair and hadn't lost my femininity," Miss Custin once told an audience of bankers in Cleveland. "But can you imagine a newspaper reporting that a man who had just been made president of a store wore Brooks Brothers suits and hadn't lost his masculinity?"

Mildred Custin is a New Englander who is keenly aware that she is blazing a new trail. She says that she deliberately taught herself to be objective by analyzing herself and concealing her ambition ("I was quietly aggressive"). The result of this self-schooling is evident in her carefully controlled manner. She never raises her voice, but the underemphasis is sometimes as dramatic as a scream.

Her start in retailing was inauspicious, but characteristic. When she was refused a job on the Macy training squad, she made up her mind to get a job somewhere in the store and work up to the point where she could fire the head of the training squad. She got a job at Macy's and was ten months on her way to this objective when her mother, a proper Bostonian, decided she was too young to live in New York City and she had to start over in Boston.

She thinks that women can rise in retailing if they are willing to take responsibility, but "most aren't trained to think in these terms." For that reason, she doesn't believe that the law against discrimination in employment will make much difference. Men on the Bonwit Teller training squad are paid more than women because the men come in after getting experience on other jobs and training from Genesco, where they are presumably being groomed for managerial positions, while the girls are hired right out of school, for on-the-job training.

"Of course women have to work harder to get ahead than men," she admits, without rancor. "Of course a man will always be preferred over an equally competent and experienced woman. But when people try to compliment me by telling me that I 'think like a man,' I tell them that in retailing it pays to 'think like a woman.' "

"Thinking like a woman" is the tried and true way to sell women, but it can sell men, too. In 1966, the Madison Avenue advertising world resounded with news of the exploits of Mary Wells, the blonde miracle worker who left Jack Tinker & Partners to set up her own shop with writer Richard Rich and art director Stewart Greene. The Braniff International Airline account soon followed her. Within months, Madison Avenue gossip created a superwoman image for Mary Wells: after hours, a swinging play-girl, jetting to fun places in Europe, South America, and Switzerland; in her office, a fabulous idea-and-work girl rolling up billings of $80 million her first year in business for herself.

In 1964, Mary Wells had already reached the top. She was earning $80,000 a year as vice president of Jack Tinker, Interpublic's division devoted to developing new forms of advertising. She had helped sell millions of dollars worth of Alka-Seltzer with television commercials poking fun at flabby stomachs. In those days, she impressed Eugenia Sheppard, a sharp-eyed reporter of the New York scene, as a "highly intelligent but wholesome type in a leopard vest and tweed skirt, with close-cropped, prematurely graying hair." Six months later, after the formation of Wells, Rich, Greene, Miss Sheppard was shocked to encounter her, at a fashionable ball—a "fragile, blond creature in a low-cut, Empire-waisted ballgown on the arm of designer Emilio Pucci."

"I used to be purely a hard-working type at places like Macy's," she explained to Miss Sheppard. "Suddenly I found people who thought I was attractive, and it changed my whole life." She did not say who "those people" were, but their impact was highly visible. At her orders, the entire fleet of Braniff planes was repainted in seven different pastel colors and the airline hostesses regarbed in space helmets and harem pants designed by Pucci. Other accounts battered down the door—Western Union, Benson & Hedges cigarettes, Personna razor blades, Wesson Oil, a General Mills line of snack products imaginatively christened Bugles, Whistles, Daisies, Buttons, and Bows.

"The prime force of my life is work," she told the newsmen who constantly interviewed, pictured, and analyzed her. "Few women are single-minded about a job. Work comes second to catching a man." So many men flocked around her that her name was not linked to any single one. But her business and her fame mushroomed from week to week. President and Mrs. Johnson invited her to stay at the White House and help entertain President Ferdinand Marcos of the Philippines. In 1967, American Motors, deep in the red, put the fate of the fourth automobile company in the country in her hands. Her first confrontation with their management was reported by *Life* magazine.

In a childishly short dress, her straight blonde hair flying, she stood up like a brave little girl and outlined her plan to the hard-bitten American Motors brass in Detroit. "Love is the key word," she told the grim-faced men. "You have to talk person-to-person with people." Before she was through, she was demanding that American Motors put air conditioning in its top model, abandon its sacrosanct logo, and film a TV commercial showing happy workmen breaking up a rival car. When Board Chairman Roy Chapin spoke up for the logo, *Life* reported that she said, "You can *order* us, Mr. Chapin, and we'll do it. But it will *destroy* the whole atmosphere of the commercials, like you *destroy* love or sex."

Chapin gave in. Agencies which had struggled for years with the ambivalent management of American Motors envied her self-confidence. "A man couldn't have put the program over," an astute observer commented. "The company had to have a miracle worker—something as far out as you could go. For American Motors, that would be a woman."

In November 1967, Mary Wells married Harding Lawrence, the president of Braniff Airways. After she left Jack Tinker, Gustave Levy, a Braniff director, helped Wells, Rich, Greene borrow $100,000 to set up shop. No one on Madison Avenue suggested that Mary Wells "got there" only by knowing the client—she has too much talent and drive to be stopped, anyway—but like most influential women, some help from a man with an interest in her career helped to boost her into a man's world.

"There really isn't much prejudice against women in this business," Mrs. Julia Walsh, general partner of Ferris & Company, Washington stockbrokers, told a reporter when she was elected to membership in the American Stock Exchange. "In fact, it's an advantage. You tend to be noticed." The value of such publicity did not escape the American Stock Exchange. When Mrs. Walsh was admitted in November 1965, Amex also admitted Mrs. Phyllis Peterson, who had long wanted a seat. A partner of Sade & Co. in Washington, Mrs. Peterson became interested in investing when her Air Force husband inherited some money. In 1965 she became the first woman to own a seat on the Philadelphia Stock Exchange, and she also applied to the Montreal Stock Exchange for membership. The two women made their ceremonial visit to the trading floor together. Both were youthful-looking, attractive mothers who earned more than $50,000 a year in commissions on sales. As anticipated, the event attracted national publicity.

When both the New York Stock Exchange and the American Stock Exchange were formed, the idea of a woman trading on the floor was so unthinkable that their constitutions never mentioned the possibility. The New York Stock Exchange had long fended off inquiries by stating that no woman had ever applied for membership, but Sylvia Porter, the financial columnist, and other forward-looking Wall Streeters predicted that a woman would sooner or later appear who would meet the strict qualifications. In December 1967, glamorous 38-year-old Muriel Siebert was admitted to membership. She paid $445,000 for her seat, all of which she had earned herself. The daughter of a Cleveland dentist, Miss Siebert went to work at Bache & Company in 1954 as a $65-a-week trainee, made herself an expert in aerospace and aviation stocks, and worked up on the basis of her ideas for institutional investors.

Like many members of the Exchange, Miss Siebert arranged to have her orders executed by another member. She denied persistent press reports that the decision was part of a secret agreement with the Board of Governors to keep a woman trader off the floor. "I'm doing it this way because I can have more freedom and make more money than if I traded personally," she explained. She has a male secretary, as does Jane Trahey.

Mrs. Walsh and Mrs. Peterson did not trade on the floor of Amex after their initial visit together, but they, too, denied that they were barred by any secret agreement not to trade. In 1967, neither exchange had a ladies' room near the trading floor, but Amex was planning a powder room for its two women members and others who might be admitted.

Mrs. Walsh made an ideal "first woman." In addition to earning close to $100,000 a year, between commissions and income on her own investments, she was running a household of twelve children. In 1963, she had married Thomas Walsh, a well-off Washington real estate man whose first wife died leaving him with seven children. They decided to marry, she says jokingly, when she accepted an invitation to speak in Hawaii and it occurred to them that it would be a good place for a honeymoon. Both are devout Roman Catholics, and Mrs. Walsh believes that it takes a strong spiritual foundation to carry responsibilities the size of theirs. "She talks so fast because her mind's going faster than she can talk," Mr. Walsh says of her admiringly. "She's a compulsive planner." The Walsh household is programmed for efficiency. With the help of two secretaries, two housekeepers, and extra help as needed, the birth of her daughter Peggy in 1964 kept Mrs. Walsh out of her office for only a month.

Newspapers love to write up people like Julia Coburn, Anna Rosenberg Hoffman, Mary Wells, Mildred Custin, and Julia Walsh. A certain amount of publicity is essential for the many famous successful women who have used their femininity to slip through the sex barrier. Their noncompetitive roles ensure them the goodwill of men, and, as we have seen, they are, with few exceptions, staunch defenders of the traditional sex roles on which their careers depend. They are the most visible and the most lively women at the top.

But they are not the only ones. Some women do make it strictly on job performance, the hard way. *Rate Busters* don't duck the competition. They beat it. These are the women who are hired by struggling firms because they will accept lower salaries. These are the women doctors and lawyers whom thrifty women patronize because "you get more for your money in a woman." Rate busters are motivated by a number of reasons, and many men and women distrust as well as fear them. However, several of these women simply like their careers and are willing to do the kind of work they want even if it means less pay and less prestige.

A good example is Lu Retta Stasch of Oakland, California. A small woman who wears high heels, tall hats, and carries impressive handbags custom-tailored to hold file folders, Mrs. Stasch is a business management consultant, a field so closed to women that when she once applied for a job with a national management consulting firm the receptionist told her to go away. Although her client list was long and distinguished, consulting firms would not hire her because she was "over-qualified for any opening we have for women." She regularly earns $1,000 a month or more in fees, less than half the compensation of men doing the same work. Her overhead is low because she works from her home.

Mrs. Stasch is a natural-born rate buster. During World War II, she was working as a secretary-bookkeeper for the Mare Island Ferry Company in Vallejo, California. The company could not find a ferryboat captain to take war workers from Vallejo to the Mare Island Shipyard, so she volunteered and became the first woman licensed to run a ferryboat by the Federal Bureau of Marine Inspection and Navigation. After the war she got a job teaching veterans how to run business machines. Rather than have them work on make-believe problems, she assigned them to do the office work of local businessmen and collected fifty cents an hour for their services.

"I know it sounds corny," she says, "but when I see a better way I just tell the person who can profit by it." As a teacher of business machine operations she had a lot of ideas for business machine manufacturers, and her innovations created a career for her as a trainer and office system troubleshooter. Like good management consultants everywhere, she often discovers that the solution of one bottleneck uncovers another.

On one occasion, a young man from a nationally known management consulting firm was investigating a series of problems. He grilled Mrs. Stasch for two days, then turned her suggestions in to the president of the company with a bill for $1,100. "Even if you don't get the credit for your work, you get the experience," she says of occurrences like this. "You can't get the money if you are a woman, but you can have the fun." Her dream is to found a business school that will really train women for management work.

Rate busters accept the rules of the game. "I know women have to be better and try harder," Helen Meyer, president of Dell Publishing Company, says. "They can't swing deals on the golf course, so they have to persuade colleagues by sticking to business, which is harder. I know a man in a job like mine would not have to worry about getting someone to wash the windows when he went home. But I am not sorry."

Helen Meyer has no reason to be sorry. A slight woman

with short black hair and an unassuming manner, she is so little known even in her own field that a woman in publishing who noticed that she was always reading galleys on the commuter train to New Jersey once asked her if she wanted a job as a copyreader.

"Equal pay for equal work is a fine idea," she told us, "but I might never have had a chance if they had had that law when I started out here."

Born Helen Honig, she was a bright math student who whizzed through high school in Brooklyn and went to work at the age of 15 as an adjustment clerk in an office distributing magazines to newsstands. Her job was to handle complaints from dealers who didn't get their magazines on time, or weren't credited for payments. Soon she was working for George Delacorte, a Harvard graduate who owned Dell Publishing, then publishing pulp magazines. Delacorte had no circulation manager, but he had Helen Honig, and by the time she was 19, he had her traveling all over the country checking on newsstand distribution.

In the 1920s, magazine circulation was a rough business. Mrs. Honig insisted that Helen's older sister or a girlfriend travel with her whenever possible. Many nights she locked herself in, after ordering dinner in her room. But in the morning she would get out again and visit distributors to make sure that Dell magazines were out where they should be.

At the end of each trip she would bring back suggestions to Delacorte. Movie fan magazines were selling. Shouldn't Dell start one? Magazines were always late in reaching the stand. Shouldn't she look into the plant to see what was wrong? Little by little, Helen Honig learned the business. On one occasion she edited two issues of one of the magazines, drawing on her sales experience to guide her on editorial content. On one of her trips she met a Harvard boy on a train. He was Abraham J. Meyer, and in 1929 she married him, but she kept on working after the birth of their two children. George Delacorte discovered that it paid to listen to her suggestions. Today Dell Publishing is a far-flung empire encompassing magazines, soft- and hard-cover books, reprints, book distribution and warehousing, all of it built by George Delacorte and Helen Meyer.

"A woman has to have a strong personality and a great

deal of dignity," she says. "She must never let the bars down. And she must be careful never to let a man reach her through flattery. Men use sex in business, too, when they work for a woman and think it will work. Yes, it used to happen here. But no more. I once had an advertising manager who made more money than I did. I was told that advertising managers always made big money. Of course, nothing like that happens here any more." Mrs. Meyer speaks quietly, but she is one of the few women managers who exercise undisputed authority without interference from above or below.

Most rate busters see only opportunity where others see exploitation. "I would have built the building if they had asked me to do it," Mildred Custin says of her early days in the retail business.

One of the few women to see the inequity is a public relations executive who prefers to remain nameless. "What I'm working for," she quipped, "is the day when a mediocre woman can get as far as a mediocre man."

6

THE NEGRO PARALLEL

Early in the 1960s a male professor of anthropology at Vassar College startled his class by listing the parallels between the disabilities Negroes suffer by virtue of their skin color and the disabilities women suffer by virtue of their sex. To begin with, neither women nor Negroes could hide the respective facts of sex or race. Generalizations about Negroes and women as workers relegated both groups to inferior status on the job. Both groups were regarded as a labor reserve, denied equal hiring, training, pay, promotion, responsibility, and seniority at work. Neither group was supposed to boss white men, and both were limited to jobs white men didn't want to do.

Negroes were supposed to be better able to stand uncomfortable physical labor; women, boring details. Both had emerged from a "previous condition of servitude" that had denied them the vote, schooling, jobs, apprenticeships, and equal access to unions, clubs, professional associations, professional schools, restaurants, and public places. Strikingly similar rationalizations and defense mechanisms accommodated both denials of the central American ideal of equal opportunity.

Both women and Negroes were held to be inferior in intelligence, incapable of genius, emotional, childlike, irresponsible, and sexually threatening. They were supposed to be all right in their places, and were presumed to prefer staying there. (If they didn't they were shamed, ridiculed, or slandered.) Both were viewed as treacherous, wily, "intuitive," voluble, and proud of outwitting their menfolk or white folk.*

Most people didn't see these similarities, because they did not think women were unfairly treated. "Discrimination" meant Negroes and, to a lesser extent, Jews. In 1967, for instance, the Public Affairs Pamphlet, *Job Discrimination Is Illegal,* made no mention at all of sex and described the Civil Rights Act of 1964 as outlawing discrimination on the basis of "race, religion, creed, or national origin," although the law read, "race, color, religion, sex or national origin."

But career women began to mention the parallel, if only as a bitter joke. "Like the Negro in our land, we [women] may be off the chains, but we're not off the hook and, by no means, off the plantation," Jane Trahey declared. "If you take James Baldwin's *Another Country,* and substitute the word 'woman' every time you come to Negro, you will simply have another very true book."

"Well, at least they don't say that women have a fine sense of rhythm," another woman said during a discussion of the jobs regarded as appropriate for women in her organization. The analogy was close enough to the surface to keep a classic "Pat and Mike" type of joke going the rounds.

"Have you heard the news about God?" the first man asked.

"No, what?" the straight man replied.

"She's black."

Marian Trembley, store manager of Macy's San Francisco, said she was able to "get down to brass tacks" with a Negro executive on her staff who complained of discrimination on the part of colleagues. "Look here," she told him, "I'm a minority, too. Let's sit down and talk about it."

Surprising as it sounds, Negroes up to now have had a broader choice of occupations than women. Because 11 percent of the labor force has been Negro, equal rights leaders have argued that 11 percent of the payroll of every big company ought to be Negro, too. In 1967, Dr. Edward Gross, Professor of Sociology at the University of Washington, applied this principle to test discrimination against women.

* Helen Hacker, "Women As A Minority Group," *Social Forces,* December 1951.

There are nearly two men working throughout the country for every woman, so if women were to demand their fair share of the jobs in each of the hundreds of occupations listed by the Census, there would be a woman engineer for every two men engineers, a woman company president for every two men company presidents, and a woman secretary for every two male secretaries. Obviously, of course, neither women nor Negroes are getting their "fair share." But when Dr. Gross studied the statistics he discovered that the sex ratios were more lopsided than the race ratios. If women were to be fairly represented in every occupation, two-thirds of those now working would have to change jobs. Thousands of secretaries, for instance, would have to become engineers. Race equality would be much easier to achieve. Less than half the Negroes would have to change jobs in order to give Negroes their fair share of every occupation. Part of the difference, of course, was that there were "bonafide sex qualifications" for some jobs. The EEOC maintained that there wasn't a job in the occupational list for which a Negro could not qualify, but it permitted employers to specify women for modeling or attending women's washrooms. Nevertheless, the jobs for which sex was a "bonafide qualification" were much too rare to account for the difference Dr. Gross found in segregation by race and sex.

The minority status of women went unnoticed because they are, as Helen Hacker said, "the only minority in history which lives with the master race." In comparing the two "minorities," she said that women are more important to the "master race" of white men than Negroes, and they arouse more ambivalent feelings. Men, after all, have to live with women, but whites can choose to live with Negroes or deal with them at arm's length as they please. Hostility between the races can, after all, be managed, if only by such morally repugnant devices as South African apartheid, but hostility between men and women threatens family solidarity. Historically, principled opposition to woman suffrage has come from people who sincerely feared that families would break up if wives were given a chance to vote independently of their husbands at the polls.

The comparison between women and Negroes is suggestive in many areas. For instance, the conspicuous absence of women in certain fields seems proof that women just don't care about them. But something more than sex may be involved. Chemical, steel, and railroad companies which limit women workers frequently turn up on lists of companies charged with discrimination against Jews and Negroes. One of the few things Negroes, Jews, and women have in common is that they rarely head industrial enterprises. Could it be that for some reason or other these industries put more emphasis than others on employing people who "look like us"?

Or take the moves under way to make men's and women's colleges coeducational. Usually these plans are discussed in terms of changing relations between men and women. Issues of sex morality are argued. But Negro colleges are beginning to recruit white students, and Ivy League colleges are going out of their way to recruit Negro applicants. Can it be that there is a rebellion afoot against "face validity" of every kind?

Comparison between women and Negroes sheds new light on the handicaps they both face in the job market. Both are fired before white men and hired after them. Both are arbitrarily limited to the lower-paying, least productive, less-skilled jobs and sometimes the same ones. For many years, for instance, Southern textile mills reserved for white women those jobs that were filled in the North by Negro men. It is not surprising to learn from the Bureau of Labor Statistics that women average 2.4 years less than men on the jobs they hold, while Negro men average two years less than white men. The gap between the races in job tenure is similar to the gap between the sexes. The similarity is worth noting because it suggests reasons why neither Negroes nor women gravitate to steady work. Both are fired before white men, of course, but both are also more apt to quit because they move away or can't get transportation to the job. Women and Negroes often do not have as much control over where they live as white men.

The frequent moves that rising executives have to make are a special hardship for Negroes; it is much easier for white men to find a convenient place to live in a new town. Career women have the same problem. If they are married, they are rarely in a position to choose a residence on the basis of convenience to their work.

Gunnar Myrdal, the Swedish sociologist, has pointed out that Southerners used to claim that Negroes had a definite biological ceiling beyond which members of their race could not be educated. More Southerners believed this, of course, in 1944, when Myrdal wrote the classic analysis of the Negro problem, *The American Dilemma*, than in the 1960s, but the notion of a ceiling on the pay a woman can be worth remains widespread. In a little-read appendix to his monograph, Myrdal specifically drew the parallel between the treatment given women and that given Negroes. In 1968, when the word "women" was substituted for the word "Negroes," and "men" for "whites," the book still made perfect sense.

"In practically all industries where Negroes are accepted," he wrote, "they are confined to unskilled occupations and to such semiskilled and skilled occupations as are unattractive to white workers." Myrdal summarized three ways in which race prejudice and discrimination kept Negroes down at work:

(1) Many *white* workers, even if they think that *Negroes* should have a fair share in the job opportunities in this country, are opposed to *Negro* competition in the localities, industries, occupations, and establishments where they themselves work.

(2) Some customers object to being served by *Negroes* unless the *Negro* had an apparently menial position.

(3) Many employers believe that *Negroes* are inferior as workers. . . . Perhaps even more important is the fact that they pay much attention to the anti-*Negro* attitudes of both *white* customers and *white* workers. (Italics ours.)

A race map of the work world would look surprisingly like the sex map we have sketched. Negroes, like women, do better in the Civil Service, where performance is rated objectively and Government policies on entry and promotion tend to preclude discrimination. Like women, Negroes and Jews rise in work that is objectively measurable, such as scientific research, show business, the arts, or journalism; in staff positions requiring special knowledge rather than in line positions of direct authority over others; and in specialist, backroom, backstop, and detail jobs "inside" organizations rather than in policy-making or in representing organizations to outsiders. Negroes and women who are exceptions to the "inside-outside" role are usually hired as tokens and so are not really exceptions at all.

Negroes who get ahead in white organizations encounter the psychological and social difficulties of women. They are excluded from the office grapevine and, until very recently, from clubs where quasi-business events are held. Their work is scrutinized more closely. Their authority over subordinates is constantly tested. They may be put through an initial "trial by fire" including deliberate attempts to undermine their confidence. Like women, Negroes are resented if they assert themselves and criticized if they don't. Negroes and women have found some of the same routes up: Like "women's women," Negroes who have risen in white organizations are usually "race men" hired to supervise or sell to Negroes.

Ambitious women are hazed, obstructed, and isolated in the same way as "uppity Negroes," while the favors of the power structure are lavished on the "real woman" and the "good Negro." The tone in which women workers are praised for their tact, courtesy, loyalty, and tractability is a warning that the praise itself is a form of culture policing. According to Myrdal, "Almost all Negroes are agreed that some of the traits for which they are praised by Southern whites (loyalty, tractability, happy-go-luckiness) are not the traits of which they should be primarily proud." Myrdal goes on to state:

> . . . the *Negro* is more gifted in music, the arts, dancing, and acting than *whites;* that he is better in handling animals, or, sometimes, children; that he is loyal and reliable as a servant (often, however, the opposite is asserted); that he is on the whole, a more happy and mentally balanced human being; that he has more emotional warmth; that he is more religious. All such favorable beliefs seem to have this in common, that they do not raise any question concerning the advisability or righteousness of keeping the *Negro* in his place in the caste order. (Italics ours.)

Negroes who fit the Southern stereotype used to be approved, by Southerners, as "good Nigras." Myrdal found that leading whites sometimes consulted "old, practically illiterate ex-servants while cold-shouldering the upper-class Negro."

"Uncle Tom" Negroes who accept these favors often criticize the Negro race more harshly than do whites.

"Good" or "real" women enjoy the same dubious advantage. Office "housekeepers" are often treated with much greater deference than women who make independent contributions to an organization. The opinions of a good secretary are frequently solicited and treated with a respect seldom accorded the opinions of professional women on the staff who are, of course, less apt to mirror the boss's opinions. "Most males do not enjoy working relationships on an equal basis with women who may bring additional talents to the task at hand," said a woman librarian. "It has been more comfortable to accept ideas if they come from women at the clerical level," she went on. And women who rise as office wives or housekeepers believe in the limited role of women in business as firmly as the remaining old-fashioned Uncle Tom Negroes accept the inferiority of the Negro race. Like the Uncle Toms, these "Aunt Janes" are often used by the management to keep their own kind in line.

Myrdal has pointed out that upper-class white men frequently praise Negro college presidents and other white-appointed Negro leaders quite beyond their reasonable deserts, merely for their humble demeanor, and he believes that this misplaced praise has corrupted Negro ambition. Have women been corrupted in the same way? His analysis is disturbing when applied to women.

"The Negro worker has less definite obligations as well as more uncertain rights," Myrdal writes. "He comes to be paid not only for his work, but also for his humility, for being satisfied with his 'place,' and for his cunning in cajoling and flattering his master." Men bosses admit they expect less of the women than of the men who work for them. Women notoriously "get away with murder" on the job. Almost every big office has at least one woman who holds her job only because she flatters the man for whom she works. As Myrdal put it, "Deference is bought for lowered demands of efficiency."

Hypocritical insistence that opportunity is really equal is the cruelest form of discrimination. It implies that the loser in any contest has lost through his own inabilities. And while women and Negroes realize that the cards are stacked against them, they are compelled by the prevailing rhetoric to act as if they had actually lost out in fair competition. Negroes and women who maintain their mental health develop some kind of defense against the imputation of incompetence. As employers complain, both groups need continual and massive injections of praise and attention—injections that become a burden to the supervisory staff.

Myrdal has described sympathetically the efforts of superior Negroes to keep their emotional balance without "falling into the bitter complacency of the inferiority doctrine or by overdoing the equality doctrine and trying to build up a case that black is superior to white." A third temptation, Myrdal has said, is "to exaggerate the accusation against whites and so use caste disabilities to cover all personal failings." Women have used all three defenses against the doctrine of intrinsic inferiority. As their critics maliciously point out, career women gloat over every instance in which a woman outdoes a man, and blame most of their shortcomings on discrimination, yet they can be easily trapped into conceding that they are not as good as men.

Negroes and women both are popularly supposed to be troublesome employees because they tend to "take things personally." But so, of course, does anyone whose status is uncertain. The consolations of religion, the petty satisfaction of sabotage, withdrawal from competition ("I don't care"), mockery of the powerful boss and contravention of his purposes, and the pursuit of small advantage by devious means are characteristic outlets for resentment. Women clerical workers and Negro domestic or menial workers often exasperate their employers by their unwillingness to "see the point," and at some level of consciousness this provocation is deliberate. The tragedy of this response, immediately satisfying as it might be, is that it provides a rationale for discrimination.

The intuition ascribed to women and Negroes can be fully explained by the closer attention these groups are compelled to pay to the personal responses of their superiors. "Most middle- and upper-class whites get satisfaction out of the subserviency and humbleness of lower-class Negroes," said Myrdal. Most men in middle and top management got satisfaction out of the subserviency of the women who waited on them at home or work.

The "separate but equal" distinction between the sexes is

drawn with all the ambiguities and ambivalences that mark the distinctions between the races, as well. The profusion of Negro organizations impressed Myrdal, and as a Swede he was inclined to attribute it in part to the over-organization of American life in general. He pointed out that Negroes excluded from professional organizations formed their own, and that the ones that were Negro could be distinguished by the term "National," where the white organizations called themselves "American."

But for every Negro counterpart organization there also seems to be a woman's counterpart organization, too, setting up an unbelievably awkward apparatus. There is a National Medical Association for Negro doctors, and an American Medical Women's Association for women doctors, in spite of the fact that the American Medical Association admits both Negroes and women. There are women's associations for accountants, architects, engineers, journalists, and on down through the alphabet of professions. There are social, fraternal, professional, political, and business organizations for women paralleling every kind of organization set up for men, and many of the men's groups have women's auxiliaries for their wives, as well.

The very names of women's organizations suggest all the ways in which women have felt themselves segregated. There is an Advertising Women of New York and a Women Leaders Round Table, although women are admitted to the Advertising Club of New York and the Million Dollar Round Table of high-producing insurance salesmen. There is the Society of Woman Geographers, the Women's National Press Club, and Women World War Veterans, Inc.

The New York phone book yields Women for President and Other Public Office, Inc., Federation of Women Shareholders in American Business, Inc., Women's Architectural Auxiliary, Women's Association of Allied Beverage Industries, Women's Metropolitan Golf Association. There are the American Women in Radio and Television, and the American Women Buyers' Club. Semantically speaking, one of the most arresting is the organization of utility company home economists who call themselves the Electrical Women's Round Table.

The time-honored argument for segregated organizations has been that they give minority leaders and professional workers a chance to develop. Negro schools provided employment for Negro teachers, and women's colleges provided employment for women scholars. Women are sometimes accused of wanting to get into men's colleges or men's clubs because they want to get close to men in a sexual way or become men themselves. When psychological testers ask people which sex they would like to be if they could be born again, many more women than men want to change their sex. This need not be taken as evidence of rampant penis envy. It may simply reflect a desire to achieve male *status*. No one would look for murky psychological explanations if a similar survey should demonstrate that many more Negroes than whites wanted to change race. Straightforward economic reasons provide ample motivation.

Whites—and particularly white men—continue to impute a sexual motive to the ambitions of Negroes and women because they themselves see demands for equality as a sexual threat. If men are driven to success by the necessity to prove that they are "men," they're likely to feel that women who aspire to success are out to unman them. Psychiatrist John Dollard of Yale analyzed the complex sexual basis of white prejudice against Negroes in his *Caste and Class in a Southern Town*. The point here is that the sexual aspect of segregation or integration is much more important to men than to women.

The evasions, denials, and hypocrisies that arise whenever men discuss—or more often, pointedly ignore—the possibility of women assuming high-level jobs all have certain sexual implications. There is an etiquette to discussion of women in business that is akin to what Myrdal has called the "etiquette of race relations." If the topic is discussed at all, for instance, it is lost in clouds of verbiage. No one seems willing or able to speak plainly or see it as a simple moral issue the way Myrdal taught people to see the Negro "problem."

More often, the etiquette prescribes silence. If you don't talk about a situation, the presumption is that it does not exist or will go away. But as Freud has said, the repressed idea returns. The censored problem enriches gossip and speeds along the organizational grapevine. A major cosmetic company, for instance, was known to have few women above the secretarial level. Women knew about the company and passed the word to each other, but the company officers denied the charge. They had no written, formal policy about women, they insisted. It was just that "for some reason no qualified girls seem to have applied to us." Some companies used to complain that Negroes did not apply to them, either.

As long as the subject is taboo, complaints can be blamed on somebody else. Negroes who complain are "bad apples"; women who complain are dismissed as psychiatric cases or sexually unattractive. The party who brings the charge is expected to bear the burden of proof: Would *you* want your sister to marry a Negro? Would *you* let a woman operate on you? "Our Nigras were happy, it's those outside agitators who are stirring them up," some Southerners still maintain. "Women were contented until Betty Friedan got hold of them," Old Masculinists grumble.

Responsibility is frequently shifted to third parties, most of whom aren't asked to give an opinion. Manufacturers allege that Negro storekeepers would rather buy from white distributors. Employers say that women would rather work for a man than a woman. "*I* would be willing to put a Negro or a woman on the job. *I* am not prejudiced. But fellow workers or customers wouldn't stand for it." Women can thank students of racial and religious discrimination for pointing out that policy-makers usually have the power to overcome these third-party objections if they are willing to take a stand.

Another advantage of ignorance is that motive can be safely imputed to the victims. Thus there is no Negro problem because Negroes love us. There is no woman problem because women love us. Women executives wouldn't be comfortable in the executive dining room with all those men. Women don't want to sell outside the office. Negroes would rather go to "their own" church than mix with the whites. Women and Negroes don't want better jobs because they seldom ask for them. Women "like" detail work.

Myrdal accused white Southerners of turning a deliberate blind eye to the Negroes they claimed to know and love so that they could maintain their view of them. Men were accused of the same wishful thinking. "It has always been a part of male vanity to contend that marriage is the only real goal of a girl's life," Pauline M. Leet, Director of Special Programs at Franklin and Marshall College, a men's college in Lancaster, Pennsylvania, told a meeting of students. Mrs. Leet was pioneering a strenuous program of coaching high-school dropouts to get them into college and keep them there. She intended to stir up the complacent Franklin and Marshall undergraduates, and drew an analogy between attitudes toward race and sex to make her point. "If you could be privy to some of the feelings girls have when they exchange names, you might not be so smug," Mrs. Leet warned the students. Her speech moved some undergraduates to demand the admission of women to a college that has been educating men only for 179 years.

Both women and Negroes have been ignored when they step outside their "places." Legislators turned aside the demands of early suffragettes by refusing to lift their eyes from their desks when the petitioners appeared. Southerners discussed the Negro problem before Negro waiters because they were not supposed to hear table talk. Myrdal told the story of a Negro waiter who answered the obvious questions by saying, "No, I don't mind, I'm just a block of wood." Women complain that bosses and husbands accept them as "part of the furniture." The complaint that Southerners treated Negroes as "work objects" could be paralleled by the complaint that many men discuss women primarily as "sex objects."

Mrs. Leet advised the young men of Franklin and Marshall College that it was both difficult and important for them to understand women. Charging that anthologists have been "sexist" in omitting women poets, just as historians have been "racist" in ignoring the contributions of Negroes, she urged them to learn about women in the only way open to them—by associating with them as people. She said, in part:

> You learn about male attitudes and anguishes from your reading *and* your experience, but when and where are you going to learn something of significance about the culture of this other nation? . . . the girls you date are too wise to tell you what they really feel. Not how they feel—but what.
> . . . It has always been a source of puzzlement to me that an emancipated, progressive, young man who would immediately detect the phoniness of inviting a token Negro to a party to show his broad-mindedness will, without any awareness of the analogy, or the pun, invite a girl about whom as a human being he cares not at all, and he will know her no better in the non-Biblical sense

by the end of that day or evening than he did at the
beginning. She is present as an object, an ornament, a
decoration for his weekend and, if he can "manage" it, as
some*thing* more, but not as some*one*.

Men aren't usually impressed by such commentary. Women
are different, they say. Women have a "special place," so
different from the place of men that the very concept of
equality is treacherous. Wherever that place is, even if above,
as men sometimes maintain, it is always located with reference to the needs of men. "Who will do the cooking?" an
alarmed member of Congress cried out when the draft of
women was suggested in World War II. Southerners used to
object to higher education for Negroes because educated
"Niggers" wouldn't do dirty work.

And if the special place of women has disadvantages, there
are supposed to be compensations. "Miss Jones is probably
being treated unfairly (and stupidly) when she is passed over
for a job in favor of a man with less ability, but I don't think
she is morally wronged the way a Negro is wronged when his
race is held against him," Sandford Brown, a senior editor of
The Saturday Evening Post, wrote us after a lively conversation on the subject. "Our social mores relieve Miss Jones of
certain economic obligations on account of her sex as well as
assigning her certain disadvantages—and I don't think equality of opportunity for women can be a moral absolute unless
there are changes to equalize the burdens between the
sexes."

"Women have a better life as it is," another man put it.
"Would you do away with chivalry?" Negroes are in a
different situation, he said, because they have no compensation for their disabilities in the job market.

There is, of course, a compensation for Negroes, but it goes
by the dirty word "paternalism." Southern traditionalists used
to maintain that it was all right to keep the "Nigras" down
because "we" take care of them. "It is a sign of social
distinction to a white man to stand in this paternalistic
relation to Negroes," Myrdal reported. Chivalry, too, was
upper-class. Class leveling has made both attitudes suspect.
The advantages of the carefree Negro existence are no longer
a conversational staple of the South, not even among Southerners who call women "ladies."

Women can thank the Negro rights movement for alerting the literate population to the self-serving attitude that has imprisoned women as well as Negroes.

Like Negroes, women have been denied training, and then denied work on the grounds that they are not skilled. Both have been confined to low-paid, monotonous jobs which carry a high rate of absenteeism and turnover on the grounds that both groups have been too unstable to trust with more responsibility. Then when they have stayed away from work or quit in disgust or defeat, the charge of instability was proved. The hypothesis was confirmed.

Sexist and racist job assignments are similarly self-confirming. Negroes are allowed to become entertainers because they are supposed to be naturally funny. They are allowed to become firemen on trains because millenniums of exposure to the tropical sun are supposed to have conditioned them to withstand excessive heat. When they took the only jobs offered them, the lowly work they had to do was cited as evidence of their instability, just as the success of women in the monotonous clerical jobs to which they have been confined is cited as proof of a special aptitude for enduring boredom.

Most people now understand that Negroes who are not ambitious were responding rationally to the fact that ambition doesn't "pay" a Negro as it does a white, self-defeating as this attitude is. The Negro analogy helps contemporary feminists to see that what early suffragettes deplored as the apathy of women won't be overcome until society rewards women for trying instead of punishing them for their efforts to achieve.

"As long as American Negroes consciously or unconsciously saw themselves as an inferior race, they inevitably collaborated in their own exploitation," Ellen and Kenneth Keniston began their article "The American Anachronism: The Image of Women at Work" in the Summer 1964 issue of *The American Scholar*. But like Negroes, women sometimes refuse to collaborate in their own exploitation. On December 14, 1967, New York City women picketed the office of the EEOC with sandwich boards reading: WOMEN CAN THINK AS WELL AS TYPE and SEX SEGREGATION IS AS UNFAIR AS RACE SEGREGATION.

Meanwhile, of course, most women continued to rate themselves on how well they were accepted by men, just as

Negroes used to rate each other on how close their skin color was to white. Both Negroes and women realized that things being what they were, the royal road to success lay in winning the favor of "The Man," as Negroes called the white boss. They saw more clearly than he that his favor was more important than their performance when it came to winning pleasanter work assignments, time off, minor points of prestige, and other small but realistic advantages open to workers in dead-end jobs.

Adoption of the dominant stereotypes doomed most Negroes and women to self-hatred. Any minority which takes most of its power, prestige, and values from the majority cannot organize in its own defense. There are anti-Semitic Jews, anti-Negro Negroes, and anti-women women. Negroes who rise because of extraordinary talent and application tend to think that most Negroes don't get ahead because they don't really try. "Upper-class Negroes are inclined to minimize the handicaps the Negro caste labors under," Myrdal wrote in *The American Dilemma*. "They are often as overbearing to common Negroes as they are weak and unassertive to whites." Achieving women solve the problem of differentiating themselves from the unaspiring women in their organizations in much the same unlovely way.

"Give women time!" gradualists urge when the disabilities of women are pointed out. "They're newly up from slavery!" These conservatives expect women, as they expect Negroes, to thrill to their escape from the literal and figurative slavery that would have been their lots if they had been born a century earlier. And if this is cold comfort, the gradualists promise a bright future for grandchildren, provided that no one upsets the applecart in the present.

Over the past century and a half, Negroes and women have had the same friends and the same enemies. Their enemies were conservatives, Southerners, male legislators, literal interpreters of the Bible, and Establishment politicians fearful of upsetting the known balance of power. Their friends were Marxists, intellectuals, the city-bred, preachers of the social gospel, and politicians looking for new votes.

On most fronts, the Negro rights movement was one step ahead of the feminist movement. Negroes got the vote before women. ("*He* can vote," a suffragette poster proclaimed, showing a rather unattractive Negro. "Why can't you?") Race discrimination in employment was outlawed before consideration was given to outlawing discrimination on the basis of sex.

The full employment of the mid-1960s brought the possibility of equal work opportunities to increasing numbers of Negroes and women. Acceptance of Negroes and women in jobs they had not previously held tended to break down the prejudice against them so that it could never again be quite so formidable a barrier. In World War II, white men got used to fighting and working alongside Negroes in the armed forces and in war plants. In 1968, the shortage of clerical help gave thousands of office workers the experience of working happily and cooperatively alongside colleagues of an unexpected race or sex.

In the executive talent shortage of the 1960s, some organizations encouraged women in the patronizing way they had encouraged promotable Negroes when the Negro rights movement was popular, but the efforts to see that qualified women were promoted were much more half-hearted than those promoting Negroes. In 1967, for instance, 15 percent of a group of companies queried by the Bureau of National Affairs said they had undertaken aggressive recruiting of promotable Negroes in response to Title VII, but only one company reported an aggressive policy of recruiting women.

"I'm not ready for a woman," a frank management consultant confessed in 1966 when a woman executive recommended a woman for a job he had open. "But boy, would I love to get hold of a good Negro!"

7

GRADUALISM:
THE NEW MASCULINISTS

"The whole education of women ought to be relative to men, to please them, to educate them when young, to care for them when grown, to counsel them, and to make life sweet and agreeable to them," Jean Jacques Rousseau wrote in *Emile*, his novel describing the ideal way to bring up children.

Although Rousseau's language may be quaint, there is nothing obsolete about defining the duty of women in terms of the needs of men. Not so many years ago, Anne Heywood, the late employment counselor, received a letter from a woman who wanted to know whether she was qualified to help her husband in his business. After describing her experience in household budgeting and buying, she added:

Also, I am an extremely fast typist. I worked as a typist in an insurance company before we were married, and kept up my typing speed ever since. I am really a very good, fast, accurate typist. In order to maintain my typing speed, I have written a lot of short stories and poems through the years, one hundred and thirty-seven of which I have sold. Do please let me know if you think I could help my husband.

Women are better off than they were in Rousseau's day. They have jobs and earn money they can keep or spend as they please. This is indeed a giant step. But it has not changed the role of women as radically as the early feminists hoped. Instead of doing unpaid woman's work for their families at home, they earn money for them by doing the domestic work of "outside" organizations. "Women are the servants of business," declared Erica Hansell, a New Zealander who runs an employer-paid employment agency in San Francisco.

David Riesman, the Harvard sociologist, has accurately stated the prevailing American view of women's work in colloquial terms. "It's right for you to have a job," he imagines society saying to a young woman. "You have a job when you get out of college and until your first child comes. And you go back and have a job when your youngest has grown and flown, or at least entered school. But your job, which may bring in a fair amount of money, is to serve the family's menage, and *not to compete in any way with your husband*." (Emphasis ours.)

Women are still expected to work for men, to make life "sweet and agreeable" for them at home and now at work, but their chores have changed with the needs of men, and they have more choices because men need them in many more ways. Most women frankly say they are working for money because that is what their families need most, but a woman may also work to make herself a more stimulating companion ("I charge her job to mental hygiene," a millionaire told us), to keep out of her children's hair, to clean up local politics as she would clean up a messy house, and to take care of the unfortunate. But never for herself first. Never for personal power or prestige.

This attitude is a New Masculinism. It recognizes many motives. It does not prescribe specific feminine duties. It does not define a specific woman's "place." It charges her instead with the duty of finding the task the men around her need done from moment to moment. The nature of the task doesn't matter. She may shoot a gun or drive a truck or serve out a husband's unexpired term in the legislature—providing only that she does it in the name of somebody else and not for the greater glory of herself.

This New Masculinism is the prevailing view, but it is not the only one. People are not consistent on this subject, but most of them hold to one of four views:

Old Masculinists believe that woman's place is in the home, that her work is prescribed by her anatomy, and that she is mentally and physically unable to do man's work. Sigmund Freud was an Old Masculinist. So are most legislators, lawyers, doctors, small businessmen, farmers, and self-employed craftsmen. Most women are Old Masculinists, especially nurses, executive secretaries, company housekeepers, and married women who don't go out to work. So are Southern segregationists, small-town people who have not gone to college, and members of the lower middle class who say, "Boys should be boys and girls should be girls."

One of the most influential defenders of Old Masculinism is the American Bar Association. Late in 1967, the ABA opposed the United Nations Human Rights Convention on the Political Rights of Women on the ground—startling for lawyers—that laws won't guarantee women equal rights in countries where they haven't demanded them. They cited a referendum in some cantons of Switzerland in which "the women voted overwhelmingly against the right of women to vote." Education for these women, rather than political rights, was what the learned lawyers advised. ABA opposed U.S. ratification of the Convention stating that the right to determine the qualifications of voters was a state's right, and thus outside the Federal treaty-making power. Morris B. Abram, president of Brandeis University and former United States Representative on the United Nations Human Rights Commission, pointed out that the Federal Constitution had an amendment guaranteeing the right of women to vote, but to no avail. That Old Masculinist club, the United States Senate, took ABA's advice and turned down a convention for which dedicated women of all nations had worked nearly four years.

New Masculinists are for updating women's traditional role. They are all for women working, providing their jobs don't change the lives of men. They often talk about "expanding the horizons" of women, and "exploding the myths" about their limitations. But they think that the celebrated difference between the sexes in temperament is so valuable that if it did not exist it would have to be invented.

David Riesman, Margaret Mead, and many other thoughtful observers believe that women have a characteristic intellectual style—that they see things that men do not see, and that the problem is not to make them more like men, but to train men to understand the contribution women have always made. Educators who have thought systematically about women's education are tempted to encourage girls to do the community-minded, idealistic work that men have neglected in their rush for status and power. These are the high-minded New Masculinists.

Others are more practical. Women who have succeeded in business as Women's Women are New Masculinists out of self-interest; their jobs depend on the notion that women have a special place in life. Women who have achieved in men's fields reach for ways to make their sex work for them.

"As an architect for schools," Marion Yahn told *The Detroit News,* "it helps to look like 'just any other mother searching for a kid.'" Women often feminize a job in this way to get it. In March 1967, J. Klatil, the first woman designer assigned to passenger car exteriors at General Motors, confessed that although she signed her sketches with initials to get an unbiased judgment, she chose for a demonstration design the problem of making a car convenient for a woman shopper.

New Masculinists lead Government, education, and the more forward-looking big businesses. President Johnson is a New Masculinist: he wants to make better use of the special talents of women. Professor Eli Ginzberg, Columbia University's manpower specialist, is a New Masculinist: in his 1966 book, *Life Styles of Educated Women,* he painted a rosy picture of the many options open to women and even envied them their new freedom. He hoped that men, too, would someday be able to choose "whether to devote their energies and seek their satisfactions in work, at home, or in activities off the job."

New Feminists think sex roles are obsolete at work and should not be revived. They see no use in ascribing special advantages or handicaps to women in most jobs. *Old Feminists,* on the other hand, are out to prove that women can be like men, if necessary by remaining single. "Anything you can do, I can do better" remains their theme song.

There is, of course, a little bit of each viewpoint in everyone. A New Feminist husband who cheers his wife's honors may be an Old Masculinist who expects his wife to sew on buttons. An Old Masculinist housewife can be a triumphant Old Feminist when she straightens her husband out on an airline timetable, a progressive New Masculinist when she volunteers her services to the Community Chest, and a radical New Feminist when she hires a man to clean the house because he is the best cleaning "lady" she can find. But the distinctions are useful. A woman college professor has little to say to the wife of a doctor at a party because one is an Old Feminist and the other an Old Masculinist. Women executives dependent on the New Masculinist managements of big corporations emphasize the femininity of their contribution, while women protected by unions, academic tenure, or Civil Service rules are often New Feminist in demanding their rights as workers.

The view a woman holds influences the way she answers a question for which tradition has not prepared her: "What shall I do with the half of my life that my family can't use?" It is all very well for society to tell her that she may have a job before and after her children are born, but the rules of hiring, scheduling, and promotion penalize her.

"We certainly don't mean to discriminate against women, but our hiring policies don't fit very well with their lives," admitted a lawyer who recruits for one of the best-known big law firms. "We hire all our lawyers right out of law school and we never hire any part-time lawyers. If you want to be a partner in our shop, you have to start young, work longer and harder than the other juniors, and stick with it." A lawyer who is looking for a job ten years after his graduation from law school is assumed to be at best a reject from one of the big firms. It's the same in the big companies. Increasingly, comers make it early.

Can the rules of hiring, scheduling, and promotion be changed to accommodate women?

No answer. That, says society, is a woman's personal and private problem. Educators try to help her cope. They advise her to prepare for a career which can be broken into three distinct stages: full-time work right out of college, little or no work while her children are young, then increasing school and work until she is back to a full-time career in middle life. If graphed, such a woman's career would form a U. Her advisers think of ingenious ways in which she can get around the set-up, but they always assume that it is up to her to "adjust."

Mary Bunting, president of Radcliffe College, encourages undergraduates to plan careers in two parts. In 1966 she proudly reported that one Radcliffe girl was majoring in economics and planning to go on to law school, not to practice, but to prepare for a career in urban redevelopment after her children were grown and flown. Another economics major was planning to go on to medical school so that she would be able to go into medical economics in her forties. Still another girl was planning to go through medical school and become a school doctor so that her working hours would coincide with those of the children she hoped to have.

Mrs. Bunting did not think these girls were trying to avoid competing with men. On the contrary. "Women are freer of some of the pressures of the 'rat race' than men," she wrote in 1967. "They have greater opportunities to use their capabilities in work that may not at the moment have the recognition of high pay. Many young men envy them this freedom. Neither they nor the women of whom I am thinking consider that they are choosing secondary lines of endeavor. Certainly in scientific work, and, I am sure, in other fields of creativity it is the carefully selected by-road that leads to new discovery."

Mrs. Bunting's program puts rather heavy demands on the imagination and talent of college girls. Most girls find it hard to plan what they are going to do when they have reared children whose fathers they have not yet met. And there is, of course, no guarantee that careers projected that far in the future will be practical when the time comes, anyway. Some women have had to make heroic adjustments to changing circumstances in order to stay in the fields they have chosen. A woman pediatrician who married a man in the U.S. consular service had to go back to medical school twice after getting her license in the United States, to qualify for practice first in England and then in Italy. In spite of this handicap, she was able to build flourishing practices in each of the countries to which her husband was assigned.

With obstacles of this kind in mind, some vocational guidance counselors are still encouraging girls to consider occupations a woman can follow no matter where her husband takes her. They point out that a trained nurse or elementary-school teacher can get a job in any city to which her husband might be transferred. They also plug occupations that can be scheduled around family duties, such as teaching, nursing, social work, real estate, psychiatry, psychological testing. They point out that many professions can be adapted to family schedules: a woman accountant, for instance, can do the books of neighborhood stores on a free-lance basis. A girl interested in architecture can work at home as an interior decorator. The brightest and best girls get the message: don't try for the really challenging work.

In a 1964 article in *Redbook,* entitled "Are We Minimizing the Difference between the Sexes?" Dr. Benjamin Spock grudgingly conceded that women who have grown up under influences that make them want to be "automobile racers or brain surgeons should have the opportunity to do so," but he clearly regarded ambitions of this kind as unfortunate and gave detailed instructions for rearing little girls to become women who would take so much satisfaction in motherhood that they would not be tempted into "unconscious competition with their husbands."

During the 1950s, talented women rusted conspicuously in every suburb. Many of the brightest and best young women had been hauled off to the new real estate developments to rear children before learning skills or even finishing school. After years of isolation with small children and neighborhood women similarly occupied, they had no idea how to look for a job or even what to wear to a job interview. Glowing newspaper accounts of women lucky or ingenious enough to create satisfying second careers only added to the frustration of women who were at loose ends because their children no longer needed full-time mothering.

Educators and community leaders tried to rescue them. Seminars, conferences, short courses, and job-finding clinics sprang up all over the country. At first the objective was frankly occupational therapy. As late as 1963, for instance, the Carnegie Corporation funded a Seven College Vocational Workshop at Barnard College to counsel married women into potential employment or at least "re-evaluation of their lives." Unpaid service was strongly recommended.

Volunteer welfare work has always used the services of women who wanted to do something constructive—and non-competitive—with odd hours of spare time. Feeling has some-times run high between paid professional social workers and the unpaid volunteers who aid in hospitals. But as the 1960s progress, welfare services really need hands. In 1966, the Carnegie grant to the Seven College Vocational Workshop was not renewed, but a Community Workshop was set up in its place under a grant from the Federal Higher Education Act of 1965 to steer mature, educated women into areas of acutely needed community service. "The time has come to focus on fulfilling the community rather than individual women," Jane Schwartz, Director of Barnard's Office of Placement and Career Planning, said in 1966.

Politicians earnestly woo women with time on their hands for their unpaid services in getting out the vote. American politics runs on womanpower. A candidate for elective office has to enlist women to organize meetings, keep lists, operate offices, and for love of a good cause or a candidate do chores which elsewhere would command substantial pay.

By the 1968 election, every state and several cities will have some sort of Commission on the Status of Women. A few are obviously political payoffs, but most of these commissions are honestly trying to find out what women voters want. One of the most elaborate is Governor Rockefeller's, which in 1967 grew into a full-time "Women's Unit." It aimed to bridge the "communications gap between government and women," and "explore solutions" to the problem women face "of keeping self-respect as a person—a person who can't, in most cases, honestly play only a role as wife and mother from age 18 to 80."

Paid employment is the solution most women want. Surveys of volunteer workers have always indicated that a high proportion—sometimes half—would really rather work for money, particularly if part-time work or work on schedules permitting home duties could be arranged. Employers used to resist the idea. They distrusted the commitment of part-time workers and saw no reason to reorganize their work to make jobs for newcomers who did not look as if they would become permanent assets, but somewhere between Sputnik and Vietnam businessmen began to shift their ground.

At conferences on how best to help older women, members discovered, to their delight, that employers were becoming more sympathetic to the plight of housewives trapped at home. Leaders of business enterprises which sold to women shared the new concern. They welcomed opportunities to get up in public and boast about the wonderful women who worked for them. They sometimes suggested that paying work made a woman a better home manager and a more understanding wife, as well as a financial asset to the family. Woman's place, it developed, was no longer always in the home. For part of her life, or part of her day, her place was helping out at the office or in the store. Editorial writers, business leaders, educators, and other Establishment types began to applaud and publicize the few women in policy-making jobs as evidence of the progress women were making. Businessmen were being converted to New Masculinism.

There was a simple explanation for the change of heart. As a *Time* headline of November 1966 put it, "A Good Man Is Hard to Find—So They Hire Women." Shortages in manpower had been cropping up in various parts of the country during the 1960s. Early in 1966, manpower specialists in the U.S. Department of Labor had insisted that the problem could be solved if employers would only make the effort. The Administration did not want to admit that the war in Vietnam was creating a boom. In March 1966, President Johnson asked employers to explore whether jobs for which they were seeking men could be done by women, teen-agers, the handicapped, and immigrants.

Companies deeply involved in the war effort had already begun to recruit women. Early in 1966, for instance, IBM had mounted a publicity campaign in Denver, Colorado, to lure 2,000 married women out of their kitchens and into its new plant by using what one state employment official called the "Rosie the Riveter idea all over again." By summer, Texas Instruments was advertising over the Dallas radio for women with school-age children.

Educators who only a few years earlier had worried about finding jobs for older women now worried about women who really wanted to stay at home but were being made to feel guilty because they were not earning. In 1966, Roslyn Loring, of the University of California Extension at Los Angeles, opened a well-attended conference on women called "Exploding the Myths" by warning that a great many women were happy to be housewives and should stay put.

But the hunt for womanpower intensified. Starting in 1966 and even more aggressively in 1967, women were recruited for jobs they had never before been encouraged to try. At the University of Minnesota, for instance, food processing companies interviewed women graduates in the liberal arts for sales jobs. In a take-off on "The Man from U.N.C.L.E.," the National Association of Real Estate Boards advertised "The Lady from N.A.R.E.B." as "absolutely relentless when it comes to spying out exactly the house you're looking for" in an effort to interest women in real estate careers. "Help Wanted" ads alerted women to the possibility of running a gas station ("We are interested in your ability, not your sex").

By 1966, the services supplying temporary office workers had grown so fat on the labor shortage that they decided to lure more housewives into the labor force. "Convinced that 26,000,000 married women who are *not* working constitute a 'gold mine' of potential skills for an industrial boom in which jobs are begging, Manpower, Inc., embarked on a massive all-out recruiting program," began a release from the company's public relations counsel in 1966. "First, we must overcome the married woman's prejudice against returning to work, and this prejudice, in most cases, boils down to her conviction that a mother's place is in the home so long as there are children there. Second, we must develop a desire for all the advantages of the 'Two-Income family.' "

Manpower retained Dr. Joyce Brothers, a psychological consultant, to help women over their fears about returning to work. She advised women how to deal with recalcitrant husbands. "Be sure to emphasize the positive, rather than the negative. 'Darling, I think I've figured out a way for us to get that new station wagon' is obviously a lot easier to take than 'If you can't get us the things we need, I guess I'll have to.' "

The company also retained Social Research, Inc., a motivation research organization, to help identify the appeals most likely to attract women. It discovered that the best potentials were married high-school graduates 35 to 39 years old with grade-school children old enough to fend for themselves or stay with neighbors after school. They saw working as "added income, a means of self-development and self-improvement and a way of combining a woman's desire to be a person in her own right with her primary (self-subordinating) function of being a wife and mother." The survey confirmed that women with children were willing to take less money and waive fringe benefits "in exchange for the flexibility of days and sometimes hours of work and for the freedom of saying 'no' when work interferes with the care of children."

Stores and service businesses such as restaurants had always saved money on temporary workers who did not qualify for vacations and other benefits and could be easily laid off when they were not actually needed. Employers did not save money, per hour, on the women office workers supplied by the temporary-help services once their fees were paid and the legally required benefits such as Social Security and unemployment insurance contributions were added to the going rates of pay. But by 1967, office help was so short that some employers were running on "permanent temporaries" in order to get help at all. The advantage the services emphasized was the money employers could save by hiring help when, as, and if needed. Their brochures hammered away at the rising cost of fringe benefits and the profitable aspects of the very flexibility which they were playing up in their recruiting literature. The temporary-help services had every reason to be spokesmen for New Masculinism. They couldn't exist in an Old Masculinist world of stay-at-home wives or a Feminist world of wives with full-time permanent jobs.

The business of exploiting feminine impermanence became one of the nation's most explosive growth industries. The temporary-help industry expanded ten times in ten years and in 1966 placed more than a million workers who performed half a billion dollars' worth of services—just about as much as a Stanford Research Institute study of 1963 had projected for the industry in 1970.

Manpower, Inc., the biggest temporary-help contractor, was listed on the New York Stock Exchange in 1967. American Girl Service, founded in 1964, projected 200 offices for 1969. Most people knew the Kelly Girls. Western Girl, a Denver organization, moved east to invade New York. These and a half-dozen others were thriving—and they all knew that expansion would not be limited by demand, but by the supply of women who could be persuaded to go to work.

In 1967, a New York City firm called Staff Builders was using a mobile truck and loudspeaker on 42nd Street and Lexington Avenue in New York City during lunch hour to lure secretaries, typists, and office workers. The barkers passed out cards urging women to "come in and talk over: how to EARN MONEY at *your* convenience, temporary— part time." At the other end of the spectrum were high-minded conferences which produced news stories intended to encourage women to look for jobs. Many of these conferences sounded very much like the university workshops offering adult education, or Government-assisted seminars directed to better utilization of womanpower. The same people appeared and they said the same things, but the conference lunch was paid for by recruiters who wanted to *hire* women.

Techniques varied. In 1967 American Girl Service held a symposium in the auditorium of Stern's department store in New York City. The program featured Mary Keyserling, Director of the Women's Bureau of the United States Department of Labor, and leading psychologists who discussed the problems of mature women returning to work. The auditorium was jammed with 900 well-dressed, elderly women, many of them pathetically eager for the stimulation of a job. It was so successful that they repeated it in 1968 featuring Faye Henle, an authority on family money management. In October 1966, Kelly Girls and *The Ladies' Home Journal* sponsored a conference in New York entitled, "Quo Vadis, Today's Women?" Mary Keyserling, Eli Ginzberg, the sociologist, anthropologists Ashley Montagu and Ethel Alpenfels, and Bruno Bettelheim, a child psychiatrist, encouraged women to raise their vocational sights.

Employers restructured work in order to get help. The Veterans Administration and the Atomic Energy Commission pioneered part-time work for specialists, and in December 1967, John W. Gardner, Secretary of Health, Education, and Welfare, appointed 22 professional and executive women to work 25 hours a week. Banks were using women tellers on a part-time basis, not only to help at rush hours but to get the services of women who wanted to be at home when their children returned from school. Although hospitals had resisted part-time nurses—supervision is more expensive when two nurses have to be clued in to a shift formerly worked by one—they finally gave in. As early as 1962, most of the nurses at the Lawrence Hospital in suburban Bronxville, New York, worked part time and by 1967, New York City Hospitals, after running for years without the number of nurses provided for in the budget, were hiring women who could work only four hours a day.

In the 1950s some well-known companies moved their offices to the suburbs to get space, quiet, and clean air. In the 1960s they discovered that nearby suburban wives were delighted to work for less than office workers of comparable skill in the city. Small companies making electronic parts settled in affluent Connecticut suburbs where educable womanpower abounded. Inevitably, town fathers used their cheap womanpower to lure the industry needed to broaden the tax base supporting the schools. One advertisement featuring five charming office girls said, "BOSS WANTED. Move your office to Nassau County—and get all the help you need." The fine print was explicit. It offered all this eager service . . . "at salary rates that tell you you're getting your money's worth."

In reasonably normal times, professional workers resist the intrusion of nonprofessionals into their work. But in 1966 the shortage was so desperate that the professions were helping to organize a nurse reserve and a teacher reserve in New York State and elsewhere. Nurse's aides and teacher's aides were recruited among housewives willing to take a short course; professionals were saved for work that required their higher training.

Employers were taking a new and more respectful measure of the talents of housewives. Department stores eagerly recruited trainees from among their customers in the suburbs who, store officials sometimes said, should know what shoppers want. But the most radical suggestion came from the Federal Woman's Award Study Group on Careers for Women. In March 1967, this group recommended that the Civil Service change its rules to include "participation in community, cultural, social service, and professional association activities" among the qualifications for Civil Service jobs.

Women stockbrokers and women computer programmers became publicity staples. A breathless genre of "Why Not?" article predicted endless vistas for women in such unlikely places as the Vatican, polar expeditions, baseball umpiring, and heavy construction, often on the basis of a single example. But there was no doubt about it. Women were on the job in force, and they were branching out. In 1967, Professor Jacob Mincer of Columbia University figured that the "elastic female labor force" accounted for *all* the extra hands industry put to work in 1966 above and beyond the young people going to work for the first time.

In 1967, as the war boom accelerated the economy, the most visible New Masculinists were employers who were drawing on the labor reserve of dispensable women workers.

To women of a certain age, it all had a faintly familiar ring. The United States was in a war economy. Women with even longer memories recalled the old World War I slogan: "Woman's place is in the munitions factory."

8

THE ANDROGYNOUS LIFE

People talked New Masculinism in 1968, but a growing number of young couples were living New Feminism.

People noticed, with distaste, that men seemed to be growing more feminine and women more masculine, and they feared for the moral fiber of the country. The fact of the matter was that trends in marriage, education, and employment conspired to make the lives of men and women similar, so that they found themselves reacting in ways associated with the opposite sex in spite of conscious efforts to be "masculine" or "feminine." Androgyny seemed to be one of the dismaying consequences of progress.

The most obvious reason was the contraceptive pill, which more than the other methods of birth control made it possible for women to be as uninhibited about sex as men. At first, this possibility was hailed as an unadulterated blessing. Sex would at last be really free from both fear and bother. Marriages would be happier.

In 1960, when the pill first became generally available, married couples offered themselves as subjects for experiments to test the theory, and the initial results confirmed the happy forecasts. In reporting the first long-term study of the impact of the pill on marriage, Dr. Frederick J. Ziegler of the Cleveland Clinic Foundation noted that after four years on the pill, wives in the study not only felt freer sexually, but actually wanted sexual intercourse more frequently than husbands. This seemed all to the good.

For generations, marriage counselors had been urging husbands to consider the lesser sexual appetite of their wives. In the 1950s, studies of marital adjustment reported that college-educated women thought that they should enjoy sex, but few of them reported that they really wanted it as much as their husbands. Psychiatrists, psychologists, and even endocrinologists had explanations. Psychiatrists found that sexual response required a modicum of self-confidence and self-esteem which many women lacked. Psychologists discovered that women who scored high on "masculinity" in written psychological tests achieved orgasm more frequently than women who scored high on "femininity." Endocrinologists reported that sexual response in both sexes depended on androgens, the male sex hormone, which women only secrete in small quantity. Women treated medically with synthetic testosterone, a male sex hormone, were sometimes troubled by unaccustomed sexual urges.

Then in the 1960s the idea that sexiness was somehow masculine began to fade. Women were no longer penalized for seeking sexual satisfaction. On the contrary, they were being brought up to enjoy sex, and they did. In 1967, Robert T. Bell, a sociologist from Temple University, reported a study of 196 college-educated young wives which showed that a fourth wanted sex more frequently than their husbands, while only 6 percent said their husbands wanted sex more frequently than they. "The results may be far more serious for the sexually inadequate or uninterested male than they were for the personally unfulfilled female of the past," he warned.

By late 1967, psychiatrists were genuinely worried about reports of this ironic switch from the patriarchal past. "Women aged 40 to 50 now expect—in fact, it would be more precise to say they *demand*—sexual satisfaction," Dr. Ralph Greenson, professor of psychiatry at the University of California, complained. "It is not rare to find men who act in bed as though the sexual act is a dangerous obligation." Dr. Richard E. Farson, director of the Western Behavioral Sciences Institute, told a conference of leading women that educated career women enjoyed sexual relations more than women of lesser attainments or women of their kind in the past, but he did not seem to think they were happier for it.

"Women really want to be dominated by men," he said. "The trouble with women is weak males."

This shift in sexual interest challenged the traditional foundation of marriage itself. How can a woman expect a man to support her in exchange for sex if she wants sex relations more ardently than he does? The answer is that an increasing proportion of college-educated, career-bound young wives simply don't think that they are trading sex for financial support. A surprising number don't even know they are entitled to support.

We discovered this curious blind spot by accident. We were trying to explain to a friend why some employers think it is right to pay men more than women. "It's because men have to support women," we reminded her. She looked so puzzled that we jokingly repeated the Old Masculinist answer to pleas for equal pay: "After all, *you* don't have to support your husband, but *he* has to support you."

"Does he?" she said with transparent innocence. And it turned out that she really did not know the laws of family support.

"You just ask your husband," we told her. "It's really so. He has to support you. By law."

For several weeks afterward we told the story to working wives as a believe-it-or-not anecdote. But many of them found nothing peculiar about her question. A surprising percentage just had never thought about marriage in terms of legal support.

"What about alimony?" we asked one newly married girl. "Why do divorced wives get alimony?"

"Do they still?" she asked, with enormous indifference. "I thought that had been abolished."

Her comment reflected the increasing opposition to alimony. The proverbial golddigger who takes a divorced husband for all he is worth is giving way to the woman who would rather support herself than accept money from a man she does not love. As one talented divorcee put it, "Who cares about money? You can make that." Young college-educated couples do not expect a wife to press her legal right to alimony unless there is some reason why she cannot support herself.

Family-support laws are being challenged in the courts. In 1966, Mary McLeod, president of the National Association of

Women Lawyers, warned that wives and mothers had been required to pay alimony to divorced husbands if they were financially able to do so. Some local welfare laws make an employed wife responsible for the support of a husband who would otherwise become a public charge. And support works both ways, theoretically at least, in some European countries.

One of the young brides we queried thought the family-support laws we told her about were reciprocal in this country, too. "If my husband supports me," she reasoned with us, "don't I have to support him, too?"

For these young women, at least, the sex-for-support bargain is a thing of the past. They have not married for money. Their husbands have not married for sex. These young couples do not think they have a vocational relationship. They think of themselves, rather, as companions, carrying the androgynous pattern of school life into marriage, family, and work. They marry almost as early as the girls who expect to make marriage a career, and like them they get a job or go on studying. But they work or study for different reasons.

Instead of waiting on table to put a husband through medical school, these young, college-educated brides seek out jobs which pay in experience and opportunity rather than in cash. They work for token pay or no pay at all on small-town newspapers, in nonprofit organizations, in the Peace Corps or poverty programs. They make jobs for themselves in museums or in local government or community colleges. Like alert young men beginning careers, they are working for the work itself, for what it can teach them, or where it can lead.

Because her work is important, this kind of young woman often marries a man in her own field, often a fellow student or fellow worker. Graduate students marry each other. Law students marry law students. Medical students marry medical students. College faculty members marry each other. Research workers marry each other. Actors and actresses marry each other. In 1966, one of the engineers inspecting telephone installations in Orange County, California, was a woman married to another telephone company employee. These wives are not helpmeets of their husbands. If they happen to have the same employer, they are colleagues, even competitors.

The first home these couples live in is temporary, and they readily accept barracks-like public housing for its convenience, or even a furnished room for the duration of the course, the project, or their first, trial jobs. Housework is minimized and shared.

They often head for the big city where both can find work. One may go to school while the other earns, but the earner is not always the wife, and the arrangement is short-term.

If they are in the same profession, they are tempted to work together, like the famous French scientists Marie and Pierre Curie, who discovered radium, and the English social reformers, Sidney and Beatrice Webb. Some contemporary couples have become famous, among them the theater team Lynne Fontanne and Alfred Lunt, Oregon Senators Richard L. and Maurine Neuberger, historians Will and Ariel Durant, Lila and DeWitt Wallace, founders of the *Reader's Digest*, and Robert and Helen Lynd, the sociologists who immortalized Muncie, Indiana, in *Middletown*. Thousands of less celebrated couples have demonstrated that two can combine marriage and a career more successfully than either might have done working alone. Many pediatricians are husband-and-wife teams who can spell each other on phone calls and office hours so that they both have time to spend with their own children. Anthropologists who marry each other make a handy team for field work which needs investigators of both sexes.

Usually, however, it is impractical for the couple to work together, and as both careers develop, it may be hard for them to stay in the same part of the country. But it can be done. In 1967 Bob and Barbara Williams were serving as Army nurses within enemy mortar range in Vietnam and living together in a hut made out of materials Bob had scrounged. They met and married while studying nursing at the Columbus State Hospital in Ohio. When Bob was drafted three months after their marriage, Barbara volunteered and joined him overseas a few months later. Both were First Lieutenant Army surgical nurses.

Sometimes it is the husband who moves. Men teachers have found jobs in Los Angeles or New York to be with actress wives. Henry Luce accompanied Clare Boothe Luce when she was Ambassador to Italy and spent most of her term with her, managing Time, Inc., from an office in Rome. In 1966, Ambassador-at-Large Ellsworth Bunker took up official residence with his bride, Carol Laise, the U.S. Ambassador to

Nepal, Asia, because residence was a requirement of her job but not of his.

For the affluent, air travel can solve the geographical problem, at least temporarily. When Rosemary Park, president of Barnard College in New York, married Dr. Milton V. Anastos, professor of Byzantine Greek at the University of California at Los Angeles, in 1966, she kept in touch with her new husband by cross-country jet until Barnard found a new president. Then she got a job near her husband's as vice-chancellor for educational planning and programs at UCLA. That same year, Senator Maurine Neuberger of Oregon was jetting between her constituency on the West Coast and her new husband's home in Massachusetts.

Two-career families may have children, but they do not build their whole lives around them. "It's simply not true that they are as involved with their families as women who want to stay at home," Alice Rossi of the Department of Social Relations at Johns Hopkins University reports after studying 15,000 women three years out of college who planned careers. She found that the career-committed women didn't want as many children, on the average, as the homemakers, and that they were far more willing to let others care for their children. One of Dr. Rossi's tests for career-commitment was a woman's willingness to postpone having a baby in order to stay in graduate school.

In two-career homes, the babies do not come all at once, at the beginning of the marriage, but in phase with the wife's work commitments. Teachers can plan to have their babies during vacations; Professor Ilse Lipschutz of Vassar has had four children without losing time from class. Almost every graduating class now has pregnant wives in the procession, and sometimes a husband and wife are graduated together while their small child looks on. In June 1967, for instance, Stephanie Beech and her husband Charles were graduated from Park College, in Parkville, Missouri, five months after their baby was born. Stephanie was able to make up the month of classes she missed and to do her part earning the money needed to keep them both in school. She and her husband shared her job on the early-morning shift at a cafeteria. He did it while she was in the hospital, and after the baby was born, they took turns, one doing the job, the other the baby's three o'clock feeding.

Many employers believe that pay isn't an inducement to a woman worker because "you can't compete with a baby." The fact is, of course, that you can. With money. The more money a woman makes, the more likely she is to come back to work after a baby. "You can afford to stay home with your baby," a woman executive once told her secretary. "At my salary, I can't." The better-paid a woman, the more apt she is to keep working.

Fathers in two-career homes are often closer to their children than men whose wives make a career out of motherhood. They share child care in various ways. A woman television director in New York who is married to an optometrist spends her days off with their two boys while he keeps his office open. On the days she has to work, he closes his office and takes care of the boys. In 1966 he took them over alone while she tested a job in California. In another family, the mother is a public relations executive and the father is a teacher. Like mothers who teach, he uses his shorter day and longer vacations to spend more time with the children. Husbands with flexible schedules cook, run errands, baby-sit, and shop for wives who have less control over their time. Two-career families either forgo the social life wives usually arrange or share the work of organizing it.

Two-career homes undoubtedly form the character of children in a different way than homes where mothers do most of the rearing alone. Mother-child relationships are cooler than the early Freudians advocated, and parents have more rights than they have recently enjoyed in America, particularly rights to privacy and a shared adult life. Dr. Rossi speculates that wives in two-career families are more interested in a relationship with their husband than the homemaking women, who tend to seek their major satisfaction from their children.

Sociologists report that they can't find any important difference between the children of mothers who work and the children of mothers who stay at home. In fact, in some cases they discovered that the children suffered in homes where the mothers wanted to work, but stayed at home out of a mistaken sense of duty. They also found that the children of working mothers were sometimes more self-reliant than children reared by full-time, child-centered mothers.

Two-career couples are New Feminists, but they are not

militant. The women are more friendly to men than the pioneer career women, partly because they have undisputed control over the timing of their children and no longer need to fear the strength and spontaneity of their own sex drives. They are not missionary about their life style, and tend to minimize and even ignore their departure from the traditional pattern.

New Feminists' husbands tend to be academic or professional men who for one reason or another are out of the rat race of middle-class suburban life. Some are graduate students. Some are handicapped. Some are artists or scholars. And a good many are gentle and sometimes charming souls who aren't ambitious themselves, but wholeheartedly admire their energetic wives. Women married to these departures from the standard pattern are freed—and sometimes goaded— to pursue goals and make money of their own. Dr. Rossi found that the career-committed women she studied in 1964 did not see their husbands as driven, career-oriented men. "Many of the males in this room are businessmen who may make erroneous appeals to employed, college-educated women by assuming that the husbands of those women are like themselves," she warned a workshop on the "Homemaker Who Earns" organized for clients of the New York public relations firm Dudley-Anderson-Yutzy in January 1967. "Women who have married businessmen or professional men —doctors, lawyers, ministers—are far less apt to show a high degree of career commitment than women who are married to academic men, to men in any of the applied aspects of the humanities or the humanities themselves, the social sciences, or the people-caring professions."

How many women are leading this kind of life? The idea of self-determination is aristocratic. New Feminist women are so often frankly upper-class that they seem snobbish. Advertising, television, and popular magazines ignore them on the ground that there aren't enough of them to matter. But if you want to know what's going to happen in the future, you must pay them very serious attention indeed. Their life style will become more common when more women are given a chance to do what they want to do.

What do these girls want? It certainly seems as if they are reacting against the preoccupation with personal relationships that characterized the 1950s and choosing instead an almost

Puritanical commitment to causes such as peace, the poor, science, art, or even scholarship. *Newsweek* reported that for women graduating from college in 1966, the "career drive exceeds the mating drive." This impression can be tested on the changing values of Vassar alumnae. Although Vassar was drawing students from a much broader base than formerly—in the 1960s, a majority of freshmen came from coeducational public high schools instead of private preparatory schools—the alumnae group has remained unusually homogeneous. In 1967, this remarkably stable population was the subject of a bigger and more intensive study than has ever been made of any group of American college women.

Vassar alumnae of all ages were asked to choose one of four patterns to describe their lives after college. Most chose the life style that could be labeled "Home with some outside interests," but the classes of 1954 to 1958 indicated a shift to "Home with whatever career could be fitted around it." The real surprise, though, was in the youngest alumnae. The classes of 1964 to 1966 voted for "Career with as little time out for family as possible," and there was even a notable rise in the number of girls who said they were pursuing a Career, period. Many of the younger graduates were just founding families, so their lives were likely to change. But these brides who described themselves as career-oriented seemed to be marrying, as their husbands did, for a meaningful private life rather than to enter the vocation of wife and mother, as their older sisters had done in the 1950s.

All the measurable data—vital statistics, education, and job patterns—indicate that women will increasingly find themselves living in ways that parallel rather than complement the lives of their husbands. Even fashions in clothing, homemaking, recreation, and social life are emphasizing the similarities between men and women and playing down the differences. The signs pointing to the future are clear if you examine the trends, one by one.

First, the *vital statistics* of birth, marriage, and death are changing to give women more years of life during which they are not bearing or rearing children. Birth control has upset patterns that demographers regarded as inevitable. Before birth control was standard practice, men waited to marry until they were well enough established to support wives and children. When they could afford to marry, they could and often did choose brides much younger than themselves. This age gap reinforced the patriarchal authority of husbands over wives and confirmed the impression that men were wiser, calmer, and less "emotional." But this is no longer true. Husbands and wives average closer to the same age, and to older people today's young couples sometimes look like Hansel and Gretel toddling hand in hand into the woods, both equally inexperienced.

In the mid-1960s, the birth rate began to drop sharply from its post-World War II high. Demographers at the U.S. Public Health Service and the Population Reference Bureau, a foundation devoted to warning against the danger of overpopulation, give two reasons: young wives may be planning smaller families than the young wives of the 1950s, or they may simply be postponing their babies.

In 1960, the foundation survey *Growth of American Families* reported that young wives then 18 to 24 said they wanted only three children instead of the 3.4 average that wives 25 to 29 years old said they wanted. It was no secret, at least to obstetricians, that the fertile wives of the 1950s were not as eager to have the third and fourth babies as they thought they ought to be.

By the middle of the 1960s, young couples were realizing that they had time for everything if they planned ahead. Young mothers spoke of spacing their children so that they would have more years in which to enjoy watching them grow. More mothers talked about having babies at times that fitted into specific plans they had for their own or their husbands' careers, instead of getting their babies "over with" as fast as possible.

Postponing babies gives young wives a chance to look around at a time of life when careers are being established. Even a year's breathing space is important. Most successful women did not bear children in their early twenties. The reason why is not as important as the fact.

In 1967, young women in the peak marrying ages were experiencing involuntary delays. Girls born in 1946, 1947, and 1948, the baby boom years, outnumbered boys born during the war. Since girls usually marry men a few years older, this created a problem. According to Robert Parke, Jr., and Paul G. Glick of the U.S. Bureau of the Census, this "marriage squeeze" will be resolved in several ways: more boys will marry at younger ages; more girls will marry later, or not at all; or more of them will marry older divorced or widowed men. However it works out, these girls in their early twenties will be marrying later, and what they do with their waiting years can make a lot of difference in their lives.

Some of them, of course, have been swept into the booming job market. But some stayed at school. Fewer girls dropped out of college, and more went on to graduate school. "When a girl doesn't get married right away when she is graduated from college and she can't find a job that she thinks is worthy of her, she gets her father to send her here for a year," one dean of a graduate school said. He may, of course, be right about her motives. But there is always the chance that once she gets to graduate school, she will be hooked on her field of interest. Women students are not quite as impervious to education as some college professors pessimistically declare.

The second powerful influence that is working to make the lives of women more like those of men is *education*. As we have seen, we educate boys and girls together so that women are conditioned to work with men. Not unexpectedly, the more years a woman has spent in school, the more likely she is to get a job. Mary Keyserling startled the Dudley-Anderson-Yutzy workshop on women by asking the participants to guess what percentage of women over 45 with five years of college held down paying jobs. Even the sophisticated market researchers in the audience could hardly believe that 84 percent of these privileged women were out earning money. The percentage and the surprise it occasions are significant because women with postgraduate education will be much more common in future. As recently as 1956, for instance, less than 15 percent of the senior class at Vassar College went directly to graduate school. In the mid-1960s, about a third were moving directly into a fifth year of college. The trend has not lasted long enough to raise the proportion of doctoral degrees awarded to women to the high prewar levels attained in the Depression, when many women went on to graduate school because they could neither marry nor earn, but the proportion as well as the number of higher degrees awarded to women is increasing.

Meanwhile, more women than ever before are staying in school through high school and beyond. In 1966, half of the white women in the United States over 25 years of age reported more than 12 years of school, almost a whole year more than in 1960. The trend must be interpreted with caution. College may not mean as much in future, when "everybody" goes, as it has meant in the past; girls may be staying in school because their parents can afford to keep them there and college is now where all the boys are. But whatever her intent, a girl increases her chances of working as she increases her schooling. In 1966 Mary Keyserling put her slide-rule to work on the relationship and reported that schooling was a stronger pull to work in 1966 than in 1952 or 1962. Education pulls women into the job market not so much because it makes them dissatisfied with the home—although it may well—but because it increases their earning power.

The third factor making women's lives more like those of men is the *experience of employment* itself. Nine out of ten women will now earn at some time in their lives. Census reports predicting the number of women who would be working in 1968 have generally fallen short of the fact. Before World War II, economists assumed that wives worked only because they had to. In their experience, a wife who had to "go out" to work was either lower-class or the victim of misfortune. They discerned what they rather snobbishly called a "respectability pattern," and they assumed that it operated quite simply and universally: the richer the country, the better the times, the higher a husband's income, the less likely it would be that a wife would work. In 1946, home economist Hazel Kyrk listed forces dissuading women from working: ". . . movement upward of men's real earnings, a longer period when children are in the home, higher standards of child care, and a standard of living that requires a large amount of home-centered time." Another analysis of the time gave "inadequacy of income of male members of the family" as the number-one reason why married women worked, and emphasized the "opportunity presented to employers to obtain cheaper labor."

This reasoning simply did not account for the rising tide of women workers during the affluent period that followed World War II. On the contrary, the women who flocked to work were not the unfortunate but the best-off.

The young women college graduates whom educators criticized for "throwing their educations away to raise families" surprised everybody. According to a study made by the Women's Bureau, 85 percent of the class of 1957 married soon after leaving college. By 1964, seven years later, two-thirds of them had children. According to every rule and all the professional advice, these privileged mothers should have been out of the job market, yet more than a quarter of those with children under 6 were working. The mothers of preschool children who were most likely to work were not the poorest, but those with five or more years of college whose husbands could presumably support them.

Economists began to re-examine their old theories. As family incomes increased into the five figures, wives began to retire, as predicted, but nowhere near as fast as the "respectability pattern" suggested. In 1963 the Labor Department reported that the highest proportion of working wives was in families which enjoyed a total income of $12,000 to $15,000.

The figures accorded with everyday experience. Almost everyone knew some wife who was working in spite of the fact that her husband could keep her. Far from a shameful necessity, earnings have become a point of pride for wives of the frankly rich. Society pages herald their ventures into business and the professions.

In the 1960s, two economists, Professor Jacob Mincer, of Columbia University, and Dr. Glen G. Cain, of the University of Chicago, constructed mathematical equations to weigh the influence of such factors as the presence of children, husband's income, the education and earning power of the wife, and even the value of her home services on her decision to go out and get a job. Both reported that the most important influence in her decision was not her husband's income, as the old attitudes toward her role assume, but the amount of money she herself could earn.

This financial "pull of the job" is a sufficient reason for the educated young mothers to go out to work. It isn't necessary to assume, as some social critics have done, that they are "pushed" out of the home because they find it boring. As long as every additional year of schooling increases their earning potential, education will continue to motivate women into employment. And since workers with education are in such short supply that their wages are rising, it is not surprising that the percentage of educated women working outside their homes is rising.

Women themselves have known this, all along. When asked why they were working, wives always said "for money." In April 1964, 42 percent of working wives told the Bureau of Labor Statistics they were working out of "financial necessity," and 17 percent more said for "extra money," but they did not seem to be propelled by the stark necessities the Women's Bureau implies when its spokesmen insist that working women "have to" work. "Husband lost job" was one category, and it accounted for fewer than 7 percent. Almost 20 percent, on the other hand, said they were working for "personal satisfaction," and 10 percent simply because they were "offered job."

Financial "necessities" vary dramatically with families. For some wives, the necessity is a boat, a second car, a vacation, camp for children. Many work to send a child to college. Many volunteer to breadwin for their men. One reason that the Census forecasts erred was that they did not expect so many men to drop out of the labor force. When young men go to college instead of to work, employers are more receptive to women, many of whom are now working so that their husbands can continue their educations. And since 1955, the percentage of men who continue to work after they are 65 has declined one or two percent a year as more men covered by pensions reach retirement age. Wives of men eligible for Social Security are often young enough to get jobs so that their husbands can afford to take early retirement. Most people are surprised to learn that in 10 percent of all American families the husband does not work at all. He may be disabled, retired, or going to college. Without his earnings, the income of the family is often low, but the family may not be living in poverty. (The absence of the father is one of the salient features of the "culture of poverty," described by Michael Harrington as the way the poor live which dooms their children to poverty, too.)

All of these influences snowball. The temporary-help agencies know that a woman who has worked previously is more likely to work again in the future and to want a permanent rather than a temporary job when her children are grown. Every time opportunity widens for women, some women escape into employment never to return home. The Hudson

Institute, a private social science research organization, figures that by the year 2000, a majority of women will work at every age between 18 and 60 except during the heavy child-bearing and child-rearing decade from 25 to 34 years of age.

The daughters of women who work are more likely to work themselves. Dr. Rossi thinks the daughters feel less guilty about working when their children are young because they do not think that their mothers hurt them by working. The snowball effect is, of course, an answer to Old Masculinists who insist, somewhat hopefully, that women "don't want to work." The proposition can only be tested when a woman is offered a well-paying job and turns it down in order to pursue a home role. It happens, of course, but not as often as claimed. And the fact that a woman is staying home at the moment does not mean that she is going to stay there indefinitely. Some surveys report that half of the full-time homemakers say they expect to get a job at some time in the future.

A fourth force that is making women's lives more parallel to men's is the growing *desegregation of work*. The sex labels remain, as we've pointed out, but a number of influences are whittling them down in certain areas. Most hopeful, perhaps, is the rise of *new* jobs that have not been sex-typed, and that have cropped up and had to be filled—with anyone qualified—during a period when employment is tight. Skill is more important than sex in computer programming, so girl mathematicians are being recruited to learn the work, even though men dominate the big jobs and the repair work in the field.

Meanwhile, the increasing use of machinery in offices is giving office jobs more status for males at a time when many young men need temporary or part-time work to stay in school, so the "girly" atmosphere of many offices is changing. At the same time, the mechanization of office work is reducing the number of supervisory jobs for which men have been preferred. When work that formerly required a roomful of girls under a straw boss is done by one highly skilled person operating a special machine, the sex of that person is of no consequence, and if the job is new, it is likely to be filled by the first qualified applicant of either sex.

The fastest-growing occupations are in services such as teaching and government work where women have always been more welcome than in business. Rapidly expanding research programs need talent too desperately to discriminate against women.

Even in business organizations, the new jobs added are likely to be "inside" jobs providing special services to salesmen or executives and so off the direct ladder to promotion. In spite of the word "public," public relations is really a staff service to managers; in 1967 about a third of those in this explosively growing field were women. Mechanization and the addition of new services created new jobs in telephone troubleshooting and internal research. In 1966, an official of the New York Telephone Company estimated that more than 10 percent of its jobs paying $10,000 or more were held by women, double the percentage of women in this salary bracket generally.

The slowest-growing occupations, on the other hand, have been those generally reserved for men. The number of farmers is declining, fewer workers all the time are needed for factory production, and fewer jobs are developing that require physical strength or exposure to the weather. Engineering, for instance, is no longer primarily concerned with heavy construction in the field but is directed to design and research.

"There is nothing inherently feminine about mixing a given batch of materials, exposing it to a definite temperature for a definite time, and producing a cake," Dr. Rebecca Sparling, of General Dynamics, declared. "There is nothing inherently masculine in mixing a batch of materials, exposing it to a definite temperature for a given time, and producing *iron castings*. I have done both and find them satisfying occupations."

Opportunities for women in occupations once reserved for men were publicized by banks, governments, and companies that were having a hard time finding qualified employees. Newspapers cooperated by giving publicity to any "first" for a woman that her organization's public information officer could verify. In the summer of 1967, we clipped, at random, news of the "first" woman assistant vice president of the New York Federal Reserve Bank, "one of the first" woman court psychologists in New York State, the "first" woman pilot to be hired by a French Government airline, and the "only" woman to be elected to the board of governors of the American Oil Society. Publicity exaggerates the progress women are making, but it also weakens the psychological barrier against them.

The fifth trend toward androgyny is a general *desegregation of the sexes*. Stag sanctuaries are being challenged, most often by their own members. Luncheon clubs in most cities are quietly beginning to admit women or are making it easier for them to use their facilities. In 1967, the National Press Club invited women to its traditionally stag "Congressional Night" honoring members of Congress. Previously, even women members of Congress had been excluded. In February 1968 the U.S. Military Academy at West Point appointed its first woman faculty member.

Professional and special-purpose organizations formed by women when the barriers against them were high are rethinking their reasons for existing. Members of the National Association of Bank Women, Theta Sigma Phi, the women's journalistic fraternity, and American Women in Radio and Television began to wonder if they should not try to join the men's organizations. Many distinguished women simply did not bother with *Who's Who of American Women*. If they weren't well-known enough to be in *Who's Who in America*, they didn't want to be in a woman's *Who's Who*.

The Medical Women's Association addressed itself to public issues on which it felt women doctors could make a special contribution, such as sex education and medical education for women. Women were, of course, admitted to the American Medical Association, which represents the profession as a whole, without question, but they were underrepresented in its House of Delegates and on its committees. In June 1967, the Episcopal Church Women of Iowa disbanded because they felt it would be "more efficient" to work with the men of the church. In September 1967, the National Secretaries Association, a formerly all-female organization, broke with "one of its basic precepts" and admitted C. J. "Bucky" Helmer, Jr., a man who had been trying to get in for years. When he was rejected in 1964, he had formed the Male Secretaries of America and built it up to 315 members.

Other customs which separate the sexes are also being challenged. The most dramatic example can be seen in the liberal wing of the Roman Catholic Church. Nuns are no longer invariably hidden away from the world, as traditional wives used to be. Some are doffing their habits. "I have come to believe that the notion of cloister—in physical enclosure or in social regulations or in dress—is not valid for some of us who must live our lives as dedicated women in the public forum," Sister Jacqueline Grennan told reporters when she left the Order of the Sisters of Loretto in order to secularize the college she heads.

During the 1960s, the notion of cloister has been breaking down so fast on college campuses that graduates of the 1950s can hardly recognize their own alma maters today. Rules restricting the hours and activities of women in college dormitories are being relaxed and even abolished. Girls are rebelling against the whole idea of living under supervision, and on many campuses have taken apartments together "off campus," and, on some avant-garde campuses, even with men students. College authorities have tried to avoid the issue with parents or the press, but many have given up any attempt to regulate the private lives of their students. In 1967, Stanford University converted four dormitories into "demonstration houses" mixing men and women in the hope of reducing "distracting social pressures" and enhancing "more natural relationships between men and women."

As recently as thirty years ago, pretty girls were warned not to go to Radcliffe, the first woman's college to be affiliated with an Ivy League men's school, because no Harvard man would look at a girl who went to school just across the street. In order to preserve their chances, many girls entered Vassar or Wellesley instead. But relations between affiliated colleges such as Radcliffe and Harvard, Barnard and Columbia, Tulane and Sophie Newcomb have grown more intimate. In the 1960s, a Radcliffe girl was made editor of the Harvard *Crimson,* and a Barnard girl became editor of the Columbia *Daily Spectator.*

Admissions statistics for the Seven Sister colleges reflect the changes. Radcliffe is currently the most popular college, while women's colleges unaffiliated with men's colleges have been complaining that they are not getting the cream of the freshman crop. In 1966, Vassar and Yale announced a joint study to determine whether and how the two might affiliate. Yale students had long been for the merger, and although older Vassar alumnae feared that the presence of men might deprive women of opportunities for campus leadership or class discussion, Vassar undergraduates of 1967 saw no difficulties.

Although outsiders ribbed Vassar for its apparent eagerness to join Yale, it was Yale who first suggested the merger. Harvard's sociologist David Riesman, a staunch supporter of his Radcliffe students, warned that without girls Yale would lose the brightest young men (presumably to Harvard, which had Radcliffe) and might even attract "boys who are frightened by women and who prefer to see them only on weekends." Gone was any thought that the presence of women might lower standards.

In the end, Vassar turned down Yale's proposal. After a year of soul-searching, the Vassar trustees decided in November 1967 to stay in Poughkeepsie and explore the establishment of a coordinate men's college on Vassar-owned land that formerly had been operated as a college farm. In February 1968, Sarah Lawrence announced it was admitting men. Meanwhile, in May 1967, President Robert F. Goheen of Princeton announced that it was "inevitable that, at some point in the future, Princeton is going to move into the education of women. The only questions now are those of strategy, priority, and timing."

The whole trend is encouraged by the rising proportion of college faculty that has been educated in coeducational colleges as well as by the number of students who come from coeducational high schools rather than sexually divided prep schools.

Segregated recreation is dying out along with segregated education. Most men no longer stop at bars to drink together after work; instead, they hurry home to help with the children, have a drink with their wives, or watch television. Poolrooms, once refuges for men, have had to try to attract family groups in order to stay in business. Girls are going on camping and biking trips with men friends, as they long have done in Europe.

The de-emphasis on sex is also altering supposedly immutable feminine biology. Now that her sex no longer determines a woman's social destiny, now that she chooses whether to conceive or even bear a child already conceived, she has fewer miscarriages, menstrual pains, and "female" troubles, real or imaginary, than when her status depended on her sexual relationship to a man. In their places, however, doctors are noticing a rise in the proportion of women afflicted with ulcers, asthma, respiratory diseases, and alcoholism—health problems formerly considered male.

Hormone therapy is expected to increase radically in the future. It is already being used to overcome some of the traditional handicaps of female physiology. Estrogen replacement can compensate for the irregular output of hormones which causes some menstrual and menopausal disturbances. Women athletes sometimes take male hormones to increase their strength.

These trends to the androgynous life—longer years for women without childbirth, more education for women, more work outside the home, less segregation of the sexes—are all part of a more general trend to individual choice. We are affluent enough and command sufficient technological knowledge to be able to live in many different ways. There will be more styles of life, and more people will be able to enjoy the style that fits them best. The choice is especially rich for women, if only because their old role is breaking down and no single new role is taking its place

9

REVOLUTION:
THE NEW FEMINISTS

Former President Johnson really believes in women. "The two brightest people I have ever known are my wife and my mother," he told Anna Rosenberg Hoffman, the manpower specialist, when she reminded him, early in his Administration, that the country could always use women in a manpower pinch.

She thought at first that he was paying her sex a gallant compliment, as former presidents had always felt obliged to do. Merit promotion regardless of race or sex had long been a Civil Service principle, but women in Government continued to complain that they were passed over for promotion solely on the basis of their sex. Martha Griffiths says that when she was working in Washington during the war she actually saw a directive from the President reminding Government officers of their duty to promote regardless of sex with a penciled notation, "This is not to be followed."

But official Washington soon discovered that Johnson was serious. The day after his conversation with Mrs. Hoffman, Federal officials phoned her to ask her to find women qualified for top posts. At a well-publicized Candlelight Dinner in March 1964 he announced that he was going to appoint 50 women to top posts and make the Federal Government a "showcase" of opportunity for both Negroes and women. He appointed so many that Washington correspondents speculated that he might become the first President to appoint a Negro or a woman to the Supreme Court, and eventually he did appoint a Negro, Thurgood Marshall, but no President ever tried harder than Johnson to give women an equal chance at work.

The President of the United States has many resources to implement a pet policy, and President Johnson drew on most of them to open opportunity for women. He made news. As the head of the Federal Government, the largest single employer of women, he set an example to other employers. He reviewed Federal policies affecting the status of women in scores of agencies, initiated investigations, and encouraged laws intended to help women overcome barriers.

He used, first of all, his own visibility. He and Lady Bird asked outstanding women to the White House and arranged press coverage for the visits. He created other newsworthy occasions. He invited all the former winners of the Federal Woman's Award for outstanding contribution in the Federal service to the White House for a ceremony in honor of the six winners for 1966. "The under-utilization of American women continues to be the most tragic and the most senseless waste of this century," he told them. Then he asked all 40 holders of the award to form a Study Group to advise him on ways to enlarge career opportunities for women in the Federal Government.

He encouraged his official family to make speeches. Vice President Hubert Humphrey made news by calling women "an underprivileged majority" whose talents "this nation has for many years squandered in shameful fashion."

He appointed Mary Dublin Keyserling Director of the Women's Bureau, and encouraged her and her boss, U.S. Labor Secretary Willard Wirtz, to dramatize the handicaps of women in employment more aggressively than had been customary in Women's Bureau reports of the 1950s. Dr. Keyserling was a former professor of economics at Sarah Lawrence College and for many years partner with her husband, Leon H. Keyserling, Chairman of the Council of Economic Advisers to President Truman, in their economic consultant and research organization. She used her talent for statistical analysis to demonstrate that the gap between the median pay of men and women was widening, not narrowing as people glibly assumed; that the percentage of women in the professions had declined, and that there was, to use her words, an "increased concentration of women in the lesser skilled, less rewarding, and less rewarded occupations." She made frequent talks pointing out that the under-utilization of women's skills represented a serious waste of human resources.

Johnson followed up his words with deeds. Instead of waiting for women in the Federal service to complain of discrimination, he went looking for cases by requiring all Federal departments and agencies to report every three months on the progress of their women employees. The attention produced results. In 1966, 36 percent of the new college graduates entering the Federal service through the Federal Service Entrance Examination were women, an increase of 7 percent from the year before, and the proportion of women assigned as management interns almost doubled.

Although President Kennedy had issued a directive to Federal agencies to promote without regard to sex, the Federal Woman's Award Study Group wanted an Executive Order, which is much stronger. President Johnson issued it on October 13, 1967. He commanded the Civil Service Commission to hear complaints of discrimination in the Civil Service and ordered the U.S. Department of Labor to investigate complaints of discrimination by Federal contractors. A similar Executive Order forbidding discrimination against Negroes by Federal contractors had been issued by President Eisenhower. It had moved big companies to employ more Negroes in order to qualify for Government contracts. The new order could do as much for women.

The example of the Federal Government influenced the policies of state and local civil services across the country and alerted unions representing local Government workers. In California, for instance, women clerks won a suit against the City of Richmond for a rise in salary on the ground that their classification and consequent pay scale was unfair.

The poverty program recognized that many families were poor because they were headed by women, and the Manpower Development and Training Program employed a higher percentage of women than private industry.

The Job Corps was set up to teach a trade to girls who were unemployed and out of school, as well as to boys. When administrators were slow in providing residential centers for women, Representative Edith Green got a law passed requiring that women should comprise 23 percent of the trainees by

June 1967, but her attempt to get a third of the places reserved for women in 1968 was turned down by the House. "Some men believe that woman's place is barefoot and pregnant and in the kitchen," she explained. "Actually, half the Job Corps should be for women." In January 1968 more than 9,000 girls in the Job Corps were being trained for work in electronic plants, offices, hospitals, schools, and libraries.

Professionally trained social workers had long deplored Old Masculinist welfare laws which restricted "Aid to Dependent Children" to mothers who stayed at home. Many workers felt that these children would be better off if their mothers got jobs that gave them a chance to grow and meet new people. In 1967, some local welfare laws were revised to give deserted mothers a financial incentive to work. And as the tide of illegitimate children began to outnumber the couples who want to adopt, agencies began to relax the rule against placing children in homes where the wife works.

Congress moved to bring sex equality to the women's armed forces. In 1967, Congress removed legislative limitations on women officers so that they theoretically could become generals and admirals, and the President could appoint them if he wished. In March of that year the National Advisory Commission on Selective Service recommended recruiting women volunteers into the armed services to hold down draft calls. The new draft law which took effect in July 1967 permitted women to serve on draft boards, and several were appointed.

Federal agencies revised policies that seemed discriminatory. In 1965, the Federal Housing Authority announced that it would give "more consideration" to the income of working wives when considering married couples for FHA mortgage insurance. Bankers generally disregarded the earnings of wives on the ground that they were too uncertain to count as a basis for long-term loans.

In 1965, Secretary of Labor Willard Wirtz recommended that the National Conference of Commissioners on Uniform State Law include a prohibition on sex discrimination in the model Uniform Civil Rights Act that they were drafting. New York State had already added sex to its long-standing Law Against Discrimination. By the end of 1965, 10 states and the District of Columbia barred sex discrimination on the job; they were Arizona, Hawaii, Maryland, Massachusetts, Missouri, Nebraska, New York, Utah, Wisconsin, and Wyoming. By the end of 1967 Connecticut, Idaho, Michigan, and Nevada had followed suit.

Even courts responded to the new climate of sex equality. On February 7, 1966, a three-judge Federal court in Alabama ruled in *White* v. *Crook* that the Alabama statute denying women the right to serve on juries was a violation of the Fourteenth Amendment, which forbids any state to "deny to any person within its jurisdiction the equal protection of the laws."

Negro rights decisions turned the attention of lawyers interested in women's rights to reconsider the Fourteenth Amendment. The American Civil Liberties Union sponsored a suit on behalf of male *and female* Negro citizens of Lowndes County, Alabama, against a commission which had excluded their names from the jury list. The five lawyers who wrote the winning brief included Judge Dorothy Kenyon, a peppery former suffragette, and Pauli Murray, an equally spirited campaigner for the legal rights of Negroes and women.

In holding that the Fourteenth Amendment applied to discrimination on the basis of sex, *White* v. *Crook* was a legal milestone in the fight for sex equality. The Alabama setting demonstrated the Negro parallel. So far as jury service was concerned, the most racist states were the most sexist, too. Alabama, Mississippi, and South Carolina were the last three states to limit jury service to men. In January 1968, Mississippi was the only state which excluded women from juries, and the constitutionality of its law was being challenged.

The traditional pattern in the United States has been to permit but not require women to serve. In 1966, for instance, a court refused to require the Board of Education of New York City to reimburse a teacher for the days she spent on jury duty, because she could have refused to serve and stayed in the classroom. Men teachers in New York City receive their pay while serving, because they cannot get out of it. New York State still lets women decline to serve, but the trend is to make jury service obligatory for women, too. At the end of 1967, jury laws were the same for men and women in 27 states.

Johnson's campaign and the legal moves to equalize the status of women were not front-page news, but they served to alert some women to the inequities of their job situations.

Response to the sex equality laws was hesitant at first. Women who complained in private often shrank from formal protest for fear of looking like troublemakers. A typical reaction is reported by Martha Griffiths. A girl who worked for a utility company in Louisiana wrote to her, evidently in response to a speech she had made on women's rights, to ask if there was anything she could do to keep her job after her impending wedding. Mrs. Griffiths wrote her employer, pointing out that the company might violate the sex provision of Title VII. Like many other employers, the company had not realized that Title VII applied to sex as well as to race. After an interval of time, Mrs. Griffiths wrote the girl to see what had happened to her. "I'm married," the girl wrote back. "I still have my job. But please don't write me again, because the company has been just wonderful. They never intended to fire me in the first place."

Slowly at first, but in increasing numbers, women began to write in to the Equal Employment Opportunity Commission to complain or to inquire about their rights. The rising volume was a surprise to many employers and others who insisted that women were content with existing job opportunities, or so preoccupied with their private lives that they didn't care. Before quitting the Commission to run for Governor of New York State, Franklin D. Roosevelt, Jr., admitted that he had no idea that so many women would complain.

At times, and in some parts of the country, complaints of sex discrimination ran as high as 50 percent of all charges filed, and they were so intricate that they monopolized the time of the Commission's lawyers. During the first year, 40 percent of the complaints that looked solid enough to warrant investigation charged discrimination on the basis of sex. There were 1,600 in all, far more than the Commission could handle. Layoff, recall, seniority, and job classification accounted for about a third of them—in one way or another, all issues challenging traditional practices reserving some jobs for men and others for women. "Can a woman bump a man?" an incredulous reader asked a Detroit newspaper.

Employers wrote the Commission for advice:

Do we have to consider a woman for a factory job that requires her to climb up to get small parts in bins?

Yes, said the Commission.

Do we have to consider a woman for a job in a department

of men with whom she may have to "engage in argumentative discussions"?

Yes, said the Commission.

Do we have to consider a woman if the job requires interstate travel with employees of the opposite sex, in violation of company policy?

Yes, said the Commission.

We don't hire mothers of preschool children, but we take them if they are putting their husbands through college. Doesn't that comply with the laws?

Not unless your rule applies to men, too, said the Commission. To comply, you would have to exclude the *fathers* of preschool children unless they were putting their *wives* through college!

During 1965 and 1966, the Commission informally answered hundreds of inquiries of this kind, but it did not have the manpower to investigate the rising tide of formal complaints. It was not until late in 1967, after several reorganizations, that the Commission began to cut into the backlog of charges of discrimination by sex.

Women who worked in offices proved less tractable as employees than women workers were traditionally thought to be. As they learned about the law, they compared notes on vacations and benefits with their husbands. They checked into the fine print of pension, insurance, and health plans and discovered that their husbands were not covered as were the wives of men with whom they worked. Most of the plans did not consider the possibility that married women might have dependents. During the fiscal year 1967, nearly a third of the sex complaints alleged a sex bias in benefits.

Employers sought Commission guidance. Do we have to provide the same coverage for a woman as a man, even though the cost to us in premiums differs?

You must either provide equal coverage, or make equal contributions toward such coverage, said the Commission.

Do we have to provide benefits for a husband of an employee who is the main support of the family?

Not if you exclude the wife of an employee if that wife happens to be the main support of the family, said the Commission. You can exclude the main breadwinner providing the exclusion applies to individuals of both sexes.

Can we retire women earlier than men?

No, said the Commission. A difference in optional or compulsory retirement ages based on sex violates Title VII.

The ruling couldn't please everyone. The question was embarrassing because the Social Security system and many private pension plans allowed women to retire early on more favorable terms than those provided for men. In 1966, a retired dental technician receiving $80.50 a month Social Security pension sued the Government for discriminating against him as a man. If he had been a woman, he would have received $92.50. The law penalizes men more than women for early retirement. When a woman retires at 62, her total earnings are figured up to the moment she stopped work and then averaged out to determine her monthly benefits. But when a man retires at 62, his total earnings are figured until age 65—including the three years with zero earnings.

The Commission was handicapped by lack of precedents. The law did not specify what discrimination meant, and the Dartnell personnel newsletter for office managers assured its readers that the law had "more holes than a lace stocking." Some employers flatly ignored it, and at the close of 1967 the Attorney General had not gotten around to bringing a single case to test the application of the law in the courts on the many important issues that remained unresolved.

Nevertheless, personnel officers of big, visible corporations took the law seriously. They knew that Title VII's provision on sex would require more changes than the better-publicized provision on race. A few big companies quietly reviewed their practices.

"Describe duties in the same manner to candidates of both sexes," Mobil Oil advised its employment interviewers in a mimeographed guideline. But if a job offer is accepted, "problems which may occur because of sex should be frankly discussed." A survey for the Prentice-Hall information service, *Personnel Management Policies and Practices,* showed that three out of ten companies regularly queried had made some changes in their practices to avoid sex discrimination by September 1966. The least frequent change was equalizing pay (most big companies of the type surveyed had uniform pay scales), and on this early survey at least, the most frequent was changing company rules on pregnancy.

Employers had neglected mentioning pregnancy in their employee policies on the theory that there wasn't any problem. A woman who had a baby wouldn't want to work for years, they thought. Perhaps not, the Commission said, but that's up to her. And if the wives of employees got maternity benefits, women employees had to get them, too.

Does that mean we have to keep a pregnant woman on after she begins to show? employers asked.

You can make her take a leave of absence, the Commission replied, but you cannot fire her or deprive her of seniority and other rights simply because she has a baby. It would be reasonable to give her leave three months before her baby was due and let her stay out five or six months.

Knottiest of all were complaints from women who felt that their employers were taking advantage of state labor laws restricting the hours and occupations of women to discriminate against them. Well over a hundred of these complaints were filed during the first seven months that Title VII was in force.

Can they refuse to hire me because the state law won't let me work nights or overtime? women asked.

No, said the Commission. They can't use the hours law as an excuse for denying you a job or a promotion, or to discriminate in any way. If the hours law for women forces your employer to pay you overtime, they have to pay the same overtime to men doing the job. If your state law permits an employer to apply for an exemption, so that you may work more than the maximum hours, then your employer *must* apply for it so that you can work overtime if you wish to.

This position leaves many questions unanswered in part because everyone wants the laws changed. "Rightsy" women interested in the principle of equality want the laws repealed so that employers cannot use them as an excuse to keep ambitious women down. But some unorganized women are still exploited. Mothers working to support their children have to get home to them on time. Without an hours law, the hard-pressed small factories which employ the lowest-paid women workers might be tempted to fire those who would not stay on after hours at little or no extra pay.

The liberal who crusaded fifty years ago against the sweatshops would be likely now to take a middle ground. The Women's Bureau, many women's organizations, and AFL-CIO policy-makers want labor standards high enough for all workers so that women won't need special protection. They argue that employers wouldn't force women to work long hours if they had to pay them extra money for overtime. But there's always a fight in Congress over proposals to raise minimum wages and extend the wages and hours laws to industries not now covered by them, so this solution will take time. Some women didn't want to wait.

On October 10, 1966, in Anaheim, California, Velma Mengelkoch, an electronics and electrical assembler, sued North American Aviation, Inc., and the State of California for violating her right to equal opportunity in employment by limiting her to eight hours' work a day under the California State labor law. The case was intended to force the court to decide the conflict of laws between Title VII and state laws, and it raised constitutional issues as well. North American welcomed the court test.

In September 1967, while the court was taking its time to make this momentous decision, the California legislature with the full support of organized labor rushed through a law extending the hours women could work. The law remedied Mrs. Mengelkoch's immediate grievance, but it denied the principle of sex equality by legislating especially for women, and it looked like an attempt to avoid a legal showdown by giving the court a chance to decide whether or not Mrs. Mengelkoch was, in fact, a victim of discrimination.

Mrs. Mengelkoch was interested in the principle of equality, and she refused to discontinue her suit. "If this law is a chain around our throats," she told women interested in her case, "we will take that chain and remove its links and make of it a 'pearl necklace' which we will wear straight to the U.S. Supreme Court of our land."

Other skilled, ambitious women saw the hours laws as a roadblock to their advance, and in 1967, women's professional and business groups in many states campaigned actively for their repeal. To save the protection for women who needed it, states were exempting women in administrative and technical jobs and setting up machinery under which a woman who wanted to work overtime could apply for a special exemption.

Support for the old laws came not only from unorganized and unskilled working women who wanted the protection until labor standards were raised, but also from Old Masculinist union leaders who wanted to keep the best jobs for men.

"Rather than protective of women," Governor Nelson Rockefeller of New York told his 1966 Conference on Women,
"such laws have proved protective of men. If you saw some of
the opposition we get to modifications of these laws, you
would be even surer that these conclusions were right."
Although the United Auto Workers officially favors repeal of
the protective hours laws, Mrs. Mengelkoch says that her
union local did not help her challenge the eight-hour law in
California.

Ideally, of course, men should not be permitted to lift
heavy weights, work long hours, or expose themselves to
unnecessary hazards. At his Conference, Governor Rockefeller called for an overhaul of the labor laws of the state to
make them protect "working *people*" rather than *"working
women."* After his speech, Assemblywoman Constance Cook
drew his attention to a bill in the state legislature obliging
factories to hire girls 18 to 21 years old on the same basis as
boys, thus opening night shifts, the traditional beginning job,
to girls as well as boys. With the Governor's support, the bill
passed both houses of the New York State legislature and
became law a few days later. In 1967, the New York law was
further changed to permit women over 21 to work at night in
taverns.

Many states were reviewing old laws limiting the occupations in which women might engage. These ranged from an
obsolete Texas state law which attempted to control traveling
burlesque shows by forbidding women to dance in tents, to
Ohio's 19 laws forbidding women to work in shoeshine
parlors, read electric meters, or rum emery wheels. In Dallas,
Texas, a woman lawyer protested an old state law that barred
the employment of women under unspecified "immoral conditions" on the ground that men deserved such protection,
too.

The bitterest charges of discrimination under Title VII
came from women who alleged, essentially, that they were
required to serve as sex objects rather than as workers. More
than a hundred airline stewardesses charged that they were
fired on marriage or on attaining the age of 32 or 35, while
male flight attendants drawing higher pay for overseas flights
were not subject to age and marriage limitations. One man
charged that he was denied work as an attendant on domestic
flights because of his sex.

Airlines defended these policies by claiming that sex was a bona-fide qualification for a stewardess. They relied on the sex appeal of young "hostesses" to promote travel on their lines among middle-aged businessmen. And there were economic as well as promotional advantages to the age limit. Under the age and marriage rules, about 40 percent of the stewardesses could be expected to leave every year, reducing the number who stayed long enough on the job to demand raises or qualify for retirement and other benefits.

Some airlines contended that marriage interfered with the duties of an airline stewardess and sometimes that the duties of an airline stewardess kept her away from home overnight and so interfered with her duties as a wife. Actually, many stewardesses were so eager to keep their jobs after marrying that many of them concealed their marriages and some even installed two telephones in their homes, one under a married name and one under a maiden name.

"If the bonds of matrimony have such tender threads, I am sure our Government would never assign duty to our service men which would separate them from their wives," Colleen Boland, the militant President of Transport Workers Union Local 550, told a Commission hearing. Prominent women, including Senator Maurine Neuberger and Congresswoman Martha Griffiths, agreed that there were elements of sex exploitation in making flight attendants serve as "sky bunnies." Men don't buy airline tickets so they can be served coffee by young women, Mrs. Griffiths pointed out.

"There is only one aspect of life in which the youthfulness demanded of an airlines stewardess has in practice been desirable," Colleen Boland told a Senate committee in March 1967. "That is when an organization hoped for profit by selling flesh and sex." Her testimony continued:

> In years past, the airlines hoped to give the impression of having your private nurse along—and dressed the stewardesses appropriately. Today some airlines like American are contemplating uniforms of the mini-skirt style. Last week I read the latest quip, "I hope United will follow suit—then we could really fly the friendly thighs of United." If this is to be the portent of the future, then this competitive-minded industry will soon be pleading to throw out or be exempt from such prudish laws as might

prevent topless or bottomless outfits for their stewardesses. While this may appeal to the predatory male
more than last year's movies, does it really warrant
government subsidy? The purpose of the airline is supposed to be Interstate Commerce—not sex.

In May 1967, after arbitration, American Airlines offered
to hire back 75 stewardesses dropped on account of marriage.
American planned to challenge the arbitration finding in
court, but many airlines were relaxing the rule and finding
other work on the ground for stewardesses when they married
or grew too old for flight duty under company rules. New
York City's Commissioner of Public Events suggested that the
grounded stewardesses be employed as guides to foreign
travelers bewildered by the complexities of their arrival at
Kennedy International Airport.

Some airlines began to liberalize their policy, but the EEOC
withheld decision on marriage, age, and sex limitations on
flight attendants. In September 1967, the Commission held
public hearings on this important issue and gave the airlines
an extension of time to file their statements. While awaiting a
decision, the airlines were recruiting Indian and Japanese girls
to serve as stewardesses on world flights outside Asia, and
TWA announced it would hire 150 Asian girls for duty on
domestic U.S. flights, to be paid at U.S. wages. The Asian
girls were expected to provide "better service" and were a
"colorful and pleasing addition to the aircraft décor."

Finally, on February 24, 1968, after five months of deliber-
ation, the Commission decreed that "although a number of
different approaches can be taken to the question of whether
sex is a bona fide occupational qualification for the position of
flight cabin attendant . . . the Commission concludes that
these duties can be satisfactorily performed by members of
both sexes," but it reserved decision on the validity of limitations on marriage and age.

Outside the airlines, the women most likely to speak out
were young, college-educated wives and mothers who were
just far enough along in their careers to discover that barriers
still existed. Women personnel specialists in a position to see
how promotions were actually made were especially indignant. But some of the most radical remedies were proposed
by men. "Just throw women into good jobs and let them sink

or swim," Leonard Sayles, a professor in the Columbia Graduate School of Business, advised a conference on executive opportunities for women sponsored by Teachers College, Columbia, in 1966. "That's the way we broke the barrier against Negroes." Evelyn Harrison, of the U.S. Civil Service Commission, pointed out that a study of attitudes toward women in the Federal service showed that men who had worked under a woman boss were more inclined to favor women in management than those who had no experience with them. This finding suggested that if women were just "thrown in," and supported by management fiat, co-workers would get used to them.

"Promote the girls faster," a woman vice president of a department store suggested. "Get them hooked before they have babies, and you may get them back." Personnel specialists called for integrating employment services so that both men and women candidates were considered together, and for making a special effort to identify girls who wanted to get ahead and giving them extra help.

There were more radical suggestions. Equal opportunity won't help, some women said, if the whole set-up is biased. Like Negro rights leaders, they demanded a basic change in the whole society. And like the Negro rights revolutionaries, they wanted to begin with the concept of the world presented to little children.

"Revise the primers to show women doctors as well as women nurses," Rita Stafford, of Hunter College, suggested to a panel of the New York State Conference on Women in 1966.

"Change the school curriculum," Alice Rossi urged. "Teach boys how to be husbands and fathers, as well as how to earn a living. Teach girls how to earn a living, as well as how to be wives and mothers." This was public policy in Sweden, where the schools taught boys child care and cooking. (The Swedes also controlled the sex ratio of students admitted to normal schools so that there would be teachers of both sexes in the school system to serve as models for the children.)

New Feminist men and women quoted and debated the revolutionary theses of Alice Rossi in her "Equality Between the Sexes: An Immodest Proposal," published in the Spring 1964 issue of *Daedalus*. "No society can consider that the disadvantages of women have been overcome so long as the pursuit of a career exacts a personal deprivation of marriage and parenthood," she wrote. She called for revamping the school system to take sex-typing out of occupational and family roles; better city housing so that the families of women now trapped in suburban female ghettos could live closer to the mother's work or school; and day-care centers or the creation of a new, skilled child-care profession.

More and better day-care facilities were proposed by everybody who thought seriously about female employment. New Masculinists were almost as favorable to group care for the children of mothers who wanted it as Feminists both old and new. Business spokesmen approved such centers. Michael O'Connor, executive of the Super Market Institute, thought that American supermarkets would have to follow the example of European supermarkets and operate day nurseries in order to get enough women clerks for the expansion ahead.

State-supported day-care centers are taken for granted abroad, although even the advanced Swedes don't think they have enough of them, but the institution has an interesting history in the United States. Except for a small group of social workers, most Americans deplored public day-care for children as one of the sadder devices of the Soviet Union to extract labor from mothers at the expense of their little children. In World War II, a little Federal money was appropriated to support nursery schools for mothers working in war plants, but it was withdrawn at the end of the war on the ground that mothers ought to be at home. Welfare workers under the influence of Freudian doctrine on the importance of mothering became so worried about the large numbers of mothers who wanted to continue earning that they mounted long-term studies to "prove" that a mother's outside employment hurt her children. The studies, when they trickled in during the 1950s, proved no such thing, but the reassurance was not reported in the popular magazines and newspapers.

The issue arose again during the Korean War, when San Diego aircraft plants called back some of the women who had been trained in World War II and then settled down to rear families in the area. Private day-care centers sprang up to serve them, and there was talk of Federal help or at least regulation to ensure standards. Alarmed at this threat to the home, *The Ladies' Home Journal* dispatched a writer from

New York to report what was happening to the children while the mothers worked. She found nothing very dreadful, but her factual report was supplemented by an editorial urging mothers to consider their maternal responsibilities before rushing into paid employment.

During the 1950s, women's magazines had devoted a lot of space to articles glorifying breast-feeding and the mystical relationship between mothers and children. A reaction was, perhaps, inevitable. At any rate, it came. By the middle of the 1960s, thousands of conscientious but stifled mothers had taken their inevitable guilts and worries to psychoanalysis and emerged, in many cases, far more self-assertive. Psychoanalysis lost some of its glamour. In 1959, Mills College in California abandoned President Lynn White's experiment with a "truly feminine" higher education for women in child care, homemaking, and such womanly vocations as occupational therapy, medical library work, and domestic science, and reverted to an androgynous, pre-professional liberal arts curriculum under President C. Easton Rothwell.

In 1963, Betty Friedan's book, *The Feminine Mystique,* became a bestseller. That same year, F. Ivan Nye, professor of sociology at the University of Washington, and Lois Hoffman, a psychologist who was then a research associate with the Institute for Social Research at the University of Michigan, published a book entitled *The Employed Mother in America,* which drew together much of the scattered information about working mothers. *The Ladies' Home Journal* reversed its previous opposition to day-care centers and set up as its public service of 1966 a campaign urging Federal support of them. *The Journal* criticized Congressmen who did not understand the need for child care as being old-fashioned. In 1967, *Woman's Day* reported the Nye and Hoffman conclusions to millions of readers who did not have access to sociological studies.

And there were other signs that domesticity was no longer considered the only feminine role. Anthropologist Margaret Mead's restatements of her views on the roles of men and women over a period of close to forty years are an accurate gauge of changes in Establishment thinking on the subject. In 1935, her *Sex and Temperament in Three Primitive Societies* was widely taken to mean that women were the victims of their culture, just as the early feminists had complained. After World War II, Dr. Mead paid tribute to women's nurturing role in *Male and Female,* a popular book which reflected the domestic orientation of her women readers when it was published in 1949. But in her many popular magazine articles and speeches of the 1960s, she exhorted young women to stay in college, delay marriage until they could find themselves as persons, and plan careers rather than four-child families which contribute to overpopulation in this country.

Margaret Mead was, of course, not alone in this shift of emphasis. A check of book titles under the heading "Women," in *The Book Review Digest* shows that there is a steady rise in the number of books on the Feminist movement, and on women in other than family roles.

In October 1966, a new and militant woman's organization emerged. At the invitation of Betty Friedan, 300 men and women set up the National Organization for Women, "to take action to bring women into full participation in the mainstream of American society *NOW* [emphasis ours], exercising all the privileges and responsibilities thereof in truly equal partnership with men." The signers were educators, advertising copywriters, business women, editors, and Government officials. Dr. Kathryn Clarenbach, Director of Continuing Education at the University of Wisconsin, became the first chairman of the board, and Betty Friedan the first president.

In clarion tones reminiscent of the Declaration of Independence, NOW proclaimed its purpose:

> We believe the time has come to move beyond the abstract argument, discussion and symposia over the status and special nature of women which has raged in America in recent years; the time has come to confront, with concrete action, the conditions that now prevent women from enjoying the equality of opportunity and freedom of choice which is their right, as individual Americans and as human beings.
>
> NOW is dedicated to the proposition that women, first and foremost, are human beings, who, like all other people in our society, must have the chance to develop their fullest human potential.

NOW was an especially happy acronym, because it suggested that women, like Negroes, wanted their rights "now." Its militant tone and some of the proposed tactics were drawn from the Negro rights movement. Instead of urging women to demand more of themselves, which was the primary message of Betty Friedan's *The Feminine Mystique,* NOW attacked the "silken curtain of prejudice" and demanded access to the "decision-making power structure."

In the spring of 1967, NOW enlisted the support of many of the women who had shepherded the sex provision of Title VII through Congress, former EEOC staff members, and individuals interested in civil liberties. Carl Degler, professor of history at Vassar College, was on the board. So was Alice Rossi, then studying the career plans of college women at the University of Chicago. But there were also Catholic nuns, union leaders, public relations executives, lawyers, doctors, and Negro rights activists.

NOW set up task forces to plan action on a number of fronts. The Task Force on Legal and Political Rights under Jane Hart, wife of Michigan Senator Philip A. Hart, demanded, among other goals, equal participation in public offices, military and jury service, and abolition of ladies' auxiliaries segregating women in politics.

The Task Force on Employment under Dorothy Haener, of the United Auto Workers, demanded:

Assistance for women with complaints under Title VII.

State civil rights acts with sex discrimination clauses.

Overhaul of "protective legislation" to extend to men the protections that are genuinely needed and now are secured for women only.

Paid maternity leave for working mothers and the right to return to the job.

The militant note reminded older people of the early Feminists, but for the half of the population under 25, the tune was really new. In 1967, NOW attracted 1,000 members. It had chapters across the country. And like all new, evangelical movements, it was discovering opportunities for action on every side.

NOW supported the airline stewardesses' case. It circulated a petition for legalizing abortion and demonstrated against the sex segregation of "Help Wanted" ads. It demanded that the New York State constitution being drafted in 1967 define abortion as a civil right and guarantee that "the right of an individual to equality of opportunity in education, employment and housing shall not be denied because of sex, pregnancy, marital status, or parenthood." NOW even urged changing the law to prohibit the payment of alimony to a woman simply because of her sex.

NOW's indignation was paralleled, in 1967, by a new concern for the social and psychological status of men. Instead of gently ribbing Pop for his inferiority to Mom, as the comic strip chronicling the triumphs of Blondie over Dagwood used to do in the 1950s, jokes and satire underlining the degradation of men by women began to appear. Cartoonists drew husbands in kitchen aprons opening the front door to wives returning from work. "I know your salary is confidential, but you can tell ME, your husband!" cartoonist Howard Broughner makes the husband say in his gag panel, "Mrs. Bee: the Working Wife," reproduced in *Editor and Publisher*. The role switch makes husbands as supplicatory as wives.

In 1967, women's rights leaders began to discern what they called a "male backlash." In April 1967, for instance, Labor Secretary Willard Wirtz entertained a meeting of the Magazine Publishers Association in Washington with lines from a drama on the coming world without men entitled "Rome and Suffragette, or King Richard the Last." After the bit of fun, Wirtz explained that he really opposed discrimination against women in pay, but deplored sex equality because it "gave women what they didn't want and left out what they did want." Even the Secretary of Labor believed that women did not want jobs and did want husbands.

The desexing of men by dominating women was the theme of three books published in 1966. Robert Lipsyte's satire, *The Masculine Mystique*, attacked women as "sex wreckers," with chapter headings such as "The Feminine Mistake." Myron Brenton's more serious psychological study was titled *The American Male, a Penetrating Look at the Masculinity Crisis*. Hendrik M. Ruitenbeck's *The Male Myth* started with a section entitled "The Male in Peril," and went on to psychoanalyze the situation from there. Even during the domestic

1950s there had always been a few books discussing the difficulties of being a woman, but there had never been so much attention directed to the problems of being a man.

The new issue was examined by all media in 1967. In January, *Look* magazine devoted an entire issue to the thesis that American women were emasculating American men. The lead editorial was headlined like a telegram: A MESSAGE TO: THE AMERICAN MAN URGE YOU RETURN TO HEAD OF YOUR FAMILY SOONEST. That same month, Harry Reasoner staged "An Essay on Women," a CBS News Special, in which he satirized the preoccupation of women with their own problems and reminded them that they do best the jobs that can't be unionized. The demand for equality did not impress him, because "Love and dependence often thrive together."

New Feminists had psychiatric explanations for men who wanted to keep women at home. "Harmless as it may sound, a man who doesn't want his wife to work may be afraid that she may get as interested in her job as he is in his, or come to evaluate home and family as he does," Nelson Foote, a sociologist working for General Electric, told the Dudley-Anderson-Yutzy Conference on working homemakers. Such a male seems insecure.

According to Captain William F. Kenny, an Army psychiatrist in Saigon, servicemen who married submissive native girls were men who felt threatened by women. They were more likely to be divorced, come from broken homes, and suffer sexual inhibitions than soldiers who preferred to marry assertive American girls. Less educated and often older than their buddies who didn't marry overseas, they tended to see Vietnamese girls as a "magical solution" to their problems and less threatening as wives than American girls would be.

More significant and more influential than these emotionally crippled Old Masculinists were the growing ranks of male Feminists. Many intellectuals were becoming sensitive to the omission of women, and sometimes they felt guilty about it. One of the biggest and longest-haired management consulting firms was making a point of hiring some of the first women graduates of the Harvard School of Business Administration because its partners felt that they had an obligation to offer opportunity to women in management. A market analyst reminded corporate officers that they knew very little about women because social research data classified them on the basis of the education and income of their husbands rather than their own; he warned that a great deal of feminine talent was inaccessible.

During 1967, reviewers of two anthologies of biography mentioned with surprise and regret that no women were included. One was *Good Lives,* a set of six men whom George R. Stewart, the author, chose because their lives had purpose. The other was Robert Colborn's *The Way of the Scientist,* a collection of profiles. Scientists were, as a matter of fact, unusually sensitive to the charge that they excluded women. Dr. Warren Weaver, who served on the boards of foundations controlling grants for scientific research, referred to women as the "lost half" of scientific talent.

Revolutions have frequently succeeded through the efforts of a party going for them within the citadel they attacked. Intellectuals at Versailles contributed to the failure of nerve of the French kings which made the French Revolution possible. Edmund Burke argued for the American Revolution on the floor of the British Parliament. In the 1960s, ardent support for the feminist revolution came from the new companionable husbands, the new male recruiters of womanpower, the presidents of men's colleges who wanted to get girls on the campus, the political and business leaders who were actively promoting women to policy-making positions.

Some of the most effective New Feminists were men, and there were more of them than appeared at first glance. According to the American Institute of Public Opinion, there was a real increase in the proportion of men who would vote for a qualified woman President. This survey organization asked the question on a poll of 1955 and again in 1963. Over that interval of eight years, the percentage of women who would vote for a woman President dropped slightly from 56 percent to 51 percent, but the male vote rose from 47 to 58 percent.

At the last count, a majority of men saw no objection to the idea of a woman President of the United States.

10

THE CASE FOR EQUALITY

Is it a good idea to treat men and women exactly alike?

What would happen if we tried it?

Is it even possible?

"After all, men and women are different," people argue. "You can't treat them alike!"

Just as we formerly had laws that said that noblemen had certain privileges because of their names, so we now have laws that say that men and women have certain privileges because of their sex. If we think we can't treat men and women alike, it may only be because the law hasn't done it.

But it can be done. In a provocative article in *The George Washington Law Review* of December 1965, Pauli Murray and Mary Eastwood reviewed the laws affecting men and women as separate sexes and reported that all such laws would be either clearer or fairer if rewritten in terms of situations, as all other laws are written. It wouldn't be necessary, they pointed out, to say that the crime of rape could be committed only by men or that maternity benefits could be claimed only by women. By definition, these situations apply to one sex only. A woman can't commit rape. A man can't have a baby. The conditions that seem to require special treatment for men or women can all be defined without mentioning sex. If all persons were liable for military or jury service, for instance, men and women could both claim exemption because they had dependents. Women able to serve would relieve the men for whom the draft is now a real hardship.

There is no reason why women should not be drafted. The crack Israeli Army drafts all boys and single girls at the age of 18. Girls who marry during their draft terms, as three out of ten do, go into the reserves. Pregnant women and mothers are excused, but women officers in the regular army get four months of fully paid leave beginning with the ninth month of pregnancy. Israeli women soldiers have fought in bloody battles in the past, but they are now assigned to handle paperwork, communications, and medical services in units with men.

It isn't necessary to require that husbands support wives in order to protect children. Both partners to a marriage could simply be required to support each other and their children in case of need. There is nothing morally repugnant about requiring money or services from the partner best able to give them, regardless of sex.

Pauli Murray and Mary Eastwood point out that the principle of mutual support legally recognizes the value of women's unpaid domestic services, which economists estimate amounts to at least a fifth of the current Gross National Product. Domestic services are regularly included in the Swedish Gross National Product, and their domestic law specifically mentions the domestic services of the wife as an economic contribution to the marriage partnership.

This recognition clarifies the position of the traditional wife whose years of homemaking experience are not negotiable in the job market if the marriage ends. Our divorce laws now award her alimony, but as Clare Boothe Luce wrote in 1967, it would be more appropriate to recognize her past services by giving her severance pay. Courts could protect rich men from women who marry them only for their money by awarding alimony on the basis of the length of the marriage and the domestic services the wives have actually rendered.

The principle of mutual support would eliminate many other abuses. Family counselors now advise that some children, particularly boys, would be better off with their fathers than with their mothers. To date, divorce courts automatically assume that mothers should always care for children and fathers always pay for them. The reverse would be better for some families.

There is no rhyme or reason to current laws specifying the ages at which a person is permitted to marry, work, or retire. They would be much fairer if the specifications were the same for men and women all the way down the line, just as they are for voting and driving. Boys mature more slowly, so there is no reason why state child labor laws should permit boys to start working younger than girls. A really functional law might require a person to demonstrate fitness to work by physical or mental test, just as we now require driving tests. Functional tests for job-holding might allow girls to work at an earlier age and let them keep working later than law and custom now permit.

The principle of mutual support would give surviving husbands the same pension and insurance benefits that now go to widows. Employers could, if they wished, require beneficiaries to pass a means test. Under this system, wives who actually support themselves would not draw benefits any more than do husbands who actually support themselves. This would allow funds committed to these programs to take better care of wives who have no earning power because their lifetime contribution was made in the home, as well as providing support for the substantial number of husbands who, because they are older than their wives, have become disabled.

Ideally, marriage should not alter the civil and legal rights of either husband or wife. Wives should be able to choose a *legal* domicile separate from that of their husbands, if this is what they both want, without this in any way jeopardizing the marriage or rights. This would allow a woman who for business or professional reasons does not live constantly with her husband, at the residence legally his, to maintain her voting rights, as well as letting her hold public office even if her husband doesn't live in the district.

Sex equality would, of course, remove any lingering doubt that a woman has a right to use her maiden name for any legitimate reason. Other countries are more consistent than we in handling names. Spanish cultures add the mother's maiden name to surnames, recognizing both lines of descent instead of the father's alone. We call a married woman "Mrs.," but a "Mr." may be married or single. Much as the Swedes love titles, they are now moving to drop forms of address that identify the marital status of women in situations where the marital status of men is not recognized.

The most widespread changes, of course, would occur in laws affecting employment. Employers would be forbidden to discharge a woman for maternity just as they are now forbidden to discharge a man for military or jury service. If men were not required to support their wives under all circumstances, there would be no reason to protect a man's job and not a woman's. A pregnant woman who loses her job should get unemployment insurance, whether her husband can support her or not, just as a married man gets unemployment insurance, whether or not his wife can support him.

Laws limiting the weight a woman worker may lift are now used to keep women out of jobs that are no more arduous than hauling sacks of groceries from the supermarket or removing a five-year-old from mischief. These laws would be fairer if they required tests of physical ability for jobs requiring strength. Men, after all, are the sex most vulnerable to hernia. Instead of forbidding women to do jobs that are considered hazardous, a really protective law would limit dangerous work to those who had passed a test of skill. There's no reason, for instance, why a woman can't run a drill press as safely as a man, if she is taught how to do it.

Minimum wage and maximum hour laws could apply to both sexes with identical exemptions. Some foreign countries guarantee the right of a mother to time off for family emergencies. American employers expect mothers to take time off, but because it is unofficial, they tend to charge the time lost against women workers in general. It would be fairer as well as better for the children if mothers and fathers were permitted a certain number of days off a year to cope with family problems. Parents could spell each other during a long siege instead of making the wife's employer stand for all the inconvenience.

All these legal inequalities could be remedied, but the real question is: Do we want to do it? Do we really want to treat men and women alike? The only way to find out is to examine, as best we can, what the change would do. The most radical effects would be felt in the field of employment. If access, pay, promotion, and conditions of work for every job were open equally to men and women, as Title VII plainly requires, there would be no legal or moral basis for what

Pauli Murray and Mary Eastwood call ". . . the assumption that financial support of a family by the husband-father is a gift from the male sex to the female sex, and, in return, the male is entitled to preference in the outside world."

Supposing individuals were hired in all occupations without regard to sex. Women would compete with men in areas now closed to them, but they would not compete with each other as much as they now do for "women's jobs." Women who stayed in "women's jobs" would win higher wages. As the wages rose, men would be attracted to these fields. Since the lowest-paying jobs are those dominated by women, equal opportunity would have the same effect as raising the minimum wage.

Thousands of marginal jobs would go out of existence. It would suddenly be profitable to mechanize cherry-picking and sell even more standard items in vending machines. What operations could not be mechanized might well be omitted. Some of us might have to go without lettuce because no one would be willing to pay what it would cost to produce as much lettuce as we now consume if we paid a living wage to the people who cultivate it. We have, of course, survived other such deprivations. No one can afford hand-tooled shoes except the very rich, and they seldom bother with custom-made apparel because fittings take time and clothes are no longer expected to last forever.

If, along with sex equality, we expected all adults to work, women who could not show that they were earning their keep at home would have to find jobs. According to one estimate, full utilization of "womanpower" would add ten million workers to the labor force. If these women could work wherever they were needed, they would free men from the obligation to earn that injures and limits some of them as grievously as the obligation to do housework now injures and limits some women. This is no idle supposition. As we have noticed earlier, under full employment many families find it makes more sense for women to work and support their menfolk.

If women were freer to choose where they worked, they would take a good hard look at some of the chores that now keep them at home. What, for instance, is the actual money value of staying at home all day long to do two hours of cleaning? Of hauling groceries from the supermarket? Of waiting in the pediatrician's office for an hour? In 1968, mothers expect all sorts of people to waste their time. The waste is not necessary, and it is not motherhood.

A woman we know solved the problem of the doctor's waiting room by arranging for a baby-sitter to take her son to the appointment. She found that she could continue working in her office for an hour or more while they waited for his turn. She could earn more at her own trade than she could have saved in cab fare and baby-sitting fees, even though the expense was not deductible. A working woman has to operate a home in a world that assumes that a homemaker's time is worth less than the wages of the lowest-paid worker for money. Deliveries are arranged on the assumption that she can sit home all day long and wait. No one calculates the time cost of shopping, either, especially in crowded discount houses and supermarkets, where women on budgets are forced to shop. No one counts the time cost of toting shoes to and from the repairman, or exchanging goods that may have been ordered by telephone to save time, but weren't right on arrival. Purchasing departments count the cost of the time that clerks use when they check prices and quality before buying, but housewives don't add the cost of their time to the price paid for family purchases.

If all adults were required to work, and free to choose the kind of work they wanted, many women would leave their homes and thereby create more paying jobs. Baby-sitters and service workers, many of them now considered unemployable because of age or lack of education, would be drawn out of their isolation and into the labor force. But all of these newcomers would not necessarily find themselves doing what housewives used to do at home. Many would find jobs in services especially organized to do housework efficiently.

More women could afford housekeeping services that now exist for the very rich alone. More charge-and-deliver grocers would be needed to serve the growing number of housewives who would not mind paying more to save the time they now spend shopping in self-service supermarkets. Cleaning services could contract to keep a house in shape by sending in teams of machine-equipped professionals to tidy for an hour or so every day; maintenance services employing salaried mechanics could keep all household gear operating for a flat annual fee; yard services like those run by teams of Japanese gardeners in Los Angeles could contract to keep lawns mowed and garden beds weeded. Food take-out services and caterers proliferating around the country would increase to serve the growing number of women who like to entertain but don't have time to cook.

These new services would be cheaper in real economic terms, because specialists working at what they enjoy are more efficient than amateurs doing chores they may detest. But the big gain would be a better use of talent. If the born cooks, cleaners, and children's nurses were paid well enough so that they could make careers out of their talents, domestic services would attract women who now enjoy household arts but hesitate to practice them professionally because they don't want to be treated as "servants." Women who have never worked often have trouble with servants because they have never learned how to hold employees to objective standards. If most women worked, domestic service could become more attractive, since hopefully domestic workers would begin to be treated more like office workers.

For hundreds of years now, many tasks have been passing from what the economists call "customary" work, done without pay, to wage work. Canning, clothes-making, and the care of the sick now are jobs, not unpaid chores. The hired man has replaced the farmer's son, the paid baby-sitter has replaced neighborly child-watching, and young people learn to drive, skate, ski, and swim from paid instructors, rather than older relatives. The shift has always increased efficiency and improved the status of the task.

Housekeeping is the last unpaid customary job, and if most women worked, it would be professionalized, too. The errands, the repairs, the appointment-making, the bookkeeping, the snack-making, the chauffeuring and other odd jobs which make women feel disorganized and undervalued, could all be turned into professionally run services. These new businesses would create more part-time, seasonal, odd-hour jobs, which would offer men and women wider choices about when they would—or could—work than the traditional nine-to-five schedule. Odd-hour schedules of work and study beget more odd-hour jobs. Round-the-clock cafeteria workers are needed to feed round-the-clock factory workers, round-the-clock bus services to move round-the-clock cafeteria workers, and so on. In New York City, there are all-night hairdressers, garages, office services, movies, and restaurants for the "night" people. These services were set up for the theatrical community, but they now grow by serving each other.

Mechanization of many routine tasks means that the expensive computers and complicated business machines that are being used every day must be kept going constantly in order to pay their way. This is one of the reasons why Herman Kahn predicts that there will be much more flexible business schedules in the year 2000 than we now have. He foresees that professional and technical specialists will do much of their work alone at computer terminals installed in their homes. I.B.M. now trains mechanics this way. Instead of traveling to a central school, each student plugs into a nearby machine that is connected with the central computer, whenever he has a free hour, and works as long as he pleases.

Flexible schedules are increasing. More men and women than ever before do work that allows them to determine their own hours. Among them are researchers for professional lawyers and accountants, computer programmers, interviewers for opinion polls, and market research analysts. There is increasing opportunity to do independent work designing everything from radios to gardens, and selling every kind of product from housewares to job printing.

Work of this kind encourages both men and women to try out new divisions of labor within families, new programs of work-and-study or work-and-child-rearing, or work-and-retirement. Women need not retire completely from work while their children are young if work is available when and where and in quantities they can choose. And there is no reason why fathers should work traditional hours, either, if they don't want to.

Work doesn't have to be done in set eight-hour shifts, and at the office or the plant. It can be allocated so that part-time, part-year workers could be used everywhere, without making women do all the "adjusting" required. Professional women have learned to take their work home and do it after the children are in bed, or while they are in school. Many more tasks could be organized this way if employers were willing.

Real sex equality would mean that every institution depending on the "free time of housewives" would undergo radical change. Unpaid welfare work would not rely primarily on the volunteer services of women. Health and welfare responsibilities would be divided equally between the sexes, just as jury duty and military service would be done by both according to ability and availability. Organizations would not have "ladies' auxiliaries" doomed to make-work activities.

There would be fewer hen parties and stag parties, more opportunities for coeducational groupings around a common interest such as cooking, hiking, or painting. Girl reporters would not be dispatched to invent a "woman's point of view" on general news, but would have to report the human point of view in competition with men reporters. The "woman's page" would become a collection of columns for all, on food, fashion, home decoration, child care—presumably all material relating to living problems that would interest either men or women.

Desegregation of the work force would eliminate the advantage Women's Women make of their sex. If clerks were a mixed group of men and women, there would be no particular reason to prefer a woman supervisor. Achieving women would not have to feel so exceptional. If the chores of consumption were shared by men and women alike, advertising and merchandising would lose its feminine orientation. If marriage were not the only or the principal means for women to acquire status, sex appeal would not be the dominant sales appeal for advertising copy.

Real desegregation of work, real enforcement of equal opportunity, would have far-reaching economic consequences. It would threaten labor costs and management incentives. It would compel a radical restructure of work, accelerate mechanization already under way, and destroy the use of women as a labor reserve.

Women are the last labor reserve employers can take for granted; they are the only labor reserve well enough educated to do the white-collar "dirty work." What would happen to the economy of the United States if this reserve disappeared? The question is not academic. Equal opportunity laws work hand in glove with minimum wage laws to make it hard for marginal enterprises to pick up cheap help, and full employment means that there is very little cheap help left. In the 1960s some crops have actually gone to waste because low-cost labor was not, as formerly, instantly available.

More important to the economy, of course, is the effect on big companies. When they figured the cost of expanding or adding new products, they would discover that they would have to pay much more for extra hands than in the past, and this could make such projects look less attractive. Equal opportunity could raise our labor costs, make it harder for us to adjust supply to demand, and reduce the flexibility of our economy. We might slow down as did the socialized British, Germans, and Swedes.

Office work would change if it were not sex-typed. Men bosses could no longer play the role of Victorian patriarch with secretaries. A man could not relegate details to "my girl," and a woman would hardly call her male secretary "my boy." It is an open secret that men whose wives no longer wait on them at home may act like Victorian patriarchs at work. They value secretaries in part for the psychological lift of being served, and may create such work as keeping scrap-books, writing useless memos, and keeping unnecessary records, to justify their presence. Under equal opportunity, executives would have to get along without servants in the office just as they get along without butlers at home.

Real equality could have unpredictable consequences in fields like public-school teaching, where men and women are employed together. Charles R. Benson, an economist specializing in the problems of schools, analyzes one such problem in a little book optimistically titled *The Cheerful Prospect.* Equal pay, he says, has ruined the morale of the teaching profession, because it fails to recognize that men and women teachers work for different reasons. The men teachers want money and sometimes take on outside jobs after school to get it. If they were paid more, they would take on heavier teaching loads. But if women teachers were required to teach two shifts of children a day, or work through the summer, many of them would drop out. If the women who teach because they can combine it with family duties should quit, Benson writes, there wouldn't be enough men teachers to go around. So we limp along, fearful to demand the productivity from teachers that could raise their wages and reform the system.

The interesting thing about Benson's analysis, of course, is that he assumes that all women have the same motivations. It does not occur to him that some women, as well as some of the moonlighting men, would be glad to work longer and harder for more pay, while others of both sexes would quit teaching. He assumes that all women are only working for their families and cannot be counted on to work for a better school system. Improved teaching, he argues, depends on making the profession attractive to men, but what he really means is that we need more committed teachers. Sex equality, along with higher pay and higher standards, could attract ambitious men and women who now hesitate to go into a profession whose prestige is low because it has been dominated by women.

Desegregation would force companies to re-examine their motives. Frequently men commit company money to beat each other out in order to gain promotion. They are more interested, sometimes, in winning recognition in the organization than in doing what's best for it. Incentives based on brownie points, trips to Hawaii for sales winners, and the gamey pitting of one worker against another may have sold vacuum cleaners, but this warlike spirit is not productive in such modern industries as aerospace research. Even companies selling to consumers sometimes find that the aggressive, old-fashioned sales methods alienate important customers or cost too much to service.

Business is becoming too sophisticated and subtle to be played like a game of football. Men who succeed in technologically advanced work can't afford to waste energy proving that they are masculine. They are interested in responsive teamwork which may seem more feminine than masculine.

And if business is a "game," there is no particular reason to assume that men have a monopoly on the winning tactics. Pentagon researchers have been working with "games" intended to sharpen military thinking. Like poker, these games require the players to anticipate the opposition. In one experiment, John R. Bond and W. E. Vinacke pitted men players against women. They found that the men tried much harder to win, but that they used exploitative tactics, which were self-defeating. The women found ways to reward other players and they won more games.

The "masculine" style can be destructive in projects requiring flexible teamwork and in the expanding fields which provide health, education, and welfare services. American hospitals worry about their cold efficiency. Because American doctors are almost all male, hospitals in this country have become starchy, impersonal factories for processing sick people as if they were things. A patient undergoing surgery is made to feel as if he were on an assembly line.

Prophets generally foresee a world which has less use for the masculine style. The high point of the male mystique may well have been a half-century ago when the great American fortunes were carved out by men who fought each other with money instead of with swords. The enterprises they built have long since become bureaucracies headed by organization men whose main concern is smoothing relations and holding the enterprise together. Responsibility for keeping things going peacefully within the firm or family has traditionally been left to women, but internal relations are now important enough to engage the attention of men.

If there are advantages in taking the sex labels off jobs, there are even more gains in devocationalizing family life. "After all, women should make more concessions in marriage because marriage is a woman's *business*," the editor of a woman's magazine remarked in 1952. The word "business" made me want to ask, "Like prostitution?"

American brides indignantly deny that they are contracting to exchange domestic services and sexual availability for financial support. Yet the vocational obligation remains. An American working wife thinks she should pay for the cleaning woman out of her salary because cleaning the house is her "job." She may try to get home before her husband at night to be sure everything is ready for him. She insists that she is earning "for the family" and boasts that she arranges matters so that they are not inconvenienced in the slightest by her earning for them. Her husband may offer to help with the shopping and the children, but it is a magnanimous free gift. Only financial support is expected of him. One wife actually agreed not to bother her husband for any help in handling the house or children during the five years he gave himself to win promotion to vice president of his company. He was doing it, he firmly believed, because he loved his family.

Love has supplanted the notion of a contract. Marriage now has to be "for love." I heard a great deal about love in discussing the new-style marriage with men and women.

"But wouldn't you rather be loved than be equal?" many people asked, but they never seemed able to explain exactly why love and equality had to be an either-or proposition. In an attempt to find out, I spent hours trying to convince a young man that a relationship recognized as dependent could not properly be described as love. He was not persuaded. A few days later another young man put the old question, "Do you really care about all this equal rights business? Wouldn't you rather be adored?"

My answer was firm. "No, I would rather *not* be adored. It's been tried, but it just makes me nervous."

Love that simply projects a romantic ideal onto another person is not very flattering to the love object. It is irritating to be adored for what one is not, and it is dull to be constrained to serve as a mirror or screen. Furthermore, it is plain wrong for one human being to use another human being as a passive object, and if this sort of relationship is natural, it is that part of nature that civilization should alter. To set the record straight, and only because the issue keeps coming up, I honestly believe that love is a strictly private and personal relationship that cannot exist if it is harnessed to economic or social objectives beyond itself. Institutions of freedom and equality can make love possible, but love itself is not an institution, a motive, a reward, an excuse, or a compensation for giving up something else.

Working women frequently told us that they were happier when they worked, and their husbands frequently confided that they got along better with their wives when both worked. "I urged her to go back after each of the babies," the husband of a department store vice president told us. "She was happier and she was much more fun when she was working."

Women have no monopoly on whining, nagging, complaining, sniping, malingering, sabotage, cattiness, touchiness, suspiciousness, petty attention-getting. Slaves, children, courtiers, male secretaries, and assistants to the president act "just like a woman," too. So do soldiers cooped up in barracks. These unattractive postures crop up whenever people are dependent on other individuals in a close, unequal personal relationship. When husbands say their *wives* are happier when they work, they may really mean that they *themselves* are freed from the demands and, sometimes, the hostilities of emotional dependence.

Marriages have always deviated widely from the model usually presented to boys and girls, but the partners involved have always been made to feel guilty about being different. Women who are dominant feel they must conceal their strength in the interest of public relations, or, worse yet, prove to themselves that they are not unnatural monsters. Men who are constitutionally unaggressive have compensated by unpleasant blustering. The first step is to render unto Caesar those things which belong to Caesar and unto love those things that belong to love. Husbands are not employers. Children are not jobs.

Caring for small children is, of course, productive work. It is usually done by the child's mother, but it is a mistake to confuse mothering with doing the diapers, making the formula, bathing, chauffeuring, dressing, feeding, and stopping backyard fights. All this and more, others can and often do. A mother and a father provide the child with models of what adults are like. Children do not grow up to be like their nurses, but like their parents. Europeans brought up by nannies say that the moral influence of their parents was stronger because their parents were not involved in their day-to-day physical care.

A generation of over-mothered children has convinced a great many armchair advisers on family affairs that fathers are needed at home as much as mothers, although perhaps at different stages of a child's development.

Young men and women would have to be educated to accept this kind of partnership, but the strongest argument for desegregation is that the public schools treat boys and girls in much the same way until they are in their teens. Why not continue this approach into adult life? The change would have to start with retraining vocational guidance counselors who now have the embarrassing job of preparing girls for the limitations of the job market.

Desegregating all education would end schools for one sex on the ground that they overemphasize sex roles. Children who profit by boarding school—and there are always some—might profit even more by coeducational institutions like Putney, in Vermont, where girls and boys get some of the social advantages of very large families or old-fashioned neighborhoods, where children did not have to be chauffeured to each other for casual play.

But the important change in education is one that the graduate school couples are pioneering already. Ever since the GI Bill of Rights, wives have been earning while their husbands go to school. If desegregation of employment offered financial rewards to women achievers which were equal to those of men, it would encourage husbands to pay their wives back by allowing them to go back to school. A working wife is now one of the principal sources of funds for the medical education of future doctors. Even if all higher and continuing education is eventually subsidized by the Government with family allowance grants, husbands and wives will have to take turns at home if careers are going to require the amount of continual retraining that planners see ahead. The U-shaped career may soon become the fate of every first-class earner.

All this sounds fine, but do women really want it? Doesn't this radical reallocation of responsibilities overemphasize work? Won't the world of the future have to cope with leisure rather than stimulate achievement? Don't we need the special talents of women to reform business and public life, and won't we lose their special gifts if we bring them up to be exactly like men? And finally, won't there be more family quarrels and ground for conflict when men and women do exactly the same things? And what about chivalry? Doesn't the financial support men give to women catalyze something in their relationship that is valuable?

The objections are formidable. The most thoughtful idealists of 1968 often defend the contribution of womanliness on esthetic and even spiritual grounds.

"The future of mankind may well depend on the fate of a 'mother variable' uncontrolled by technological man," Erik Erikson, lecturer in psychiatry at Harvard, writes. Like many sensitive people appalled at the mechanical, crowded, impersonal society we are building, Erikson hopes that the compassion and humanity of women can save us. Idealists who look to women for salvation are often less interested in man-woman relations than in using women as a natural resource against the collapse of human values under the impact of technological advance. This is, of course, a New Masculinist attitude.

The most fervent of these idealistic New Masculinists are men. In 1964, Vermont Royster, the chief editor of the business-oriented *Wall Street Journal*, attacked the "Work Mystique" which in his opinion was misleading women into equating self-fulfillment with employment. Work is not all that important, he insisted. In 1967, a *Reader's Digest* editor, Charles W. Ferguson, articulated this New Masculinist appeal

in his book, *The Male Attitude,* which blamed the parlous
state of the world squarely on stag rule and urged society to
save itself, before it was too late, by making greater use of the
neglected insights of women.

What these people are saying is that women are better than
men because less tainted with power. They have revived the
Victorian notion of the pure woman, the madonna redeeming
an evil world. The trouble with this flattering assumption is
that women are no purer than they ever were and the history
of their behind-the-scenes or from-the-side influence is as
uneventful as their impact on politics. Women are uncom-
mitted and unorganized and hence a tempting target for
politicians and reformers, but they have, so far, resisted all
attempts to make themselves better than men. Today's women
can't pioneer leisure styles of living for men any more than
yesterday's women could appreciate art and music for men.
There is no male side or female side to the war in Vietnam. A
father's son dies for every mother's son who dies.

With us still are the Old Masculinists who argue that real
equality would leave women worse off than before. And it's
true. Laws that classify by sex are largely designed to protect
women from desertion. They date from the days when marriage, with its consequent exposure to child-bearing, was the
only way a woman could earn a decent living. But family-
support laws are becoming dead letters, and in any case they
bear more heavily on the rich who own property than on the
poor who don't have assets worth attaching. Desertion is the
poor man's divorce.

More serious is the possibility that real desegregation would
develop conflicts of interest between husbands and wives that
now occur only rarely. In 1962, the London Stock Exchange
turned down the application of Elisabeth Rivers-Bulkeley for
membership because her husband, a Lloyd's insurance broker,
was "at business in risk" and she might have a "moral
obligation" to meet his debts. But such problems can be
solved. If Carolyn Agger, the Washington lawyer, had a case
that went to the Supreme Court of the United States, her
husband Justice Fortas might elect not to hear the case, or she
might get another lawyer to argue it.

A more serious problem for two-income families is our
increasing mobility. Salaried workers are frequently moved by
their organizations or offered better jobs elsewhere. In Asiatic

cultures, separation of the husband and wife for periods is not regarded as serious. Family ties are not personal but legal. In our American upper classes, as in others, husbands and wives often go on separate trips and do not feel that they must be together all the time in every phase of their marriage.

But in a society where men and women are treated equally a wife would not be forced to follow a husband if he were better able to make the sacrifice of location than she, and the move made sense for the partnership, as well. In some cases, key men have refused to move to a new place unless suitable jobs could be found for their wives. Employers could do more of the accommodating than it occurs to them to do now. Federal and state services might lead the way by adopting a policy that the spouse of a transferred worker be given priority on appropriate job openings in the new area; that husbands and wives employed by the service be transferred, insofar as possible, together; and that refusal to move because of employment of a husband or wife may not be held against a civil servant in considering him for promotion.

Finally, there is no avoiding the fact that there are drawbacks. If boys and girls are not to form their characters around the need to be "manly" and "womanly," they will need other models, other motivations. It is realistic to urge a boy to do a dull job because it will benefit him in the future, but it is easier to get him to "act like a man." And because of its visibility, sex difference is a handy way to decide small matters, such as who gets named first in a social introduction. The brave new world of sex equality would be a world of frequent divorce. Divorces increase in good times and decline in bad times, suggesting that many more couples would like to separate than are financially able to. Regardless of cause or effect, the marriages of career women are less stable than the marriages of women financially dependent on their husbands.

Vanguard couples have taken turns working and going to school, but all pioneering requires thought and planning which tradition and habit settle with less effort. The answer is easier to find when the answer is the same for all; if grandmother's marriage seemed calmer, it may have been only that it required fewer personal decisions and women had to make more accommodations. The colleague marriage may be "better" if it comes off, but it takes more energy. It's risky, and it fails noisily.

Parallel to the dangers of choice in family roles are the uncertainties of choice in vocation. When asked why they marry, men often answer "to have something to work for." When asked what they would do if they had enough money to live without working, they say they would continue to work. In the Old Masculinist morality, women symbolize the goal. When a man has a woman to work for, he doesn't have to think any further. Without her, he has to examine his real feelings and motivations.

American women are already confused by the choices they now have of work and home and various combinations of each. Are we to impose this kind of choice on men, too? There is evidence that the intrinsic interest of the work is more important to girls choosing professions than the money they can earn. If boys as well as girls were free to choose work that interested them, we might have a hard time getting dull jobs done. What if everybody wanted to act in television, an occupation which need not increase proportionately to population, while fewer and fewer wanted to become nurses and teachers, occupations which parallel population growth?

The real argument for equality cannot be made on the basis of expedience. The compelling reason is equity. The little jokes the New Masculinists love to make about the New Feminists imply that the difference between the sexes is so beautiful, so rewarding, so deeply rooted, so innocent, and so much fun that it is worth enhancing at the expense of considerable inequity.

Yet equity is not to be dismissed so lightly. It is the sort of blessing that doesn't count when you have it, but ruins everything if you don't. Most Americans are now aware of the enormous social, psychic, and economic cost of Negro slavery. These costs became widely apparent only when the inequity of slavery aroused indignation and set people thinking.

Billions of words and hours of thought have been expended on the complexities of race relations. Progress, said the sophisticated, will have to be slow. You cannot change a way of life overnight. Yet today it is clear that however agonizing the changes have been, the problem has never been all that complicated. What we did to the Negroes was just plain wrong, and everybody knew it.

So with the employment of women. Relations between the sexes are complicated, and change is hard, but the way women are treated is just plain wrong.

It is wrong to make aspiring women prove they are twice as good as men.

It is wrong to pay women less than men for the same work just because they will work for less.

It is wrong to exclude women from work they can do so that they have to work for less in the jobs open to them.

It is wrong to make aspiring women pay the penalty of women who are content to be used as a labor reserve.

It is wrong to assume that because some women can't do mathematics, *this* woman can't do mathematics.

It is wrong to expect women to work for their families or the nation and then to step aside when their families or the nation want them out of the way.

It is wrong to deny individuals born female the right to inconvenience their families to pursue art, science, power, prestige, money, or even self-expression, in the way that men in pursuit of these goals inconvenience their families as a matter of course.

It is wrong to impute motives to women instead of letting them speak for themselves.

It is wrong to ridicule, sneer, frighten, or brainwash anyone unable to fight back.

It is wrong, as well as wasteful and dangerous, to discourage talent.

All these things are wrong, and everybody knows it. And just as "separate but equal" schools limited white children as well as Negroes, so the doctrine that women are different but equal limits men. Mary Wollstonecraft, John Stuart Mill, George Bernard Shaw, and President Goheen of Princeton were all concerned, and some of them primarily with the damage inequity does to men. David Riesman points out that every boundary we impose on women we impose on men also.

Equity speaks softly and wins in the end. But it is expedience, with its loud voice, that sets the time of victory. The cotton gin did not make slavery wrong, but it helped a lot of Southerners to *see* that slavery was wrong. The immigrant vote did not make woman suffrage right, but it frightened politicians into enfranchising women on the theory that the educated women of politically conservative old American stock would vote more readily than the submissive women of politically unpredictable ethnic groups.

So with equal opportunity for women. Conditions conspire to help people see the inequity and the advantages of ending it. First the pill gives women control over their fate so that they can be as responsible as men. Then modern medicine prolongs the lives of women so that all now have decades of potential working life, beyond child-rearing age, during which none of the limitations imposed on women make sense. Next, modern technology takes their work out of the home and invites them to do it elsewhere, and for pay. It frees more mothers of the work of bringing up children, and gives it to schools. Meanwhile, the new technology is less and less a respecter of old-fashioned sex differences. It eliminated the need for physical strength very rapidly and is now eliminating the need for "detail work."

What the new technology needs is educated manpower that can learn new skills. What it doesn't need is more ordinary people without skills. Both needs strengthen the case for equal opportunity for the underprivileged majority of Americans who were born female.

CHAPTER NOTES

Foreword: The Future of Sex

The September 1967 issue of *Esquire* ran pictures of several unmarried couples living together on college campuses. Marshall McLuhan's statement was in *Look* magazine for July 25, 1967, and Margaret Mead's projection of the future of domesticity comes from a paper, "The Life Cycle and Its Variations: The Division of Roles," she contributed to the Summer 1967 issue of *Daedalus,* entitled "Towards the Year 2000."

Chapter 1—Ladies' Day in the House

The Congressional Record for February 8, 1964, faithfully reports the antics of Ladies' Day in the House. Martha Griffiths and Pauli Murray told me some of what went on behind the scenes. May Craig referred me to the script of "Meet the Press" on January 26, 1964, to corroborate exactly what she said to Howard Smith.

The breakdown of the labor force by sex and by color in 1964 comes from U.S. Bureau of the Census, *Statistical Abstract of the United States,* 1965, p. 216. The median income figures of white and Negro men and white and Negro women come from U.S. Department of Labor, Women's Bureau, *1965 Handbook on Women Workers,* p. 130. This invaluable red paper-covered "Bible" brings together the salient Government statistics on women's income, education, employment, occupation, and legal status.

Franklin D. Roosevelt, Jr., the first Chairman of the Equal Employment Opportunity Commission, was not a member of the House on Ladies' Day, but his brother James, a Democratic Representative from New York, loyally supported the coalition and told the House that he thought his mother, Eleanor Roosevelt, would have opposed the sex amendment.

Plato was the first feminist. He favored educating women like men, Book 5 of *The Republic.*

"Maternity Protection and Benefits in 92 Countries," *Women in the World Today,* International Report 6, June 1963, reprinted by the Women's Bureau of the U.S. Department of Labor, is an eye-opener for those who believe that the U.S. is just naturally more advanced than any other country. If American women are generally better off than foreign women, the credit goes to our wealth, not our laws.

Mrs. Griffiths laid the Commission out in forty shades of lavender in remarks reprinted in *The Congressional Record* of June 20, 1966, entitled "Women Are Being Deprived of Legal Rights by the Equal Employment Opportunity Commission." She reported the experience of newspapers that had desegregated their help-wanted columns.

For early guidelines and opinions of EEOC, see the Commission's *Digest of Legal Interpretations Issued or Adopted by the Commission,* October 9, 1965, through December 31, 1965.

Mrs. Blumrosen was quoted in *The New York Times* of July 27, 1965. Most of the remarks of Commission members were reported in *The New York Times,* which has kindly given permission to quote from its editorial of August 21, 1965, "De-Sexing the Job Market."

Chapter 2—Up from Slavery

Blackstone is quoted from Marg Beard, *Women as a Force in History,* Macmillan, 1946, p. 79. For contemporary situation, see "Know Your Rights," Leaflet 39, Women's Bureau 1965, or the little paperback, Richard T. Gallen's *Wives' Le-*

gal Rights, Dell, 1965, available at the checkout counters of supermarkets.

For the analogy between the status of women and the status of slaves, see Appendix 5, "A Parallel to the Negro Problem," in Gunnar Myrdal, *An American Dilemma,* Harper & Brothers, N.Y., 1944. H. W. V. Temperley, "The Sale of Wives in England in 1823," is in *The History Teacher's Miscellany,* III:66, April 1925. Carl Degler, professor of history at Vassar College, contends that the parallel, while useful, is inexact. "It is probably true that paternalism informed the *conception* of slavery," he wrote us, "but the legal status, as Myrdal himself admits, was quite different. . . . Buying and selling cannot be taken as a measure of slavery, although to the 20th century it may seem to represent it. Indentured servants were commonly sold. And one has to be careful about generalizing from examples drawn from the poor and the working of the poor laws. Women, I think, *socially* partake of the situation of Negroes, but I do not see the reality of putting them in the same category as legal slaves. The two criteria of a slave that I think are central are ownership for life and inherited status for their children as slaves."

The work done by colonial women has been documented by Elisabeth W. Dexter, *Career Women of America,* 1776–1840, Francestown, N.H., M. Jones & Co., 1950, and a paper entitled "Changes in the Status of Women: 1800–1840" read by Gerda Lerner, assistant professor of history at Long Island University, at the American Historical Association meeting of December 1966.

Eleanor Flexner, *Century of Struggle,* Harvard University Press, Cambridge, 1959, is the best authority on the history of civil rights for American women, the early suffragettes, and the politics of the women's movement down through the founding of the Women's Bureau. Andrew Sinclair's *The Better Half,* Harper & Row, N.Y., 1965, is more indignant, as books by men on women's rights tend, for some reason, to be. Sinclair elaborates the relationship between Abolition and Feminism. Aileen S. Kraditor, *The Ideas of the Woman Suffrage Movement 1890–1920,* Columbia University Press, New York, 1965, states the case of the suffragettes and their opponents and distinguishes between the early human rights basis for demanding the suffrage and the sheer political expedience of the suffragettes who actually put the 19th Amend-

ment over. A collection of "anti" pamphlets made by the
Massachusetts Association Opposed to Further Extension of
Suffrage to Women, bound under the title "Why Women Do
Not Want the Ballot," no date, is a fascinating peek into the
ideology of the Victorian lady. "Political Rights of Women in
Member Nations of the United Nations," *Women in the
World Today,* International Report 2, United Nations Report
A/5456, reprinted by the Women's Bureau, 1963, lists the
dates on which women won the suffrage in different countries
and shows that they coincide with wars and revolutions.

Elizabeth F. Baker, *Technology and Woman's Work,* Columbia University Press, New York, 1964, is a serious history
of female labor force participation, women's occupations, and
the changes in sex labeling of jobs with advancing technology.
Robert W. Smuts, *Women and Work in America,* Columbia
University Press, New York, 1959, is shorter and more indignant (the author is male), especially on the fate of women in
the early sweatshops. Gerda Lerner analyzes the role of the
forceps in the shift from midwives to male physicians, and
Logan Clendening has compelling detail about the Chamberlains in his *Behind the Doctor,* Garden City Publishing Co.,
Garden City, 1933. The quote from Sarah Hale came from
Dorcas Campbell, *Careers for Women in Banking and Finance,* Dutton, New York, 1944.

Mabel Newcomer, *A Century of Higher Education for
American Women,* Harper & Brothers, New York, 1959, is
the best source on the history of college for girls. Women's
Bureau publications keep a close watch on contemporary educational attainments of women.

Mary Elizabeth Massey, *Bonnet Brigades,* Alfred Knopf,
New York, 1967, documents the influence of women on the
Civil War and vice versa. Irene Corbally Kuhn tells how the
Congressional Medal of Honor was awarded Dr. Mary Walker, the Civil War physician, and then withdrawn in a syndi-
cated King Features column of May 11, 1963. Some of the
material on women in the U.S. armed forces came from Caroline Bird, "Let's Draft Women, Too," *The Saturday Evening
Post,* June 18, 1966. Edith Thomas, *The Women Incendi-
aries,* G. Braziller, New York, 1966, is illuminating on the
role of women in revolutions.

Baker and Flexner are good sources on the union attitude
to women workers. We are indebted to Gerda Lerner for the

suggestion that orientation of European unions made them more receptive to women than American craft unions. *Woman at Work: The Autobiography of Mary Anderson* as told to Mary Winslow, University of Minnesota Press, Minneapolis, 1951, is the absorbing story of a pioneer woman labor leader who became the first Director of the Women's Bureau. The rationale for paying women less is expounded at length in Congressional hearings, "Equal Pay for Equal Work for Women," U.S. House of Representatives, Subcommittee No. 4 of the Committee on Education and Labor, 80th Congress, 2d Session, February 9, 10, 11, and 13, 1948. It reports War Labor Board cases charging pay discrimination. U.S. Department of Labor, Bureau of Employment Security, "Occupations Suitable for Women," 1942, listed what women were expected to do in wartime. The reversal following the war is summed up in several papers on women in the May 1947 *Annals of the American Academy of Political and Social Science* and indignantly denounced by A. G. Mezerik, in an article entitled "Getting Rid of the Women," *The Atlantic Monthly*, June 1945.

The Women's Bureau kept a close watch on the postwar decline in the proportion of women in the professions, while participation of women in the labor force continued to rise. Jessie Bernard's brilliant study of the contemporary role of women in college teaching, *Academic Women*, the Pennsylvania State University Press, University Park, Pa., 1964, contends that the decline was voluntary rather than the result of discrimination.

The Old Feminists may have gone the way of the old upper class, David Riesman suggests in his Introduction to Jessie Bernard's *Academic Women*, p. xx. No one criticized upper-class women for leaving their children with governesses, and their daughters and sons were freer of middle-class sex role limitations on tomboy or sissy behavior than children groomed to rise in the world either via a good marriage or occupational achievement. Mme. Nehru, the chief executive of India, and the politically powerful wives of Mao Tse-tung and Lin Piao are explained by sociologists as products of a society in which upper-class status is more important than sex in determining behavior. The decline of feminism in the United States after World War II coincided with the wholesale induction of millions of young couples into the middle classes. These newly arrived families brought the sex role rigidities of the lower classes along with them.

The Old Feminists, well-financed and intransigeant, continued to work for an Equal Rights Amendment specifying "Equality of rights under the law shall not be denied or abridged by the United States or by any state on account of sex." See *Equal Rights Amendment: Questions and Answers Prepared by the Research Department of the National Woman's Party*, edited by Margery C. Leonard, Government Printing Office, 1963, Senate Document No. 164.

Information on recent Government moves to open opportunity for women came from Esther Peterson, Mary Keyserling, Pauli Murray, and Evelyn Harrison of the U.S. Civil Service Commission. Miss Harrison's account of the President's Commission on the Status of Women is in an article entitled "The Quiet Revolution" in *Civil Service Journal*, October–December 1962. The President's Commission issued its report *American Women 1963* plus committee reports on civil and political rights, education, Federal employment, home and community, private employment, protective labor legislation, and social insurance and taxes and four "consultations" on private employment opportunities, new patterns in volunteer work, portrayal of women by the mass media, and problems of Negro women.

The President's Commission disbanded, but its work is carried on by state commissions on the status of women and by an Interdepartmental Committee on the Status of Women bringing together representatives of appropriate Federal agencies headed by the Secretary of Labor, and a Citizens' Advisory Council on the Status of Women headed by former Senator Maurine B. Neuberger, who issues a brief and informative newsletter of progress. These two permanent groups put out a joint annual "Report on Progress on the Status of Women." Almost all the facts bearing importantly on recent changes come from these progress reports or the Women's Bureau.

Chapter 3—The Invisible Bar

The literature of the 1960s is more critical than formerly of the cultural conditioning of girls to limited vocational aspirations. See Seymour M. Farber and Roger H. L. Wilson, *The Challenge to Women,* Basic Books, N.Y., 1966; J. Davis, *Great Aspirations: The Graduate School Plans of America's College Seniors,* Aldine, Chicago, 1964; *New Approaches to Counselling Girls in the 1960s, A Report to the Midwest Regional Pilot Conference,* February 26–27, 1965, among many other sources. The "way girls are brought up" was mentioned by most of the women we interviewed personally and deplored at conferences on careers for women such as "The Woman Executive in an Affluent Society," Greyston Conference Center, Riverdale, N.Y., May 3, 1966, sponsored by Teachers College, Columbia, at which Bennett Kline made the statement attributed to him.

The confrontation between company recruiters and the first women to take the full course of the Harvard University Graduate School of Business Administration was more tense the first year than subsequently; the fine record of the pioneers and the growing labor shortage have made job-finding easier for these girls.

The man who described femininity as subservience was quoted in a column by Flora Lewis she called "The Femininity Thing," which ran in the *New York Post* of April 17, 1967. As this book went to press, she was reporting the Battle of Saigon.

The best evidence on women's careers is "A Survey of Advancement of Men and Women in the Federal Service" made in 1962 on the basis of a long questionnaire returned by 26,809 men and women in the Federal service and analyzed in the Report of the Committee on Federal Employment to the President's Commission on the Status of Women. It confirmed many impressions about career women we gathered in interviewing them, including the hopeful finding that a woman boss, like a Negro neighbor, isn't as unacceptable in practice as in prospect.

The best recent study of attitudes toward women executives is the *Harvard Business Review* survey of 1,000 male and 1,000 female executives reported in the July-August 1965 issue by Dr. Garda W. Bowman, then Director of the Merit Promotion Project, National Conference of Christians and Jews, and N. Beatrice Worthy, Personnel Practices Analyst, Bell Telephone Laboratory, Inc., and Stephen A. Greyser, *Harvard Business Review* Assistant Editor and Research Director. Significantly, we think, Beatrice Worthy is an outstanding Negro woman executive, and Garda Bowman became interested in discrimination against women while studying discrimination against Negroes and Jews. Her doctoral dissertation, "The Image of a Promotable Person in Business Enterprise," 1962, reported interviews with executives. Dr. Bowman was kind enough to lend us her original data, which contained revealing male comments on the suitability of women for policy-making jobs.

Georgina M. Smith, *Help Wanted, Female, A Study of Demand and Supply in a Local Job Market for Women*, Rutgers, Institute of Management and Labor Relations, 1964, documents that women are first fired and last hired at the factory gate. For the experience of the most privileged women, see Eli Ginzberg, *Life Styles of Educated Women*, Columbia University Press, New York, 1966. We are indebted to Audrey Saphar, Bryn Mawr 1961, for access to answers to questions on discrimination included in a survey of the experience of her class five years out of college, and to William Gifford, associate professor of English at Vassar College for the letter from a former student on her experience job-hunting in New York City. An authoritative view of the difficulties of blue-collar women is afforded in the breakdown of charges of discrimination in the *First Annual Report of the Equal Employment Opportunity Commission*, fiscal year ending June 1966; 90th Congress, 1st Sess., House Document No. 86, p. 64.

Most of the evidence for the Invisible Bar, however, came directly from the career women we interviewed, most of whom did not wish to be quoted. See the full list in notes for Chapter 5.

Chapter 4—The Sex Map

The income figures come from the U.S. Bureau of the Census, *Current Population Reports-Consumer Income*, Series P-60, No. 53. We are indebted to the courtesy of Herman P. Miller, the income specialist of the Census, author of *Rich Man, Poor Man*, Thomas Y. Crowell, New York, 1964, and his staff for patient instruction in its use, as well as to Mary Keyserling of the Women's Bureau and her staff for updating the presentation of the facts of women's income in the 1965 *Handbook on Women Workers*. None of these professional statisticians are responsible in any way for the interpretations of the facts.

The pay gap between men and women narrows in wartime. A chilling sign of the times in early 1968 has been the virtual disappearance of the pay gap between the starting salaries of men and women college graduates reported by the Endicott Survey of Northwestern University in *U.S. News & World Report,* February 19, 1968.

On pension coverage, see *Public Policy and Private Pension Programs: A Report to the President on Private Employee Retirement Plans,* January 1965, and the grilling of company executives by Representative Martha Griffiths in *Private Pension Plans,* Hearings before the Subcommittee on Fiscal Policy of the Joint Economic Committee, Congress of the United States, 89th Congress, 2d Session, 1966. Betty Martin of the Institute of Life Insurance instructed us in the theory of insurance and pension planning, particularly the ways in which current practice favors women.

Forest L. Miller, Acting Director of the U.S. Department of Labor's Unemployment Insurance Service, believes that the main conclusion to be drawn from the low percentage of women getting the top unemployment insurance benefits is that state benefit ceilings are too low. "Ironically, low wages operated to the advantage of women in the unemployment insurance program," he wrote. "A recognized unemployment insurance principle is that benefits should be wage-related; most unemployed workers should receive a weekly benefit equal to half their average weekly wages when employed, up to the State maximum weekly benefit amount." The ceilings don't allow most men to get half their wages, but it's hard to agree with Mr. Miller that this is any particular advantage to women!

On the "uncertainty" of women workers, the mimeographed summary "What About Women's Absenteeism and Labor Turnover?" issued by the Women's Bureau is a handy report on the statistical evidence. According to *Current Estimates from the Health Interview Survey, United States, July 1966–June 1967,* U.S. Public Health Service Publication No. 1000—Series 10, No. 43, employed men 17 years old and over lost an average of 5.3 days from work due to illness for the year, and employed women lost 5.4 days. For investment in on-the-job training, see Dr. Jabor Mincer, "On-the-Job Training: Costs, Returns, and Some Implications," *The Journal of Political Economy,* Vol. LXX, No. 5, Part 2, Supplement, October 1962. William H. Miller's statement is from the *American Oil Company News* of May 4, 1966.

On sex-typing of jobs, Esther Peterson tells the story about electronics assemblers and brain surgeons. For the sex of cornhusking, see Daniel Bell, "The Great Back-to-Work Movement," *Fortune,* July 1956. For sex ratios of American occupations, see *Handbook of Women Workers;* for sex ratios in Europe, see Alva Myrdal and Viola Klein, *Women's Two Roles,* Routledge & Kegan Paul, London, 1956. On sex role theory, see Talcott Parsons, *Social Structure and Personality,* The Free Press, Collier-Macmillan, London, 1965.

The earnings of physicians and dentists are those reported in the U.S. Bureau of the Census, *Statistical Abstract of the United States: 1967,* p. 232. Vocational literature issued by the Women's Bureau and others alerts women doctors and lawyers to the wider opportunities for them in Government work, and the U.S. Civil Service Commission study of 1962 shows that the Government employs higher percentages of women doctors and lawyers than do private employers. On women lawyers, see James J. White, "Women in the Law," *Michigan Law Review,* 65:1051, April 1967, for a revealing survey of the careers of recent women law graduates.

The sex labeling of specific jobs comes from the women interviewed, but is generally confirmed by vocational literature advising girls where to look for career opportunities. The metalworking president's comment is from "Women—Industry's Newest Challenge," *Dun's Review,* August 1966. The most serious study of sex labeling of jobs is one made by Edward Gross and reported in *The Public Interest,* September 25, 1967. His mimeographed paper on it was titled "Plus Ça Change . . . The Sexual Structure of Occupations over Time."

For the library sex war, we are indebted to the references and anecdotes supplied by Robert Jordan of the Council on Library Resources in Washington.

For various divisions of labor by sex see Margaret Mead's classic study, *Sex and Temperament in Three Primitive Societies,* New York, 1935, reprinted in The New American

Library paperback, 1950. For the Invisible Bar in the Philippines, see Chester L. Hunt, "Female Occupational Roles and Urban Sex Ratios in the United States, Japan and the Philippines," *Social Forces*, 43:407–417, March 1965.

On Lady Murasaki and the Japanese "woman's language" see Donald Keene, *Japanese Literature*, Grove Press, New York, 1955, An Evergreen Book, p. 73. Male clerks thought the typewriter undignified, and several women who had helped to build organizations told us that their work had been taken over by men when their companies grew in size and affluence.

The percentage of women at the top in the Federal service came from Federal Woman's Award Study Group on Careers for Women, *Progress Report*, 1967, p. 94; in the income elite, from current *Population Reports—Consumer Income*, Series P-60; in the Standard & Poor's directory of executives, from its report for the 1965 edition; in *Who's Who in America* from Patricia Klensch of Marquis-Who's Who Inc.; and in the professions from the *1965 Handbook on Women Workers*.

Chapter 5—The Loophole Women

All the women named in this chapter and many more were interviewed by visit, phone, or mail except Dr. Maria G. Mayer, who was reported from the article about her in *Current Biography*.

Needless to say, most of the women who shared their experiences and opinions with us do not agree with our conclusions, but they all contributed anecdotes, confirmation of generalizations, and biographical career material on the basis of which we set up the loopholes. We tested the loopholes by assigning every woman to one or more of them. Women who contributed, in alphabetical order:

Margaret Adams, Ruth Adler, Mrs. Gerald Ahern, Mrs. Andrew Jackson Allison, Grace J. Altemus, Dorothea I. P. Anderson, Ruth Andrus, Jane Ashby, Winifred Asprey, Edith Austin, Jacqueline Babbin, Helen Bale, G. E. Barthold, Madeline Berns Bedell, Susanna Bedell, Marilyn Bender, Shirley Bennett, Mary Birdsall, Evelyn Borning, Doris Bossen, Garda Bowman, Helen Brattrud, Jean Bromer, Audrey Brown, Marjorie M. Brown, Deirdre Budge, Lydia Caine, Florence Carroll, Nora M. Carsey, Gann K. Carter, Julia Coburn, Madeline Codding, Joaquina Conroy, Peggy Cook, Betty Cooper, Marion Corwell, Carolyn Crusius, Mildred Custin, Virginia Culver.

Kathryn Dailey, Jean Dalrymple, Dorothy Daniel, Wyona Dillard, Barbara Downer, Catherine Durrell, Helen Edwards, Marjorie Eicher, Lyn Medbury Freeman, Helen Garrett, Dorine George, Mary Girard, Nan Glennon, Dr. Elizabeth Goessel, Jane Grant, Dorothy Gregg, Martha Griffiths, Ruth Gupta, Emilie Hall, Guin Hall, Erica Hansell, Eva B Hansl, Patricia Harris, Evelyn Harrison, Mary Gies Hatch, Dr. Christine Haycock, Bernice Hemphill, Faye Henle, Beatrice Hicks, Anna Rosenberg Hoffman, Lillian Hogue, Ida R. Hoos, Bea Horner, Peggy Hubbard, Charlotte Hyams, Jane Johnson, Shirley Johnson, Bobette Jones.

Dorothy Kenyon, Jane Kielsmeier, Alice Gore King, Jan Knoop, Nellie Knorr, Leslie Koempel, Dorothy Kostka, Susan Lauer, Beth Laurence, Dory Lee, Lillie Lee, Pauline Leet, Maude Lennox, Beth Levy, Kay Lewis, Rosalind K. Loring, Jane Lounsbury, Jeanne Lowe, Margaret M. Lucas, Carol Lushear, Betty Martin, Roslyn Martin, Ruth Mayse, Sandy McClure, Edna MacMahon, Mary McMahon, Marilyn McManus, Jane McMorrine, Velma Mengelkoch, Katharine Meyer Graham, Helen Meyer, Gertrude G. Michelson, Llewellyn Miller, Kay Moore, Joan Murphy, Mary Ellen Murphy, Pauli Murray, Margaret Myers, Grace Naismith, Dr. Rosa Nemir, Maurine Neuberger, Cora Newhold.

Elizabeth Fagg Olds, Wanda Overstreet, Bette Oxboro, Arlene Palitz, Esther Peterson, Phyllis Peterson, Harriet Pilpel, Constance Pirnie, Ann Powell, Doris Pullen, Gerry Raker, Ceceilia Bessell Rauch, Virginia L. Razee, Geraldine Rhoads, Jennifer Rodman, Alice Rossi, Beatrice Rystrom, Jean Schoonover, Audrey Saphar, Kathleen Seffens, Beatrice Sheffield, Ruth Sherwood, Muriel Siebert, Dorothy Siegel, Caroline Simon, Virginia Sink, Betty Skelton, Margaret Brand Smith, Robin Smith, Jeanne Spiegel, Elizabeth Stalcup, Lu Retta Stasch, Mary Stewart, Juanita Kidd Stout, Frances Taft, Margaret Thompson, Jane Trahey, E. Marian Trembley, Julia Walsh, Lorraine L. Webb, Mary Wells, Jo Wheeler, Emily H. Womach, Beatrice N. Worthy, Kate Yutzy, Dorothy Zayar.

Chapter 6—The Negro Parallel

The American Jewish Committee's Institute of Human Relations, 165 East 56th Street, New York City, has information on studies of the incidence of Jews among the top management groups of various industries and companies. For prejudice against Negroes and Jews in business see Lewis B. Ward, "The Ethnics of Executive Selection," *Harvard Business Review,* March–April 1965, as well as Garda Bowman's doctoral dissertation, "The Image of a Promotable Person in Business Enterprise," and Caroline Bird, "More Room at the Top" *Management Review,* March 1963.

Gunnar Myrdal has kindly consented to our extensive quotation of *The American Dilemma,* Harper's, New York, 1944. His wife, Alva Myrdal, is interested in the status of women, and sex roles are more of an issue in Sweden than in the United States. One Swedish feminist told a visiting American labor leader that women were Sweden's "white Negroes." The quotations from Myrdal were taken from the convenient paperback condensation by Arnold Rose under the title *The Negro in America,* The Beacon Press, Boston, 1956. Statements that could apply to women as well as Negroes appear on pages 17, 24, 31, 35, 41, 50, 69, 70, 74, 110, 112, 124, 125, 135–138, 150, 186–205, 217, 218, 221, 228, 229, 236, 246, 247, 255, and 302.

Pauline Leet's speech, "Women and the Undergraduate," delivered on November 18, 1965, at Franklin and Marshall College, has been circulating in mimeograph ever since. We thank her for permission to quote from it. The Kenistons' article was in the Summer 1964 issue of *The American Scholar.* For Old Masculinist alarm at the prospect of drafting women, see *The Congressional Record,* March 17, 1942.

Chapter 7—Gradualism: The New Masculinists

Rousseau devotes a chapter to the education of woman, the mate for man in his *Emile or Treatise on Education.* Quote is on p. 263 of translation by William H. Payne, International Education Series, D. Appleton, New York,

1918. The typist with a problem was reported by Anne Heywood, *There Is a Right Job for Every Woman*, Doubleday, Garden City, 1951, p. 19.

David Riesman imagined "society" talking to women at a workshop for New York State university presidents, but his view is systematically presented in "Some Dilemmas of Women's Education," *The Educational Record*, Fall, 1965.

Grace C. Ferrill, of the Women's Bureau, made an illuminating analysis of the American Bar Association stand against the United Nations Human Rights Convention on the Political Rights of Women for Mrs. Keyserling dated October 3, 1967.

Women presidents of women's colleges are among the most determined New Masculinists. Esther Raushenbush (Sarah Lawrence), Rosemary Park (formerly Barnard), and Mary Bunting (Radcliffe) all seem a bit defensive against the charge that they may be encouraging girls to "compete" with men. Men presidents of women's colleges (Alan Simpson, Vassar, and C. Easton Rothwell, of Mills, for instance) seem a bit more "rightsy" in admitting that barriers exist and are wrong.

On the New Masculinists, Mary Bunting outlined her views at a talk before the Harvard Club of New York and in letters; Nevitt Sanford's position is in his *Self and Society: Social Change and Individual Development*, Atherton Press, New York, 1966; Erik Erikson's "anatomy-is-destiny" position is presented in "Reflections on Womanhood," his contribution to the Spring 1964 issue of *Daedalus* devoted to "The Woman in America"; and Dr. Benjamin Spock states his position in "Are We Minimizing the Difference Between the Sexes?" in *Redbook,* March 1964. His resistance to the Vietnam War in 1968 suggests that he hoped, like many New Masculinists, that women or womanliness might prevent wars. For a recent play on this theme, see the February 1968 eulogy of Jeannette Rankin, the old suffragette, for her pacifism in *Ramparts*. The other motive for New Masculinism, of course, is to utilize womanpower in business, government, or politics.

Governor Nelson Rockefeller of New York has campaigned to remove barriers to women in much the way that President Johnson has campaigned at the Federal level. New York State was one of the first to bar discrimination on the basis of sex. Governor Rockefeller's "Women's Unit" headed by Kitty Carlisle is lively, posh, and intellectual, and it puts out a monthly newsletter, "Women's Unit News."

Manpower, Inc., and American Girl Service both have helpful public relations counsel working on programs to identify their services with wider horizons for women. The Social Research, Inc., study is entitled "Bringing Women Back to Work: A Study of the Woman at Home and the Manpower White Glove Girl," Social Research, Inc., 740 N. Rush Street, Chicago, an unpublished report prepared for Manpower, Inc., by Richard Renck and Diane Gregart.

Ruth Sherwood of the New York State Social Services Department filled me in on the new volunteer work. The *Federal Woman's Award Study Group on Careers for Women Progress Report to the President* of March 3, 1967, advocated relaxing Civil Service rules for women returning to the labor force, and Vice President Hubert Humphrey went a step further to suggest that maybe the Federal Government should give women a "free year of re-entry education, to equip them to embark with confidence upon this new and significant chapter of their lives." Dr. Jacob Mincer supplied us with a copy of "The Short-Run Elasticity of Labor Supply," September 1966, his unpublished paper measuring the entry of housewives into newly created jobs.

Chapter 8—The Androgynous Life

Frederick J. Ziegler's study of San Diego couples on the pill was reported at the 1967 convention of the American Medical Association, *The New York Times*, June 20, 1967. An example of the fear of female sexuality is the *New York Post* feature, "What's Happening to the Male Sex?" July 8, 1967. For a short report and evaluation of the culture bias in masculinity-femininity tests used by psychologists, see Nevitt Sanford's *Self and Society*, noted above, p. 7. A good account of the hormonal basis of sexuality is in a paper by Dr. John Money, "Developmental Differentiation of Femininity and Masculinity Compared" in *The Potential of Woman*, a McGraw-Hill paperback edited by Seymour Farber and Roger H. L. Wilson, New York, 1963, based on a symposium on that subject financially underwritten by The Schering Corporation, one of the pharmaceutical companies manufacturing the contraceptive pill. Dr. Ralph Greenson has kindly given us permission to quote from his article in *Pulse* on the sexual appetite of middle-aged women. Dr. Richard Farson's remarks were made at the *Ladies' Home Journal*-Kelly Girl Seminar, "Quo Vadis, Today's Women?" New York City, October 6, 1966.

On alimony, see "Payment of Alimony by Women Proposed by Legislative Panel," *The New York Times,* December 9, 1967. The Vietnam War nurse couple were featured in *Family Weekly,* June 18, 1967; Charles and Stephanie Beech in an article "Campus Marriages . . . Can They Succeed?" in *The Kansas City Star,* May 7, 1967.

Studies on the effect of mothers' employment on child development are collected in F. Ivan Nye and Lois W. Hoffman, *The Employed Mother in America,* Rand McNally & Company, Chicago, 1963. Its findings were reported by Caroline Bird's "What We Are Finding Out About Working Mothers," *Woman's Day,* September 1967, and somewhat more briefly in the summary by Alice Rossi in *Management Review,* "Working Wives: How Well Is Business Talking Their Language?" April 1967, based on the Dudley-Anderson-Yutzy symposium on this subject for clients held January 31, 1967, at which Alice Rossi commented on the husbands of achieving women. The shift to career aspiration of college girls was reported in preliminary figures on the Vassar alumnae study reported at the Council Meeting of the Associate Alumnae of Vassar College on October 11, 1967, in Poughkeepsie.

Current Population Reports, Series P-20, is the Census Bureau publication that issues the latest news on changes in birth and marriage rates. Our figures came from "Marital Status and Family Status, March 1966," *Current Population Reports,* Series P-20, No. 159, January 25, 1967. Another faithful source is the *Population Bulletin* of the Population Reference Bureau, Inc. The report on the growth of American families came from Population Bulletin XXII, April 1966. Paul C. Glick of the Population Division of the Census Bureau explained the "marriage squeeze"; see also "Prospective Changes in Marriage and the Family," by Robert Parke, Jr., and Paul C. Glick, a paper presented at the American Sociological Association on August 31, 1966.

On the influence of education on women's employment, see latest reports of the Women's Bureau. Mrs. Keyserling's

"Trends in Educational Attainment of Women," June 1966, documents the fall in the percentage of women awarded bachelor's, master's, and doctor's degrees. The percentages graph to a rough U shape. High tide of women awarded B.A. degrees was in 1940, when 41 percent of the B.A.s were women. The trough was 1950, when only 24 percent were women; the percentage was 40 percent in 1964 and may just now be getting back to the 1940 level. The year 1930 was the high tide for master's and doctor's degrees awarded to women (40 percent and 15 percent respectively. They fell to lows of 29 percent and 10 percent in 1950), and have not yet fully recovered. However, if graduate students lose their draft deferment, as seemed likely in February 1968, educators predict that half the men in graduate school will drop out. This would leave the sex ratio of graduate school close to 50-50 for the first time in history.

On the increasing tendency of women to work, the primary source is Jacob Mincer, "Labor Force Participation of Married Women," in *Aspects of Labor Economics,* reprinted from a Report of the National Bureau of Economic Research, Princeton University Press, Princeton, 1962. Glen G. Cain carried this analysis further in his *Married Women in the Labor Force: An Economic Analysis,* University of Chicago Press, Chicago, 1966. Hazel Kyrk's explanation is from "Who Works and Why," *Annals of the American Academy of Political and Social Science,* May 1946. Dan Bell's *Fortune* article of July 1956 cited in Chapter 4 has a simple explanation of the "respectability pattern" and the doubts economists were beginning to have about it even then. Denis F. Johnston, Labor Economist for the Bureau of Labor Statistics, U.S. Department of Labor, explained that BLS projections always fell short on the number of women working because "the restraining effect of the 'baby boom' was overestimated and the attractions of work opportunities, the felt need for additional income, etc., was underestimated." The projections are reported in a series of Bureau of Labor Statistics reports that revise the future as we get closer to it. They make interesting reading in retrospect, when the actual figures are known. The propensity of mothers to work could have been suspected from the Women's Bureau report, *College Women Seven Years After Graduation,* Bulletin 292, 1966. The high labor force participation of mothers of preschool children with five or more years of college is from Women's Bureau Leaflet 37 of 1966, "Who Are the Working Mothers?" According to this report, 33 percent of them work.

Ten percent of husbands are without income, according to Herman Miller, *Rich Man, Poor Man,* cited in Chapter 4, p. 192. For women's reasons for working, see Carl Rosenfeld and Vera C. Perrella, "Why Women Start and Stop Working: A Study in Mobility," *Monthly Labor Review,* September 1965. The Hudson Institute figures that more women will work until in 2000 a majority of them will be earners except during the 25-to-34 years of highest family commitment. See Herman Kahn and Anthony J. Wiener, *The Year 2000, A Framework for Speculation on the Next Thirty-Three Years,* Macmillan, New York, 1967, Table XXII, p. 174.

On the new jobs ahead, see "Where Job Chances Will Be Best in the Years Just Ahead," *U.S. News & World Report,* January 2, 1967. Dr. Ida. R. Hoos was thoughtful on the impact of automation on the sex ratios of occupations. Ernest G. Guillet of The New York Telephone Company estimated the proportion of women in the upper brackets in his company and the growing need for them. We are indebted to Dr. Rebecca Sparling, now retired from General Dynamics Corporation, for permission to quote her analogy between cake-baking and iron-casting-making used by John W. Macy, Jr., U.S. Civil Service Commission Chairman, in a speech before the National Federation of Business and Professional Women on July 25, 1966.

Most of the news on desegregation of colleges, clubs, and associations comes from items in *The New York Times,* which is indexed, but see "Man Friday Joins 26,000 Secretaries," *The Detroit News,* September 21, 1967, and "Woman Instructor at West Point Accustomed to Breaking Tradition," *The Poughkeepsie Journal,* February 4, 1968. In 1967, Eleanor Prescott of Barnard was editor of *The Columbia Daily Spectator* and Linda McVeigh of Radcliffe was editor of *The Harvard Crimson.* "Ladies Welcome—A New Sign for Pool Rooms" was from the Montreal *Gazette* of July 24, 1967. "Sex Test Disqualifies Athlete: Six Doctors Rule on Miss Klobukowska, Polish Sprinter," *The New York Times,* September 16, 1967, reports the hormone dosage of women athletes.

Chapter 9—Revolution: The New Feminists

The legal moves to equalize opportunity for women are conveniently summarized in the annual Progress Reports of the Interdepartmental Committee on the Status of Women and the Citizen's Advisory Council, and the Women's Bureau is fast and accurate in supplying information on the changing scene, but the laws and moves are tricky. Mary Keyserling went to endless pains to straighten out the record for us, and we are indebted also to Edith Green, Maurine Neuberger, Martha Griffiths, Pauli Murray, and Sonia Pressman, legal counsel for the Equal Employment Opportunity Commission.

In addition to these sources, and the news reports available in the *New York Times* index since 1965, see "Women's Groups Fight Last Vestiges of Bias on Job, Before the Law," *The Wall Street Journal,* May 23, 1967; "Sex and Civil Rights," *This Week,* March 19, 1967; "New Jobs for Women: A Survey," the *New York Post,* August 21, 1967; and "Women Claim Job Laws 'Protect' Them Too Much," *Minneapolis Tribune,* January 15, 1967. *The First Annual Report* of the Equal Employment Opportunity Commission, House Document No. 86, for year ending June 30, 1966, is authoritative on the record of sex complaints under Title VII and should be consulted along the EEOC's *First Annual Digest of Legal Interpretations,* July 2, 1965, through July 1, 1966, of the Equal Employment Opportunity Commission. For an industry-oriented report on the impact of the law, see Prentice-Hall, *Personnel Management—Policies and Practices,* September 20, 1966.

A good account of the two attitudes toward protective legislation is in Mary Keyserling's speech "Labor Standards Legislation and Equal Employment Opportunity" before the National Conference of Commissions on the Status of Women on June 29, 1966. Velma Mengelkoch of California kindly sent clips about her case from California newspapers and kept us informed about the progress of her case. As this goes to press there has been no decision.

Colleen Boland of the Air Line Stewards and Stewardesses Association supplied copies of her statement of May 10, 1966, to the Equal Employment Opportunity Commission hearing on whether sex was a bona-fide qualification for flight attendants, and of March 16, 1967, before the Senate Labor and Public Welfare Committee. Introduction of Asian stewardesses was reported in *The Newark Evening News* of September 12, 1967.

The New Feminist statement of Leonard Sayles was made at the Greyston Conference of May 3, 1966, "The Woman Executive in an Affluent Society," sponsored by Teachers College, Columbia University. Alice Rossi and Michael O'Connor spoke at the Dudley-Anderson-Yutzy conference for clients, "The Homemaker Who Earns: How Well Are We Talking Her Language," January 31, 1967, New York.

The renaissance of feminism in the 1960s is one of the reasons for the unexpected success of Betty Freidan's *The Feminine Mystique*, W. W. Norton, New York, 1963. The writer dispatched to San Diego during the Korean War was Caroline Bird. Her report in Margaret Hickey's Public Affairs Department of *The Ladies' Home Journal*, September 1951, was aimed at working mothers, but Congress is the target of the November 1966 *Ladies' Home Journal* article by Ben H. Bagdikian, "Who Is Sabotaging Day Care for Our Children? A Ladies' Home Journal Campaign. Only the Nation's Aroused Mothers Can Breach the 19th Century Attitude of Our Lawmakers."

Margaret Mead may not have changed her basic view of the difference between the sexes so much as she has found it important to emphasize different elements at different times. In the 1960s she has been worried about overpopulation, especially in the United States, and failure of women to take political responsibility. Her article "The Case for Drafting All Boys—and Girls," *Redbook*, September 1966, is typical of her contemporary thinking.

The NOW manifesto comes from the Statement of Purpose adopted at the organizing conference of the National Organization for Women in Washington, D.C., of October 29, 1966.

On the male backlash, the Broughner cartoon was printed in *Editor & Publisher* of March 11, 1967; the Wirtz takeoff was reported in the *New York Post* of April 4, 1967; the *Look* issue on The American Man was January 10, 1967; the CBS News Special "An Essay on Women," by reporter Harry Reasoner, produced by Andrew A. Rooney, was aired January

24, 1967; the study of GIs marrying overseas was reported by Francis Spatz Leighton, in his "GIs and Oriental Girls," *This Week,* September 10, 1967. The books about the male predicament are: Myron Brenton, *The American Male: A Penetrating Look at the Masculinity Crisis,* Coward-McCann, New York, 1966; Hendrik M. Ruitenbeck, *The Male Myth,* Dell, New York, 1967.

Male feminists turn up in surprising places. The two reviewers mentioned were Alden Whitman reviewing George R. Stewart's *Good Lives,* Houghton Mifflin, in *The New York Times* of June 13, 1967, and I. Bernard Cohen reviewing *The Way of the Scientist,* Simon & Schuster, in *The New York Times Book Review,* January 15, 1967.

George Gallup, Jr., assured us that there was a real change in attitude rather than a statistical "bug" in the progress between American Institute of Public Opinion Poll # 543 of February 8, 1955, on a woman President and American Institute of Public Opinion Poll # 676 of August 13, 1963.

Chapter 10—The Case for Equality

Pauli Murray and Mary Eastwood have kindly consented to our extensive quotation of their "Jane Crow and the Law: Sex Discrimination and Title VII," *The George Washington Law Review,* Vol. 34, No. 2, December 1965, Washington, D.C. For Israeli soldiers, see Caroline Bird, "Let's Draft Women, Too," cited in notes to Chapter 2, and *The Washington Post,* October 26, 1967, for the role of Israeli women soldiers in the Egyptian War.

For severance pay in lieu of alimony, see Clare Boothe Luce, "Is It NOW or Never for Women?" *McCall's,* April 1967. For new thinking on custody of children in divorce, see Katharine Davis Fishman, "Children at Stake," *The New York Times* Magazine, December 11, 1966.

Betty Martin of the Institute of Life Insurance suggested that there might be demand for a means test of the need of a pension beneficiary if husbands were to be covered as well as wives.

The 10-million-workers estimate is from Myrdal and Klein, *Women's Two Roles,* cited in the notes to Chapter 4, p. 188. In her column of April 5, 1967, Sylvia Porter cited a study,

"Productive Americans," from the University of Michigan's Institute for Social Research, which estimated that Americans do $300 billion worth of unpaid productive work a year, but this includes male do-it-yourself projects as well as housework done by women. The Swedes incorporate housework into their Gross National Product, but we do not. Swedish, British, and Dutch feminists press for regular salaries for housewives, but as we have seen, Americans shy away from the economic bargain as a model for marriage.

Flexible hours and home-based intellectual work are discussed as future trends in Herman Kahn and Anthony J. Wiener, *The Year 2000*, cited in notes to Chapter 8, p. 194.

On equal pay for men and women teachers, see Charles S. Benson, *The Cheerful Prospect: A Statement of the Future of American Education*, Houghton Mifflin, Boston, 1965, p. 34.

For inefficiency of male game strategy, see Thomas C. Uesugi and W. Edgar Vinacke, "Strategy in a Feminine Game," *Sociometry*, 26, March 1963, p. 75.

Erik Erikson postulates a "mother variable" in *Insight and Responsibility*, W. W. Norton, New York, 1964, p. 235. Vermont Royster's editorial "The Work Mystique" was in *The Wall Street Journal*, June 24, 1964.

According to *The New York Times* of January 4, 1967, the new town of Washington planned for England provides space for light industries that will employ wives. But we must watch out lest we create female ghettos. Equal opportunity for both partners to a marriage is one of the unregarded assets of the big city.

INDEX

Protect yourself and your family!

Don't be one of the "taken"!

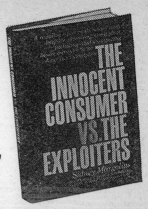

BUYER, BEWARE. Each time you walk into a store, call a serviceman, or sign a contract, you run the risk of being "taken." And not just by fly-by-night operators either. Some of the best-known and respected companies in the country lend their names to unscrupulous practices.

• Now, Sidney Margolius, leading consumer authority and an expert in financial management, shows you how to avoid being "tricked" by shady operators and operations. In his book, *The Innocent Consumer vs. The Exploiters*, you'll discover:

• How you can save up to 90 per cent on your drug bills without changing stores. (See page 195)

• The simple "instant" process that lets you calculate the real interest on a loan. (See page 37)

• Why your department store is so anxious to open a revolving charge account for you. (See page 55)

• That you are buying "balloon bread" without realizing it, fruit drinks that are 90 to 97 per cent water, and pre-sweetened cereals that are 45 per cent sugar (at $1.07 a pound.) (See page 115)

• More than an exposé, *The Innocent Consumer vs. The Exploiters* will give you the protection you need every time you open the door to a salesman. Once you've read this book, you won't be tricked—as so many have—into paying more than $400 for a TV set worth $150 which has false guarantees. And you certainly won't be one of the thousands who have their salaries garnisheed every year without even being notified.

77070

10-Day Free Trial

With all these pitfalls, one sure way to get your money's worth when you buy anything would be to bring along a lawyer, an engineer and a man from the Food and Drug Administration. Much simpler, however, is to go to your bookstore *or* fill out the coupon at right to get your copy of Sidney Margolius' revealing and helpful *The Innocent Consumer vs. The Exploiters.* If you do not believe that this book will save you many times its cost, you may return it within ten days for a full refund.

Trident Press, Dept. TP-1
630 Fifth Avenue
New York, N.Y. 10020

Please send me at once a copy of THE INNOCENT CONSUMER VS. THE EXPLOITERS. If I do not feel that this book will save me many times its cost, I may return it within ten days and owe nothing. Otherwise, you will bill me only $4.95, plus a small mailing charge.

Name_____

Address_____

City_____State____Zip____

☐ SAVE POSTAGE. Check here if you enclose check or money order for $4.95 as payment in full —then we pay postage. Same 10-day trial privilege with full refund guarantee holds. (Please add sales tax where applicable.)